OJI

Spy Girls At The Gate

W T Naud

Grovesnor Square Press

GROVESNOR SQUARE PRESS
10220 Buena Vista Road
Luucerne Valley, CA 92356

ISBN: 0615573762
ISBN-13: 9780615573762
Library of Congress Control Number: 2011918010
CreateSpace, North Charleston, South Carolina

For my best friend and wife without
whose sense of humor
and dedication this book would
have never been possible.
Special thanks to:
Bob Swain
Lillian Chutsky

Foreword

When WWII ended, Red China took over control of North Korea, dividing the country. It was inevitable that the Chinese would try to take over South Korea as well, setting its sights on restoring Korea to one communist nation. Thus, the Korean war started in 1950.

This is my story. I intended to write this book shortly after leaving the service, but somehow it took me fifty years to find a chair.

The Author

Chapter 1

Going To War

We had been sitting in the all-night diner for four hours drinking coffee, waiting for dawn and the morning fog to lift over San Francisco Bay.

"There it is, Jess," I said.

Jessie wasn't interested. He just kept drinking his coffee. He had been dreading this moment.

The outline of the berthed troop ship USS Black appeared through the mist like a ghost. On the dock four or five hundred GIs were assembling their gear anxiously waiting to board.

I wasn't looking forward to going on the troop ship any more than Jessie was. But Jessie was counting on me for reassurance that all would be well. So, I put on a brave face.

"Bill, if it's a police action, why didn't they just call in the cops?" Jessie asked. Then he added like a hurt child, "They shouldn't have lied to me."

Jessie Bonato was twenty-one, six-foot-four, built like a bull and naïve. His father was the head of the Mafia in Brooklyn. When the army recruiter in Times Square gave Jessie "his word" he would be stationed in Italy if he enlisted, Jessie signed up. "Your word" meant something to the son of a Mafia Don. The army kept their word and stationed him near Rome, for three months. Now he was on his way to Korea.

"I don't want to die in a foxhole in Korea, Bill. "

"You're not going to die in a foxhole. Stop worrying," I said, trying to ease his fears.

I was a street smart twenty-year-old from upper Manhattan. More than a year earlier I had been drafted. I could have ducked it, by going to Canada and applying for dual citizenship, since my father was a Canadian citizen from Montreal. I didn't. I took an Oath of Loyalty to the U.S. Army and became Private William Thorton Naud, U.S. 51103442.

Part of my reason for not fleeing north was the snow and the cold up there. In my view, snow and cold were two of God's lousiest ideas. But my main concern was how running away would reflect on my family, particularly my older brother, Tom, who had been awarded both a Purple Heart and a Bronze Star for fighting the Germans in World War II. Besides, he probably would have kicked the crap out of me if I deserted.

The fog lifted and I could see the troops finally funneling up the gangway. I put the money for the check on the table.

"Come on, Jess. It's time to go."

He followed me out the front door. The morning air was cold and crisp, and the passing traffic was noisy. The faithful 1937 Pontiac, with the Al Capone running boards that my brother paid 97 dollars for at a used car lot, was parked in front of the building. It had carried us coast to coast, 3,450 miles from the expansion joint on the George Washington Bridge to a run-down diner two hundred fifty feet from San Francisco Bay.

We unloaded our gear from the rear seat.

"Bill? What are you gonna do with the car?"

I had been pondering that question for the last few hours. The faithful old car deserved a better fate than being abandoned in front of a run-down diner, only to be hauled away to a junk heap.

Across the street a twelve-year-old Mexican boy was trying to hitch a ride for himself and his family. Behind him on the curb were an older man and a woman holding a baby in her arms. They were laboring people with weathered faces, whose only assets were the clothes they wore and what little dignity life had afforded them. The boy earnestly held up a sign to the oncoming traffic.

It read:

MONTEREY, PLEASE

The trucks and cars roared by, ignoring them.

"Hey, son, is that your family?" I screamed over the traffic noise.

"Oh, si, mi madre, padre, yes," he hollered back.

"Can your father drive a car?" I asked.

"Si, he mechanico," the boy said.

"Would he like to own a car?" I yelled.

The boy spoke excitedly to his father in Spanish. Then he turned to me. "Padre, no have money," the boy said apologetically.

"Well, tell him, I want to give him my car," I adamantly called back.

The mother listened skeptically as her son explained. She stared at me, as she continued to rock her baby, then said something in Spanish.

"My mother asks, 'Why you do this?'" the boy said.

"Well, come on over here and I'll tell you all," I said.

3

With the boy leading them, the family scurried across the busy highway.

"Look, tell your folks, I'm giving you this car so we'll have someone to pray for us while we are at war," I said.

After interpreting, the boy listened as his mother and father quietly spoke together.

The man frowned and shook his head.

"My father says, 'No, thanks,' but he will pray for you anyway," the boy said.

"Why won't he take it?" I asked.

The parents remained silent. It didn't make any sense to me. The boy kept glancing over at the gas station by the diner.

"The kid's telling you they don't have gas money," Jessie whispered.

I took off my left shoe and pulled out a twenty-dollar bill. It was all we had left.

"Son, tell your father the car comes with gasoline money," I said as I took the man's hand and laid the twenty-dollar bill on his palm, along with the signed pink slip for the car.

"Gracias, Senõr," the father said, with a simple dignity.

Tears welled up in the mother's eyes.

"We will all pray for you, at the war, mister," the boy said happily.

I was embarrassed.

"Stay alive, mister," the boy hollered, as they climbed into the car.

Jessie and I headed to the dock and showed our orders to the MPs at the gate.

After a quick glance the guard returned them and cleared us to go in. "You're boarding from level two. Up those steps," he said, pointing.

We started up. I took my last look back at land and was happy to see the old Pontiac was gone. I was carrying my duffel bag on one arm and had slung my golf bag full of clubs over the other. We headed up the steps.

Suddenly we were stopped by a voice. "Hey, wait a minute."

As I turned, a news photographer took my picture with a huge Graflex flash camera. "What are you gonna do with those clubs soldier," he hollered as the crowd herded Jessie and I up the steps onto the ship.

"We're gonna play the North Koreans to win the war," I called back.

'Next stop, Tokyo,' I thought as my foot touched the main deck. It felt greasy, like the floor in a mechanic's garage.

Chapter 2

The USS Black

A petty officer checked us in and gave us a map to our compartment. It was at the bow of the ship, way down on D-deck.

"Looks like they got us sleeping lower than whale shit," I quipped.

Jessie didn't laugh.

He just stood staring unhappily into the dimly-lit airless tomb, jammed with rows and rows of GI filled canvas bunks stacked four high. There was no way to escape the coughing, sneezing, snoring, farting and assorted blends of BO, from all the bodies crammed in like canned sardines. But at least we didn't need a map to find the latrine. It was right at the head of the compartment, shaped like the letter A, with evenly spaced toilets around the walls and a twenty foot long urinal trough crossing the room.

Jessie and I were hundreds of miles at sea, trying to sleep, when the late edition of the San Francisco newspaper hit the streets. Beneath the headline, July 19, 1950 TRUMAN SENDS TROOPS TO BATTLE NORTH KOREANS, was a photo of me boarding the ship with my golf clubs.

"I can't breathe, Bill," Jessie grumbled from the top bunk. "I think I'm gonna puke."

I was in the bunk below him keeping my eyes shut, trying to ignore the complaints, hoping he would eventually go to sleep.

"It stinks in here too," he moaned.

"Hey, dummy, knock it off," an angry voice cried out of the darkness.

"Yeah, keep quiet," another irritated GI echoed.

But Jessie just kept it up. "Bill, it's true what the guys at the Petaluma base said. It's like a coffin in here."

When I didn't respond he looked down over the edge of his bunk at me. "Did you hear me Bill?" he whined, like an abandoned child.

"Shut the hell up," another gruff voice screamed out.

This was the second night Jessie's whining had produced a stream of complaints and angry protests from guys in the compartment.

"Jess, try to go to sleep, huh?" I pleaded quietly.

An irate Corporal ready to tear someone limb from limb came out of the darkness and stuck his face in mine. "You the guy doing the bitching?" he demanded, shaking my shoulder.

Before I could answer, Jessie dropped down from his bunk. "No. It was me, " he explained. "There's no air and I can't sleep. "

The blood drained from the Corporal's face when he saw how big Jessie was. He was angry, but not suicidal.

I smiled. Last night, another 'angry guy' had gotten the same surprise. The corporal tempered his attack. "Yeah? Well, try to keep it down," he stuttered. "Please. Okay?"

"Okay, I'm sorry," Jessie said apologetically.

The Corporal vanished back the way he came, into the smelly darkness.

"Bill, I know I'm trouble," Jessie whispered in a contrite voice. "But I can't help it." He knew no matter how many guys disliked him, I would still be his friend. He climbed back into his bunk and lit a cigarette.

I leaned out. "Just try to sleep, Jess," I said as I watched him take a drag on his cigarette. He exhaled, blowing the smoke directly at the vent above his head. I noticed the stream of air coming out of the vent was barely strong enough to blow the smoke away, so I traced the main air duct that ran along the ceiling which brought in the only source of fresh air for the entire compartment. Just before it reached the vent above Jessie, it branched off to a wide duct and then into smaller ducts that served the rest of the compartment. I figured that was the problem. The air was divided up among so many vents that no one was getting much of a breeze. Like what happens to the water pressure in a house when all the faucets are turned on at the same time, no one gets much of anything.

"Jess? Let me get into your bunk for a second, okay?" I whispered.

Jessie lowered himself and I climbed up.

"What are you doing?" he asked.

"Never mind. Relax. Keep your voice down," I said.

Using my dog tag as a screwdriver, I removed the grate from the air duct and peered in. I was right about the cause and the solution was obvious. All I had to do was to cut off the air to all the other outlets.

"Give me your pillow, Jess," I said. I took it and jammed it into the branched-off duct, making sure it was sealed closed. Then I screwed Jessie's grating back in place and lowered myself into the aisle.

"Go ahead, give it a try," I whispered.

Jessie climbed up into his bunk.

"It's great, Bill. I can breathe," Jessie said with glee.

"Good. Now go to sleep," I said tossing my pillow up to him.

The snoring and coughing noises around us were now drowned out by the noise of the air roaring out of Jessie's vent. It sounded like a wind tunnel.

I climbed back up into my bunk questioning the ethics of what I had done. I managed to convince myself that the men might actually benefit by being deprived of fresh air. Why? Because now, Jessie would sleep. So, he couldn't possibly complain. And the guys HE had been keeping awake with his complaining, would sleep. And the guys THEY had been keeping awake with their complaining would sleep.

"Bill?" Jessie whispered.

"What now," I said with slight apprehension.

"It's cold in here. I'm freezing," he moaned.

I gave him my blanket.

"Bill? I'm a pain in the neck, huh?" Jessie said sounding like a friendless child.

I was tempted to agree. But didn't. Jessie's friendship meant a lot.

"We're friends, Jess. So we gotta help each other," I said.

"Bill, you're the ONLY friend I got," Jessie responded.

I was embarrassed. I didn't know what to say. I was still thinking about it when I heard snoring. At last, Jessie was asleep. And soon, I was too.

A couple of nights later after watching the nightly movie, *The Best Years Of Our Lives*, shown on the main deck, we headed down to the compartment. We were met by an angry mob gathered around our bunk. They had discovered the pillow I stuffed in the air vent. The staff Sergeant in charge of the compartment shoved the pillow in my face. "Try that again and I'll cut off your air," he threatened. The grumbling crowd's anger was quelled by the Sergeants actions. They dispersed back to their own bunks.

I whispered, "Come on, Jess, we had better find another place to sleep."

We grabbed our blankets and headed back up to the main deck making a bed near a lifeboat.

"I'm afraid of falling off in the dark Bill," Jessie fussed.

"Don't worry I'll stand watch," I said.

Jessie slept like a baby while I remained awake all night making sure he didn't roll off the ship, just as I had promised.

When dawn finally broke Jessie awoke refreshed, but I was exhausted.

The sky was blue, the sea was calm and the USS Black continued sailing west on its way to the war. The troops strolled about on deck feeling the warmth of the sun. Some talked or exercised or caught up on sleep. Others wrote letters or just sat on deck thinking. The thinkers were the fewest in numbers. I was one of them, busy trying to find a solution to our sleeping problem.

The officers' mess was at the hatchway nearest us. As the officers came out, I noticed they were wearing fatigues and a t-shirt without any insignia or indication of their rank. I figured it was a dress code designed to accommodate the crowded decks, eliminating the need to constantly exchange salutes.

That gave me an idea.

I changed into a clean crisp pair of fatigues and a brand new white t-shirt. I took my Bobby Jones 'Calamity Jane' putter from my golf bag.

"Where are you going, Bill?" Jessie asked.

"Fishing," I said cryptically and walked away. I and my putter headed up to the officers mess. Breakfast was almost over. The serving line ran down the left side of the forty-foot room. Seven enlisted men in aprons and hats stood behind a billowing wall of steam serving food from the trays. I got on the end of the line which stretched into the companionway and began practicing my putting stroke, knowing that someone would eventually yell 'FORE'. Right on cue, someone did. It was an officer wearing an OD-Officer Of The Day arm band. He was coming out of the mess hall.

I stopped him. "Ah, kind sir, maybe you can help me," I said in an effected tone. "Father wanted me to look up a friend of his from the Hamptons. He's a fine chap. I believe he's in charge of compartment assignments. Could you point him out me?"

"That must be Colonel Koster. He's in charge of billeting," the OD replied using the proper nomenclature. He turned back to search the crowd in the room. The officers were eating standing up at rows and rows of ten foot long stainless steel counter top tables that were bolted to the floor and a wall lined with portholes that overlooked the decks.

"That's him," he said pointing, "down in the corner by the last porthole."

I spotted him. "Thanks ole buddy," I said turning back, but he had already gone.

I made my way to a spot at the counter top directly opposite Colonel Koster, who was preoccupied reading some charts and eating a stack of pancakes.

"Those look great," I said laying my putter down on the counter top table. I think I'll have pancakes too. Mind watching my putter sir?" I inquired. Without waiting for his response I got a tray and started down the serving line. I didn't really want pancakes but I figured indebting myself to Koster was the easiest way to start up a conversation.

Koster was examining the club when I returned from the serving line. "I used to have the exact same putter," he said affectionately.

'Good news' I thought. The guy in charge of compartment assignments is a golfer.

"What's your name?" he asked.

"William Thorne Naud," I replied.

"Where do you play in the States Naud?" he asked.

"I'm a member at Winged Foot," I said, lying convincingly. I could tell he was impressed.

"What outfit are you with?" he asked.

"ASA Sir," I spewed out confidently through a mouthful of pancakes.

"ASA Huh...You must know Colonel Arrowsmith."

"Very well, Sir. The Colonel and I were golf partners for the ASA matches this year." 'I hooked a good one,' I thought.

"Good Golfer. Good man," he said crisply.

"Yes, Sir," I said awkwardly, swallowing a forkful of pancakes while yawning. "Excuse me, Sir," I said, covering my mouth as I yawned again. "Sleeping on deck is not the most restful place."

"What's wrong with your compartment?" Koster asked.

"I got aboard late. They stuck me in the bowls of the ship with a hammock. How about more coffee, Sir?" I asked through a yawn. Without waiting for his answer, I took his cup and headed for the chow line. Food service was over and the room was almost empty. I leisurely filled the cups from the self-service urn. I wanted Koster to have time to ponder my sleeping problem. I returned to the table and placed the full cup of coffee before him.

"Maybe I can give you a golf lesson, Sir," I said through a stifled yawn.

"I'm afraid you'd probably be falling asleep!" he chuckled.

I chuckled awkwardly back while taking another bite of pancake.

"Say, Naud, maybe I can help you with your sleeping problem," he started.

I stopped chewing.

"Compartment #8, just down the companionway outside the mess hall entrance, is reserved for a general staff officer. Unfortunately General Stallworth couldn't make the trip. I can't officially assign it, but nobody should bother you. I'll make sure the door is left open."

I swallowed. "Thank you, Sir," I said gratefully. I figured I had better get out while I was ahead, so I picked up my putter and tray and turned to go.

"Oh, one thing, Naud. I need to see your ID," Koster asked.

My heart sank. "Well sir. Agency people are sworn not to show their ID Card to anyone but authorized agency personnel."

"Sorry Naud. I'll have to see it," Koster insisted.

Reluctantly, I produced my ID Card, making sure the first thing he saw were the words ASA TOP SECRET stamped above my picture.

Koster was clearly suspicious. "Naud, this shows your rank as private," he said in a huff.

I had no choice but to go on bluffing, hoping Koster would buy it. I leaned in and spoke in a low toned, confidential manner. "Sir, all special missions people carry ID cards with the rank of private in case of capture."

"Just tell me your true rank," he insisted firmly.

I stood straight up at mock attention, in military fashion, figuring it was all or nothing now. Then I spewed out a slow and deliberate wooden litany of the ASA oath.

"Sir, I cannot and will not discuss . . . deny . . . or confirm anything about my present mission including my rank." I held the stance waiting for Koster's reaction.

He remained silent for a few moments, contemplating the situation. He must have concluded I presented the look and breeding of an officer, for he handed me back my ID Card sporting a slight smile.

"Maybe we'll play Wingfoot sometime, Naud," he said with a chuckle.

I relaxed my stance. "I hope so, sir," I replied, trying not to show my potent sense of relief. I excused myself and headed off to find Jessie.

Around midnight Jessie and I hauled our stuff up the narrow dimly lit stairway, making our way to compartment #8. The door was unlocked and we slipped in.

Jessie struck a match as I locked the door. There was a desk under a porthole with a bed on each side. Jessie tested one of the mattresses and laid down.

"It's like going to heaven, Bill. And we got a window," he said like a kid.

"They call it a porthole, Jess," I said. "Now go to sleep."

I figured it was a good idea for me to stay awake for a while, just in case somebody came by asking questions. It wasn't that Jessie was dumb, he just wasn't a very convincing liar.

About an hour later, still fully dressed, I laid back on the bed and for the first time since I got aboard I slept like a log.

Jessie was starting to have nightmares about dying in Korea. In an effort to keep his mind off his fears, at least for a little while, I offered to draw his portrait. He agreed, so we took a blanket, some paper and pencils I found in the desk, and we went out on deck. We found a spot near the ship's bow where the light for drawing was good. It was against a steel superstructure which looked to have fresh coat of gray paint. I checked to be sure it was dry. I laid the blanket out, both as a cushion and insulation from the heat of the steel deck. Then I posed Jessie and began to draw. Jessie was fine, for about thirty seconds. And then he started to fidget.

"Jess? You gotta hold the pose or I can't draw you," I complained.

"The ship's rocking, Bill," Jessie said, making a lousy excuse.

"Yeh, well, hold still or I'm gonna quit," I said, but I really didn't mean it. I had studied art at the prestigious Pratt Institute, in Brooklyn. I had even thought of becoming an illustrator. I knew I had some talent, but I wasn't Norman Rockwell.

A crowd began to gather.

Jessie was now the center of attention. He found it very appealing. To the onlookers, watching a portrait emerge on the blank piece of paper was something quite magical.

"Hey, you're a good drawer," a pimply Private commented.

"Yeh, it sure looks like him," a Sergeant observed, easing his way to the front of the growing crowd to get a better look.

"Let me see," Jessie insisted, breaking his pose hoping to take a peek at the drawing.

I pulled the picture in against my chest. "Not until it's done," I said directing Jessie to resume the pose. Jessie did, but like a petulant child.

"Hey, buddy," the private addressed me. "Can you draw me?" he asked.

"He might if I ask him," Jessie answered abruptly, in a peevish tone, venting his annoyance at being stuck with holding still.

"Oh, yeh? Who are you, his agent?" the Private protested.

"Yeh, smart guy," Jessie answered turning around to glare at the guy.

"Hold still, Jess," I said, sounding testy.

Jessie swung his head back.

"Is this guy you're agent, buddy?" the Private asked me.

"That's right," I said playfully, as I lightened the highlights on Jessie's lips to give them a fuller look.

The Private addressed Jessie. "Okay, buddy. What does it cost?"

Jessie struggled to answer out of the side of his mouth, afraid I would bitch at him again for moving. "If you gotta ask, you can't afford it," he said dismissing the guy.

The private pulled out a wad of money from his pocket. "How about twenty bucks?"

Jessie's eyes lit up

"Here," the private said, shoving a twenty dollar bill in Jessie's face.

The sight of the money changed Jessie's whole attitude.

"If anybody else wants a picture, better sign up now," he said sounding like a huckster. "He's not going to be doing a whole lot," Jessie said pocketing the money. Men, searching for money in their pockets, gathered around him. Ten minutes later Jessie had a fist full of money and lots of signed up customers.

I held Jessie's picture at arm's length to critique it. I wasn't sure he liked it, but the impressed buzz in the crowd told me they approved.

By the time the bells finished ringing for noon chow, I had finished all the portraits.

"No more till after we get some chow," Jessie announced.

Jessie counted the money as the crowd dispersed, murmuring their discontent with having to wait. "Two hundred forty bucks, Bill," Jessie said as he handed over the cash.

"You'd better hold the money, Jess," I said. "You're my agent, aren't ya?"

"I guess. Yeah," Jessie said.

"Watching the money is part of what an agent does. How much is your commission as my agent?" I inquired.

"I don't know. How much should I get?" Jessie asked.

"If the artist is good, they usually keep fifty per-cent," I said.

"No, Bill. The most I could take would be forty," Jessie said.

It wasn't the money but the smile on Jessie's face that pleased me.

"Hey, Bill, now we can buy anything we want at the canteen."

"Why not? We're rich," I grinned.

After lunch, we bought cigarettes and tons of candy: Milky Ways, O'Henrys, Baby Ruths, Milk Duds and Candy Corn. We sat on deck stuffing our faces like glutinous kids.

I was reading the newspaper as I finished off another candy bar. What I read was grim. There had been rumors going around the ship that the UN was losing the war in Korea. Like most rumors they were true, and the American casualties were high. I crum-pled up the paper and threw it overboard, before Jes-sie could see it.

That evening there was a horror movie neither of us was in the mood to see. Jessie went back to the cabin to sleep. While *Dracula* was sucking the blood out of the townspeople on a thirty-foot screen behind me, I stood at the stern of the ship, holding onto the rail, watching the propeller wake vanish into the horizon of the inky black sea. Above it the vast dark night sky was lit by a million stars.

Major General Hammel had a late night meeting in his compartment with Colonel Koster, his logistics officer. His aide brought the General a copy of MacArthur's Tactical War Summary, a report that was sent each day to the Joint Chiefs in Washington. General Stone read it, then handed it on to Koster.

"Take a look, Henry. It's the same grim shit. I hope to God we get there in time to make a difference," he said.

....

TOP SECRET/ASA, OJI Copy 1 of 3 Decrypted
Communiqué
Date: 13 JULY 1950
To: JOINTS CHIEFS OF STAFF
From: MACARTHUR
Subject: TACTICAL SUMMARY

Synopsis:
   Have cut 7th division to reinforce
25th and 1st cavalry.
   Now using 3.5″ rocket launchers
against T34 tanks. Proving effective.
   Desperately need more troops.
   Enemy has crossed Kum River sur-
rounding Taejon. Heavy casualties.
   We are getting our butts kicked,
pure and simple.

[Signed]
MacArthur

....

The following afternoon the sun was hot and the air muggy, but the sea was calm and a breeze came by often enough to make the deck a relaxing place to be. As usual, the troops were scattered all around, talking, writing letters, sunning or gambling.

I began to notice, the closer we got to Japan and ultimately Korea, the more the guys were just sitting and thinking.

In the afternoons I liked to relax on the hatchway by the ship's stern and watch the crew rig the giant silver screen for the evening movie.

"Hey, buddy," I called out to one of the riggers. "What's the movie tonight?"

"*Casablanca*," he hollered back.

I had spent a lot of time going to movies as a boy, often two or even three times a week. My parents worked long hours, trying to keep the family together, and movies took me to places away from the fears and frustrations of my own life. The one film I remembered best was *Casablanca*. I had seen it a dozen times, first at the RKO Coliseum, then the Coronet Theater in upper Manhattan. I never tired of it and knew most of the famous lines, including the last thing Bogart said to Claude Raines at the airport: '*Louis? This may be the start of a beautiful friendship.*' I figured I knew what the film was telling the audience: if there is ever a chance to do some good in life and you fail to do it, God might forgive you, but you won't forgive yourself.

"Hey, fellow. Is your buddy sea sick again?" the movie rigger asked. The last time the sailor had seen us, Jessie had been throwing up over the rail.

"No. He's getting rich, gambling," I said with a note of cynicism.

The remark made both men chuckle.

Jessie was off somewhere playing cards with the money he got from the portraits but everyone knew he was a terrible card player, the kind who bets on a pair of twos, sure he can draw three aces to win with a full house. I was sure he would come back broke, just as he always had at Fort Devins.

"Bill? Look," a voice said behind me.

I turned to see Jessie beaming, holding up a fist full of money. "I drew three aces for a full house, and won three hundred bucks."

"That's great, Jess," I said. It was more than great, it was a miracle.

Jessie's victory celebration turned sour when, without any warning, the ship began to vibrate violently as if it were tearing itself apart.

Jessie's alarm bells began going off. "We're sinking, Bill. I told ya we would," he said in a panic.

I looked at the faces of the crew rigging the movie screen, they weren't panicking. If there was a problem with the ship, it couldn't be too bad.

"We're not sinking, Jess. Relax," I insisted. But something was making an ugly grinding noise in the bowels of the vessel. After a few minutes the ship finally stopped shaking and came to a rest, silent and dead in the water.

A commanding voice came over the loudspeakers. "This is the Captain speaking."

Now Jessie was convinced we were about to be ordered to abandon ship.

"Gentlemen. You are now on the International Date Line. The only place on earth where you can have one foot in today, and the other in tomorrow.

Before we proceed to our destination, it's time to find out who will be crowned King Neptune."

"Who's King Neptune?" Jessie asked with relief.

I told him what I had read in the ship's paper. King Neptune was an ancient mythical God who protected ships at sea.

"You can become King Neptune," the Captain explained, "by jumping into the ocean on the International dateline, from a higher point than anybody else. The lucky winner gets to wear a crown, a cape, and carry the pitchfork. And for the rest of the journey everyone on board must bow down to him as he goes by."

A buzz of talking and chuckling erupted through the listening crowd.

"Are you ready?" the Captain called out.

Raucous cheers rang out from the GI's crowded on deck as they looked around in anticipation wondering who among them would have the guts to do it.

Jessie became alarmed. "I can't swim, Bill," he said anxiously.

"You don't HAVE to do it, Jess. It's a volunteer thing," I assured him.

We worked our way through the excited crowd, to the rail, to see what was happening. Members of the ship's crew were securing long rope ladders to the main deck's rail posts and unfurling them down to the sea, fifty feet below. Other crewmembers were in the water attaching a 'shark net' to the side of the boat. It was a flimsy looking thing, which ran about two hundred feet alongside the ship, stuck out forty feet from the hull, and was being kept afloat by a dozen or so oversized life preservers.

How many guys would be willing to bet their lives on it, I wondered. In my view sharks were smart enough to know they could just jump over the net, into the 'safe' area, to get to where the best things to eat were. I didn't want to be lunch for a shark. I was content to watch.

I was surprised to see how many GI's were excitedly climbing down the rope ladders and jumping into the water. Maybe it was the thought of being able to swim from yesterday to tomorrow, maybe some were just reacting to a dare or a bet, maybe they felt it was their one chance to swim around with more than two miles of water beneath them, or maybe they just wanted to get a King Neptune Certificate. Whatever the reason, the men swimming in the ocean below were obviously enjoying themselves.

"Looks like fun, Bill. I shoulda learned to swim," Jessie said.

"Yeh," I responded with little enthusiasm. I tried counting the heads in the water. Keeping track of the swimming bodies was impossible, so I gave up, roughly estimating the crowd at seventy five.

"Attention on port deck. Attention," a cheery, husky voice came out over a loud hailer. "This is Chief Petty Officer Fishback. Listen up, you sons of Neptune. Any of you guys in the water who wanna compete for the title of King Neptune, need to get to the rope ladders NOW. Remember only one contestant at each," he announced.

After some confusion, each of the rope ladders was finally manned by a single GI and the guys not competing swam back out of the way.

"Okay," Fishback said, as he counted the men below. "It looks like we got nine contestants. When I blow the whistle, you got forty five seconds to climb as high as your guts will take you and at the end I'll blow again, and you gotta jump or you're out. If two guys jump from the same height, the first person to hit the water wins. If you're ready, wave."

The contestants grabbed hold of the ladders and raised a hand indicating their readiness for the start.

Fishback blew the whistle. Amidst the hooting and cheering from the GIs for their favorite contestants, the contest got under way.

Jessie and I, along with the crowd, pressed tighter into the railing to get a better view of the men scrambling up the ladders that hung down the side of the ship. A muscular Sergeant was on the ladder directly below us. He was climbing steadily, rooted on by his avid supporters who had clustered around us. If there was a strong horse to bet on it was him.

A round of betting swept through the crowd. "Fifty bucks on Sergeant Darling. Any takers?"

"I'll take it!"

"Count me in!"

"I got twenty on Salley!"

The nervous contestant Salley, on ladder two, struggled up five rungs of the wobbly rope ladder. Then he stopped. He was shaking so badly with fear he leaped off, landing awkwardly in the water with a loud belly flop. Moans of disappointment came from his buddies on deck who had just lost a days pay as Sally swam for safety. Some in the crowd hooted and clucked like a chicken. "Bawk Bawk! Bawk Bawk!" they taunted, flapping their arms, adding to Salley's humiliation.

The well-built blond GI Hurgleman, hurrying up ladder four, suddenly slipped, entangling his foot in the rope ladder. Gasps reverberated through the deck crowd as his body arched out and swung in towards the ship. His head banged against the steel hull like a bell clapper. The force of the blow jarred his foot loose and he tumbled toward the ocean like a rag doll.

The other climbers were frozen, watching him fall.

As his limp body hit the water, the crowd became silent, fearing for his life.

"Holy Shit the guys gonna drown," Jessie said with alarm.

A moment later Hurgleman surfaced holding his head, obviously in pain but otherwise okay.

"YEAHH!" A wave of cheers of relief and admiration swept down the deck.

The contestants on ladders five and six resumed their efforts, attacking the treacherous climb with reckless abandon. Fishback spotted them. His voice blared with excitement over the loud hailer. "Contestants five and six are setting a new record height at the forty five foot level! " A sudden roar of approval rose from the crowd as they jostled themselves along the rail to see better.

"They're nuts," Jessie said. "Those guys are going to get themselves killed."

The daredevils reached the railing, turned and squatted down, appearing ready to jump. They looked down at their fellow climbers below and yelled out in unison "SUUCCKERS!" Then the pranksters turned and leaped over the railing onto the deck, laughing heartedly as they vanished down a gangway, chased by the tumultuous sounds of boos and catcalls from the disappointed crowd.

Darling and the guy on ladder one just shook their heads and resumed their climb. The guy on ladder one soon started pulling ahead.

"Higher! Higher!" the crowd called out.

Fishback was keeping one eye on his timing watch and his whistle at the ready. "Ten seconds," he announced.

"Gotman! Gotman! " rang out from a rowdy group of GIs further down the deck, just above ladder one.

"Gotman? "Jessie mumbled in surprise. He leaned further over the railing, taking a hard look at the contestant climbing ladder one. The suns glare was making it hard to see, he squinted hard and bobbed his head until he finally caught a glimpse of the man's face. "It's Gotman Bill," he called to me in disbelief.

I leaned over and looked down the railing. I could see Jessie was right, but I lied. "I can't tell, Jess. I can't see his face."

"That's really him, Gotman. The guy who tried to kill you at Fort Devins! Baker's GUTLESS STOOGE!"

Suddenly, a bulky staff Sergeant pushed in against Jessie. "Who you calling gutless, buddy. He's down there and you're up here," he taunted.

"Yeh, when he wins you're gonna have to bow down to him, chicken shit," another one of Gotman's buddies teased.

Jessie became livid. The thought of bowing down to Gotman was more than he could take.

A cheering battle erupted across the deck in a deafening chorus. "KING GOT- MAN! KING GOT-MAN!" Countered by, "KING DARLING KING DARLING!"

Gotman reached the top rung first. Darling was struggling to catch up. Fishback blew his whistle.

Gotman clutched the railing and turned, cocking his knees, setting himself to go. Just as he leaned out to jump, he froze, as a large object wrapped in Khaki emitting a bone chilling scream flew through the sky and plummeted fifty feet to the ocean's surface, hitting the water with a giant splash like an elephant doing a belly flop. Then the object sank. The stunned crowd held its breath until it surfaced. Then they erupted into wild cheers and laughter of disbelief. Most had no idea of what had happened.

To my horror, I realized the floundering, Khaki-colored elephant, drowning in the ocean below, was Jessie.

"He can't swim," I screamed over and over, but nobody could hear me over the noise of the crowd.

One of the GIs in the water finally realized Jessie was in trouble, so he dragged him to safety.

I was relieved.

Jessie had leaped from the main deck, sixty feet to the water, just to prove he had more guts than Gotman. Whether it was guts or stupidity, I was proud of him. Though he was not an official contestant, Jessie was crowned King Neptune by popular acclamation. Chief Petty Officer Sergeant Fishback told the men, Jessie's record might be tied, but could never be beaten. Especially since he was the first non-swimming King Neptune they ever had, and would probably be the last.

The next day, Jessie wore the crown and coral cape, and proudly carried the scepter of King Neptune. Everywhere he went on the ship, the GIs played along, making way for him with a bow, and addressing him as King Neptune. He roamed around all day in his costume hoping to run into Gotman, but he never did.

When Jessie returned to our compartment it was just after evening chow. I had gorged myself on the last of the milky ways bars earlier in the day so I had no appetite for SOS·shit on a shingle, which was being served that night at the mess hall.

Jessie laid down on the bed to rest without taking off his King Neptune outfit. "Gotman must be in hiding," he said disappointedly.

I was preoccupied, busy dropping a golf ball in a bucket of water, trying to time how long it took to sink to the bottom. I dropped it again for the fourth time, then counted out loud as the ball clunked to the bottom.

"One second," I said.

"Whatta you doing Bill?" Jessie asked.

"Remember the golf ball I hit off the stern of the ship? I was wondering how long it would take before it reached the ocean floor. One of the guys on deck told me the ocean depth was somewhere around twenty four thousand four hundred feet." I started to do my calculations out loud based on that depth. "Let's see, if it's one second per two feet, then sixty seconds a minute, then......" At that point I began struggling with the numbers, math was not my strong suit.

Jessie chimed in to help. "That's easy," he said. To my surprise he started spouting lists of numbers, multiplied and divided by others numbers, in an incomprehensible stream.

I was stunned.

"You know, Bill, you also have to factor in the water pressure and varying current pulls." After five minutes of calculations he declared, "I figure it will hit the bottom of the ocean in approximately eight hours, twenty minutes and thirty seconds from when you knocked it off the side." Then he added, "that's if a fish don't gulp it up on the way down."

I just stared. Suddenly his being drafted into the ASA made some sense, Jessie was a math whiz.

An hour later he was asleep, and I was still preoccupied with my own calculations on the ball drop.

There was a knock on the compartment door.

"Who is it?" I asked guardedly. Nobody was supposed to know we were there, except for Colonel Koster.

"Officer of the Day," a stern voice came back.

I opened the door slightly. "Oh, Lieutenant Fuchs," I said quickly reading his lapel badge. He was a thin guy with a butch hair cut, ruddy face, shifty eyes and a lieutenant's bar pinned to the shoulder of his white t-shirt.

"This compartment is reserved for General Staff Officers. Show me your ID?" he asked in a resolute tone as he tried to see past me into the compartment.

The guy was an obvious zealot. The only chance I had to get rid of him was to do something outrageous. With an obvious lisp I said, "We're ASA on a special mission. You'll have to talk with Colonel Koster, he assigned us here."

The lisp in my voice hit him like a slap in the face, he became flustered. "I don't care if MacArthur put you here," he stammered "I have to see some identification!"

In a sweet high pitched tone I said, "Now look, Colonel Koster and I are very good friends, VERY GOOD FRIENDS. Do you understand?"

The meaning of what I was implying sickened him. "I don't believe it!" he protested. "And besides he's a happily married man."

"Well, if you don't believe it, you're welcome to ask him when he gets here in a few minutes."

"He's coming here?" Fuchs was revolted by the idea.

"Why not," I said, camping it up. " Last night we used HIS place."

Fuchs finally caught sight of Jessie. "And what the hell is that?"

"He's part of our trio," I flamed.

The lieutenant gagged. "You... you... degenerate," he stammered.

"Come in and we can talk," I said opening the door wider.

Fuchs ruddy face turned beet red, as he grabbed the door handle and yanked it shut on himself. Then he marched off shivering in disgust.

I had to smile, listening to him babble down the companionway, 'degenerates! No wonder we're losing the war.'

"Who was that weirdo," Jessie mumbled. Then he curled into a more comfortable position and fell back to sleep.

At two minutes past midnight, Jessie and I were fast asleep, and twelve thousand four hundred and ten feet below, the golf ball I had hit into the water off the deck, nestled silently in the sand on the ocean bottom.

Over the next few days the seas got rougher. A crewman explained to me that it always gets that way as the ship gets closer to land, the waves bounce off the shoreline. That seemed to support the rumor that we would soon be arriving in Japan, though no one of authority would officially say when. I figured it was for security reasons. Though it was highly unlikely, there always was a chance the North Koreans had a submarine that might attack us.

A quiet settled over the troops on deck. Most of the men sat alone writing letters or thinking. Some anxiously read the newest edition of the ships news-paper, hoping the headline would say we had won the war and would all be going home. But the opposite was true. We were losing badly, and the Koreans did have a submarine.

Jessie gave up looking for Gotman, but kept wear-ing the King Neptune costume to the evening movie. It guaranteed us the best seat on the hatchway. That night they were showing Alfred Hitchcock's *Foreign Correspondent*, starring Joel McCrea and Edmund Gwen as a cockney killer.

It was difficult for me to watch. It didn't seem right for Gwen, the one and only true Santa Claus from *Miracle on 34th Street*, to be shoving an American cor-respondent to his death off a tall building in London. I refused to believe Santa would ever do such a thing.

Later in the compartment I was trying to sleep, but Jessie was keeping me awake with his snoring and occasional bouts of nightmares. I decided to go below and sleep in our old bunk on D-deck. Wear-ing just my robe and boxer shorts I headed down to the smelly troop compartment. I was settled in, just falling asleep, when I needed to go to the bathroom. I went to the nearest enlisted man's 'head', as the sailors called it.

When I arrived, I found all the toilet seats occu-pied and there was a long line waiting to get in. It was unbelievable that a latrine could be so busy at four in the morning.

Suddenly the ship rolled sharply, scattering the guys who were waiting in line. I took advantage of the confusion and rushed for the open toilet, pulling my pants down as I went.

As I sat there, I noticed nobody ever made eye contact with anybody else. It was as if they were saying, 'I'm not really here. You can't see me. I don't need to do this.'

"Hang on. This ones gonna be rough," an experienced sea veteran hollered.

Before I realized what was happening, the ship's bow rose steeply then violently crashed back down into the sea. The sudden up and down movement lifted me three feet above the toilet, then I fell back down, like a rider on a bucking horse.

No sooner had I settled down than the ship rolled left. I hung on to the handles on the side of the toilet. Then it lurched back again to the right. I was horrified to see the entire contents of the fifteen-foot long urinal sloshing down the trough. All at once, a tidal wave of golden liquid engulfed me. I was drenched. It may have been the only time in toilet history a urinal ever pissed back.

I left the drenched robe and shorts in the latrine and headed back to the compartment in utter disgust. As I started up the dark narrow stairwell stark naked, a drunken overweight officer came stumbling his way down towards me. He paused to catch his balance by clutching the railing. As I eased my way by, trying to ignore my own nudity, he confronted me in a drunken slur. "Hey soldier, you're out of uniform."

The boat rocked violently tossing him towards me. The pungent smell of urine dripping on me was so reviling he threw up on me. I found him equally reviling and puked back. Then we both staggered off like two smelly ships passing in the night.

I made it back to the compartment and washed the last reviling hour off my body in the shower. Jessie was still having nightmares, so I took two blankets and headed out on deck hoping to find a quiet place to sleep. I made a bed near a life boat. The stiff fresh breeze lulled me to sleep.

Several hours later I awoke. The ships motor had stopped. We were standing still, dead in the water. I wrapped myself in one of the blankets and went to the railing. I stood there smoking a cigarette, staring into the dense fog, waiting for dawn. When it finally broke, like a magician, mother nature made the morning mist vanish and there stretched before me was *The Land Of The Rising Sun* · JAPAN.

Chapter 3

Arriving at Oji

The USS Black anchored out in the mouth of Tokyo bay, and was still anchored there as it started to get dark. It felt like there was no end in sight to the wait, except for the occasional, pacifying, one-word rumor, 'Soon'.

Jessie and I were leaning on the ship's rail looking around, along with a boatload of other GI's who were equally impatient for the journey to end. The harbor air stuck in my nostrils, it tasted like diesel oil.

"How much longer do you think we'll be," Jessie asked the Sergeant.

The Sergeant shrugged. "No idea, fellow. I sure hope the damn war ain't being run like this."

We did too.

I spent my time looking around the harbor, hoping to catch glimpses of the ghosts of World War II. Earlier, a ship's crewmember pointed at the spot where the Missouri had been anchored during the Japanese surrender ceremony. He said MacArthur had done it out in the water for security reasons. I wondered how the Japanese felt about signing their country away. Did they hate Americans five years after we had won the war?

I could see Japanese stevedores sitting on the roof of a warehouse watching the guys on the troop ships. They seemed friendly, waving at the GI's, who waved right back. They didn't seem to be mad at anybody.

Rolling thunder sounded above as storm clouds gathered over the bay. Lights were coming on all over the harbor. It was starting to rain. I pulled my poncho over my head and watched the drops strike the water. It glistened in the light coming from the docks. I looked out to the west hoping to see Mount Fuji, but it was hidden behind the gathering storm clouds.

"Gentlemen, Good news, we're up next," the ship's Captain announced over the loudspeaker. The old gray puke bucket began to shudder and vibrate as the motors came on. The GI's on deck gave out a loud cheer.

It was shortly after two in the morning when the two tugs came out and escorted us into our dock.

The troops began to disembark. The rain was coming down heavier, making the gang plank slippery.

"Bonato and Naud," a deck officer announced over a loud hailer, "get your stuff to the last truck." We followed the orders and climbed in back. There were already a few GI's aboard who had arrived on other ships.

I knew one of them, a guy named Callahan, from New York. The other guy, Jessie knew from his short trip to Europe. His name was Kulowski and he was a brain, what the agency officers called an egghead. He had just graduated from the ASA's language school at Fort Ord in California.

We headed north as the truck bounced and skidded on the damp roads. Though the back flap of the truck was open it was too dark to see much of anything. About an hour later a wooden sign went past with an arrow pointing to the left, **Oji, 2 Miles**. We turned left onto a cobblestone road and after a couple of miles of a jaw jarring ride, the two and a half-ton army truck passed through an enchanted village lit by twinkling orange lights, it seemed oddly untouched by any war.

Then we came to an abrupt stop before a pair of twenty-foot high medieval iron gates flanked by a high stone wall. Bright search lights flooded the area making it hard to see anything beyond the gates. The lights flashed onto a dozen attractive oriental girls who were circling around our truck.

Two armed guards with carbines stepped out through a narrow slot in the giant wrought-iron gates. Both guys had stone-hard faces and steely eyes. They brusquely ordered the girls away. " Syonara. Ichi macho." The women disappointedly backed off.

One guard took the orders and the ID cards from the driver and checked them against his manifest as the other came around to the back of the truck to look over the occupants.

"I get the feeling we're trying to break into Alcatraz," Callahan quipped.

The guard glared at him.

Nobody laughed.

"Cleared to enter," he called to his buddy at the gate.

One of the wrought-iron gates finally opened and the truck proceeded onto the base, crawling along a road that circled a massive three-story rusty colored stone building that sat on a hill. It resembled a medieval castle complete with eerie lion and odd bird gargoyles. The entire roof was a forest of antennas, some of which reached one hundred feet high. It confirmed to me what I had heard about OJI, it was the most secretive base the American Army operated in the far east, handling all the top secret coded transmissions between president Truman, General MacArthur, and his field commanders in Korea. Only the top floor was lit up with the shades drawn. Men were probably in there working through the night, code-breaking was a twenty four hour a day job.

"Oji," I whispered to myself.

We continued past the building, then finally came to a stop in front of a hundred-foot long, three story high, white industrial type concrete structure with long windows. There were a lot of others just like it.

"Everybody out. Let's go," a Corporal barked. He was standing by at the back of the truck, taking charge. Everybody climbed off hauling their gear with them.

"Alright, listen up. My name's Langdon. Corporal Langdon to you," he said. "While you're here, I'm in charge. And if you screw up, I'll nail your butt, understand?" Reveille will sound in two hours and ten minutes, so sleep fast," he added. The Corporal led us up to a barracks room on the second floor of the building. It was an open factory room filled with fifty cots most of which were already filled with sleeping GI's.

The Corporal lowered his voice to a strong whisper. "All right, grab a bunk, hit the sack, and keep it quiet."

We grabbed two bunks near the door. I lay awake, half-expecting Jessie to have one of his nightmares. Instead, he went to sleep quietly. Being off the boat seemed to help.

'Next stop, Korea' I thought. Now that we were back on terra firma, I realized I was just as anxious as Jessie about going to war.

Reveille blasted out over the base loudspeakers. Sleeping bodies stirred as the grating sounds of the tinny bugle bounced around the barrack walls. Bitching and grumbling voices could be heard all over the room.

I lay on my bunk, eyes open, wishing the blaring noise would go away.

"Everybody UP! Let's go! Move," Corporal Langdon demanded, snapping on the room lights. His weak, squeaky voice undermined any authority he might have.

"Hey. We only got two hours sleep," Callahan groaned.

"I said UP. And NOW!" Langdon barked. He walked along the line, shaking the cots of the guys who hadn't yet moved.

"Aww, come on, we got in late," a deep angry voice protested.

"Hey, please don't, Corporal," a sleepy voice pleaded. But Langdon kept shaking the cot until the sleepy GI bounced out onto the floor.

Jessie still lay motionless beneath his army blanket. He looked like a giant Baby Ruth.

The Corporal scowled at his motionless body. "Wake him up," he demanded.

I was already sitting up. "Hey, Jess, get up," I called over, nudging Jessie's bed with my foot.

Jessie grunted, and pulled more of the blanket up, compressing himself into a smaller Baby Ruth. It seemed like an obvious act of defiance, which further angered the Corporal.

"Hey, get your butt UP," the Corporal demanded, picking up Jessie's bed.

Jessie rolled out onto the floor, forcibly unwound from his blanket wrapping. Then he stood up rubbing his eyes like a child, but because of his size, to the Corporal he was more like a grumbling bear.

"Ahh. Ahh," the Corporal stuttered. "Just hurry up or you'll miss your breakfast," he said and walked away.

The guys all chuckled at the way Jessie had of evoking a scared response without even trying.

The bugle call for assembly blared out over the base loudspeakers.

The members of ASA Oji's Headquarters Company began emerging from the buildings bordering the Parade Ground. It was obvious to me, which guys were company personnel, and which were the ones called "eggheads." Without their work, there would be no Army Security Agency.

The basic operating personnel, the clerks, cooks, mechanics, drivers, supply people, etc, etc, rushed out to join the morning formation. They were aware, if they didn't hustle, they would be shipped to the front lines in Korea. The eggheads, on the other hand, emerged at a leisurely pace, like honored guests at a South Hampton lawn party. There were two hundred fifty of them, at least.

The orderly room door in the building, with the ASA headquarters company sign above it, opened. Out walked a Captain. To me, he had the swagger and warmth of Jimmy Stewart.

"Headquarters Company, ATTEN-HUT!" a Sergeant barked. "All troops present or accounted for, Captain Mulvey, Sir."

"Alright, Sergeant, put the men at-ease," Mulvey said after returning the salute.

The Sergeant executed another crisp about-face and barked, "Company, AT- EASE." The formation relaxed.

"MEN," Captain Mulvey began, "as you all probably know, I'll be leaving Oji in a few weeks." He paused a moment to choke back his emotions. "In the time I've been here, I've gotten to know a lot of you personally. To be honest, when I first took over, you weren't exactly what I expected. And maybe I wasn't what you expected. But somehow we found a way to work together. Along the way we've had problems, which, I'm glad to say, we managed to work out." He paused again, then went on, "at least, most of the time."

The code-breakers snickered. Not at Mulvey, but with him. Every man in the formation, especially the eggheads, knew the risks Mulvey had taken for them and how far he had stuck his neck out.

"I can't say, I know how hard it is to do what you do, because I can't do it," Mulvey quipped.

The men laughed loud and hard, enjoying the joke.

"But, I can share the pride you must feel for what you have accomplished. I am proud to have known each of you and to have been your commander. May God bless you all. And if you're ever in Seattle, please come by and see me."

"Atten-hut," the Sergeant barked. The men crisply returned Captain Mulvey's salute and he walked off.

"TO," the Sergeant barked, ordering the troops to complete their salute.

The arms came down smartly.

"Company, At-EASE," he said.

The group relaxed.

"Most of you will be going on to units in Korea," Corporal Langdon barked out. "Your travel orders will be posted later and you'll be shipping out Monday morning at 0800 hours. If you want a day pass, contact Corporal Dehler, the company clerk.

After morning chow, Jessie, Callahan and I went by the company bulletin board, just outside the mess hall door, to check if ours orders had been posted. There they were. Our group was scheduled to leave from Haneda Air Base, Monday morning at zero-eight-hundred hours. Destination: Pusan, Korea.

"Where is Pusan anyway?" Jessie asked.

"On the Southeastern coast of the Korean Peninsula," I said. I had seen a map in the ships newspaper.

"I bet by the time we get there, it'll belong to the gooks. It'll just make it easier for us to surrender," Callahan quipped with his cynical New York sense of humor.

The fact was, the North Koreans were driving the UN's forces off the Peninsula and the casualties were heavy.

Jessie was lower than whale shit. He was convinced, now more than ever, that his premonition about dying in Korea was about to come true. Nothing I said seemed to help. It was hard to believe a guy who had the physical strength of a grizzly bear could be so emotionally fragile. The more I thought about it, the more I wondered if all the worrying I had been doing about Jessie wasn't what was keeping me from falling apart.

Callahan convinced Jessie to go downtown for some sightseeing. All of the forty-five casuals, the

GIs in transit to Korea not attached to the base, had been given day passes.

I was glad to let them go without me. 'Let Jessie cry on Callahan's shoulder for a while,' I thought. I took my clubs and I went up to the parade ground to practice hitting some golf balls. Golf always seemed to take my mind off my worries. But I couldn't prac-tice, there was a base personnel softball gaming going on so I just sat in the stands watching them play.

Late that afternoon I lay on my bunk, in an empty barracks, with paper and pen poised to write my mom a letter. I wasn't sure when I would get another chance. I wanted to write, 'Dear Mom, tomorrow we're going to Korea and I'm scared,' but I couldn't. The one thing she didn't need was more to worry about. I ended up lying there, staring into space try-ing to think of what to write, but nothing came. I was too tired from worrying about everything, to think about anything and fell asleep.

"Wake up! Bill wake up!" an anxious voice shouted at me as I was being shaken out of a deep sleep.

"Wha-a-a t's wrong?" I slurred in my barely con-scious state.

"Jessie's got a gun, he's gonna shoot himself!" Callahan hollered as he pulled me up to a sitting position.

"Keep it down," a guy bitched from across the darkened room filled with sleeping snoring GI's.

"Jessie's flipped out. You gotta help him," Calla-han begged.

"Where is he?" I said, struggling to wake up.

"He's at the Flaming Pisspot, a whorehouse in Oji," Callahan said as he dragged me to my feet. "On the way back from downtown, Jessie just kept saying a condemned man deserved a last pleasure. Come on, hurry, he could be dead by now."

I stumbled down the stairs right behind Callahan, tucking in my shirt, trying to listen to his explanation of what happened. We exited the building and hurried toward the main gate.

The chilly night air suddenly knocked me into full consciousness. Something didn't add up. "Where'd Jessie get a gun?" I asked, cutting his story off.

"It belongs to the girl he's with. She uses it for protection," Callahan said. "He just went WACKO. All of a sudden I heard him yelling he's gonna shoot himself, so he doesn't have to go to fight in Korea. I tried to talk him out of it, but he wouldn't listen." Callahan was nearly in tears reliving the event.

We arrived at the main gate. Two guards were on post. One burly red headed soldier, built like a tank, stood in front of the wrought-iron gates holding his carbine- at-the-ready. The other came out of the booth and abruptly stepped in front of us, blocking our path.

"Lemme see your passes, guys," he demanded.

Callahan handed his over as I frantically searched my pockets for mine, then realized I never went to pick it up.

The Sergeant checked Callahan's pass then handed it back.

"Sorry Sergeant, I can't find mine. We're just going down the street, my buddy's in trouble," I anxiously tried to explain.

"No pass, no go," the guard said coldly.

From the expression on his face I could see it was pointless to plead, he wasn't going to change his mind.

Callahan came to the rescue. "I saw you put it in your back pocket Bill," he said as he reached behind me. "Here it is," he said, producing a crumpled paper pass.

I took it from Callahan and held it out to show the guard.

"Alright. You're clear to go," he said with a smirk on his face, overlooking the obvious switch. Then with a stony glare he turned to Callahan. "But YOU gotta stay on base."

"You'd better hurry Bill! The Pisspot is down the street to the left," Callahan urged me, gesturing with his head for me to go on. "Maybe Jessie will listen to you."

As I went out through the gate the guard cautioned me, "You gotta be back by midnight, you only got an hour, soldier.

"Don't worry. I'll be back," I called out as I turned left and hurried down Oji's main street. All of the quaint shops of bamboo and cedar architecture were closed. Everything was dark, except for the glow of a few orange globe paper lights hanging in the windows. The smell of burning charcoal was even thicker in the cold night air then when we first arrived.

I could see a large two-story wood and plaster structure a block ahead. On the roof of the building was a giant colorful fluorescent sign shaped, like an old fashioned cooking pot, out of which three curved neon steam lines rose. Callahan was right, the Flaming Pisspot was hard to miss.

Standing in the street out front, were a couple of half dressed GI's consoling their frightened Joy-Girls, clad in thin oriental night robes. Other scared girls stood together next to a U.S. military jeep marked MP.

As I got closer to the building, I heard a gun shot go off somewhere inside. "Jesus!" I called out. I started to run flat out towards the front door. I had to get to Jessie before he hurt himself or somebody else. Then a morbid thought crossed my mind, 'if he hadn't already killed himself.'

The wooden door to the Flaming Pisspot was half open. I peered in cautiously. On the floor ahead of me was a straw matted reception area with large colorful patterned pillows scattered all around. Beyond it was a hallway leading to the back of the building. It was lined by a maze of rice paper paneled rooms.

The sound of whimpering girls emanated from a dark alcove beyond the reception area. I could see a weathered old Japanese woman and four attractive frightened oriental girls huddled together against the back wall.

To my right two MP's huddled for cover against an open sided staircase leading up to a second floor balcony. Upstairs was another maze of rice paper paneled rooms. There was a dim glow from the room directly at the top of the steps. The MP's guns were drawn as they watched the shimmering candlelit silhouettes of two people behind the translucent rice paper panel.

"More Sake Mamasan!" a garbled angry voice called out from the room.

I recognized Jessie's voice.

"No Sake GI!" the old woman's craggy voice answered back.

Bang! Bang! Shots rang out from above. The two MP's ducked down as chips of the wood beam above, floated down.

The young oriental girls whimpered in the dark and huddled closer to the Mamasan, who grumbled angrily, she was used to dealing with drunken GIs.

The Sergeant turned to the Corporal and whispered, "See if you can find a way to get behind him upstairs."

The Corporal crossed the reception area, staying low, then vanished down the hallway leading to the back of the building.

The Sergeant pulled himself onto the staircase and started to crawl up.

I crouched low, and in a Groucho Marx stoop, made my way to the base of the steps.

The Sergeant came to a stop just below the landing.

He called into the room. "Soldier this is Sergeant Hilgrim of the Military Police. Put your weapon down and come out."

"I don't need any MP's. Go away!" Jessie called out.

Bang! A shot rang out.

We both ducked, as the bullet tore through the rice paper and hit the wall to the side of us.

I dragged myself up to a place beside the Sergeant. Through a narrow slit in the wall panel, I could see Jessie. He was sitting on the floor in his shorts, holding a forty five. A pretty young oriental girl lay beside him. She was naked and crying, her face in her hands, immobilized with fear.

"Don't hurt him Sergeant," I begged. "He's my friend. His name is Jessie. "

"Get outta here Buddy," the Sergeant cautioned me.

"I'll get him out," I insisted. "He'll listen to me," I begged.

"If you don't he's dead meat," the Sergeant said to me. It was obvious he was in no rush to charge a drunk with a forty five. Maybe because he was older, he was more inclined to reasoning than action. "Go ahead try," he said.

"Jessie it's me, Bill, "I called out. " Let me in and we'll talk."

"I'm not going to fight in Korea, Bill. No gook's gonna kill me," Jessie yelled back.

I could see Jessie press the muzzle of the gun against his knee. We had both heard stories, coming over on the ship, about guys shooting their kneecaps off to avoid combat.

"Go away, Bill," Jessie said. He looked as if he was gathering the courage to pull the trigger.

The Sergeant was out of patience. "You had your chance, buddy. Now move away before you get hurt," he ordered. He could see his Corporal was positioned against the rice paper wall just behind Jessie. The Corporal signaled he was ready.

The Sergeant nodded back, then raised up his gun and took aim through the slit between the panels, directly at Jessie. "Last chance, buddy, come on out," he called.

I was out of time. It all seemed insane. Jessie was going to get himself killed in Japan, to avoid getting killed in Korea.

I heard Jessie cock the trigger of his gun. I had to DO something. So I leaped over the Sergeant's body on the landing, and dove straight at the rice paper wall, hurling my body at it like a wrecking ball. I shattered the panel and landed hard, along with a heap of debris, at Jessie's feet.

In a reflex response, Jessie swung the Forty-five around, and aimed it at my face.

"DON'T SHOOT," I bellowed, as I stared into the barrel of the gun.

The Asian girl gasped in horror, expecting to see my head blown off.

"IT'S ME, Bill," I screamed.

Jessie was so drunk; it took him a moment to recognize me.

"What are you doing, Bill?" he asked quizzically in a drunken slur.

"Put the gun down, Jess. Please," I pleaded gently.

Jessie shook his head trying to clear out the effects of the sake. "I don't know, Bill," he said. Now he wasn't sure what to do. "I'm not going to Korea, Bill. I'll die there, I know it."

"No you won't. You won't die there, I promise," I said, trying to reassure him.

"I never lied to you. Have I, Jess?" I added.

Tears began to well up in Jessie's eyes.

The gun was still aimed at my face.

"Promise on your father's life, Bill?" Jessie said, wiping the tears off his cheeks with the back of his hand. He knew how much my father meant to me.

"I promise. On my father's life," I said firmly.

The terrified girl spotted the Corporal MP easing himself into the room, through a narrow opening in the wall behind Jessie, with his gun aimed at Jessie's head. She managed to stifle her gasp, by sinking her head in a pillow.

I spotted him out of the corner of my eye.

"Please, Jess. Put the gun down," I said, knowing if either one of us made a wrong move now, we would both be shot dead.

After a long tense moment, Jessie slowly lowered the gun to the floor.

"Now, shove it to me, Jess," I asked politely.

Jessie started haltingly to move his hand, then with a decisive shove, he pushed the gun towards me.

I grabbed it and flung it out through the rice paper panel. It bounced against the balcony steps, then disappeared into the darkness below.

The Corporal MP shoved his gun up to Jessie's head. "Hold it right there."

Jessie's chin dropped to his chest. The ordeal was over. He was emotionally spent.

The girl was sprawled across the floor, sobbing uncontrollably.

"Okay, we got 'em," the Corporal called out confidently to the other MP.

The second MP entered the room through the hole in the wall, stumbling over the debris, aiming his gun at Jessie and then at me. Once he was convinced the situation was under control, he re-holstered his weapon.

"Get dressed. Move," the Sergeant barked, tossing Jessie's clothes at him.

They covered Jessie's head like an umbrella. But he didn't move. He was lost in a mind-numbing fog somewhere in sake land.

The Sergeant MP kicked Jessie to evoke some response.

"Hey. You don't have to do that to him. He already gave up!" I protested.

"Get outta here or we'll take you in too," the nasty Sergeant said.

"Look, can't you just let him go? He didn't hurt anybody," I begged.

The MP just ignored my plea. "Get up," he said, nudging Jessie's shoulder hard with his Billy club.

"Cut that out," I yelled insistently.

"Shove off, buddy," the Corporal warned me, but I didn't budge.

The Sergeant MP's nerves were strained from the whole ordeal. "Alright, cuff them both," he said.

As the Corporal MP grabbed my arms to put the handcuffs on me, Jessie went berserk. "Hey, don't," he said, yanking the Corporal's hands away. "He's my friend," he added.

The Corporal MP swung his Billy club at Jessie, but Jessie caught it in mid- swing, yanking it from the Corporals hand. Both MP's jumped on Jessie determined to subdue him, but he just tossed them around like rag dolls. The embattled bodies looked like a pile of brown scrambled eggs. Neither MP could fire his gun, for fear of hitting the other.

The scared naked girl crawled out of the room.

I dove to the floor and watched the MP's being tossed around.

Then two more MP's arrived.

It took all four men to wrangle Jessie to the floor and cuff him.

I followed behind as they carried his half-dressed semi-conscious body down the stairs and dumped him into one of the MP jeeps and drove away.

I stood in the street feeling mixed emotions. On the one hand Jessie would be in a jail, but at least he was alive and in one piece.

I checked my watch. It was one minute before midnight. I was three hundred yards from being AWOL.

Chapter 4

Off To Korea

Early the next day, all the casuals, dressed in fatigues
and field jackets, were gathered in loose formation
on the headquarters company compound. They were
waiting for a truck to take them to Haneda air base
for the flight to Korea.

The morning air was cold and the truck was long
overdue.

Cold and snow were high on my list of Gods ten
worst ideas, along with dentists and death. I fanta-
sized that the PX in Korea would have an electric
blanket, with a hundred mile long extension cord,
that I could use in whatever foxhole I wound up in. I
took a wedge out of my golf bag and started to chip
some pebbles to keep my circulation up.

Callahan was flapping his arms, hopping from
foot to foot trying to stay warm. "I wonder where Jessie is?" he said.

I wondered too. I had spent most of the night
tossing and turning, thinking about it.

Corporal Langdon emerged from the headquarters company office. He had gone to find out where
the truck was.

"What'd they tell you about Jessie?" I asked.

"Nothing," Langdon answered, blowing me off.
"They're not saying anything."

A GI sitting on a pile of duffel bags, reading a greasy wrinkled Jap girlie magazine, called out, "Hey Langdon. I'm hungry!

"Why don't you eat your girlie magazine," a wise ass voice answered.

The group exploded with dirty laughter.

"Knock it off," Langdon barked.

He was interrupted by the arriving deuce-and-a-half truck making its way along the compound road. The casuals burst into applause, as the truck skidded across the gravel to a stop.

The driver, a twenty-year-old burly blonde-haired PFC, jumped out of the cab and rushed to the back of the truck. He unlatched the tailgate, letting it slam down hard. "All aboard the Pusan express," he announced. "Load 'em up Corporal Langdon. I'm going to get some Java."

Everyone grabbed their stuff and pressed in at the rear of the truck, readying to climb aboard.

I was content to wait and let everybody else get on first. I hated lines. To me they were demeaning, so I sat on my golf bag waiting. I was watching the driver walk across the compound towards the mess hall door. As he went in, I was stunned to see who came out, First Sergeant Baker. Following right behind him was a corporal who resembled the actor Glen Ford. They stopped to talk by the company bulletin board.

I still couldn't believe my eyes. The last time I had seen Baker was at Fort Devins, he was chasing me around in the snow trying to shoot me with his forty five.

I had been at Fort Devins in Massachusetts for code breaking basic training, or lack of it in my case. The day after I arrived, by a quirk of fate, I met Colonel Arrowsmith at the base golf course. He was the head of the ASA, a dashing forty-year-old, who loved the game of golf as much as I did. He became my mentor and I became his ace-in-the-hole golf partner for the army golf matches held twice a week. My days were taken up practicing golf with the Colonel or playing in matches held at bases up and down the eastern seaboard.

First Sergeant Baker, a shit-kicker from Tennessee who grew up in a shack with dirt floors, tried to put me on regular army duties, anything resembling work. But each time he did, at the last moment, Colonel Arrowsmith took me off the detail. Baker hated my privileged position with the Colonel. He saw me as a rich kid from New York who did nothing in the army but eat, sleep and play golf. He was right about everything, but being rich.

Baker was a crook. Some of the GI's told me about his kick back laundry scam. I mentioned it to the Colonel who read Baker the riot act, threatening to court martial him if he didn't stop. After that Baker's hatred of me grew fiercer.

With the colonel as my protector I had the upper hand, until without warning, Arrowsmith was shipped to the Far-East. Overnight my life went from heaven to hell. Baker put me on every shit duty list in the army; ditch digging, KP, latrine cleaning, laundry pickup, then finally company furnace fireman on the night shifts.

A brainy near genius private, Carlyle Sohn, was put on the detail with me. He was so bright he had memorized the King James Bible and the Uniform Military Code of Justice, just out of boredom. He could take apart a Volkswagen and put it back together, blind folded. He had a 10,000 word vocabulary and an IQ that was off the charts, the only problem was, he was a wino. The army didn't know what to do with him.

We were a good match. We both hated manual labor of any kind. Together, we designed a minimalist work approach. Rather than taking the time to shovel out the debris left in the furnaces three times a night, as we were suppose to, we just sprinkled a thin layer of coal over the ashes in the eighteen buildings once a night. If anyone looked inside, it created an illusion that the furnace was ready to become a raging inferno the moment the blowers came on. We then disconnected all the fuses each night, so the blowers couldn't click on. We figured the sleeping GIs couldn't complain about the lack of heat.

It was all working great until one fateful night. Sohn and I were tromping through the snow, to keep warm I was wearing two extra pairs of long johns and Sohn was sipping from his wine bottle. We went from barracks to barracks making it look as if we were carefully checking the furnaces. There was no heat in the buildings, it was warmer out in the snow. Sohn opened the furnace room door to barracks thirteen and snapped on the light switch.

KABOOM!!

The men of the ASA training Battalion, at Fort Devins Massachusetts, were rocked out of their sleep by a horrendous explosion. The new coal warmed by the accumulated ashes had produced explosive fumes. The spark from the light switch ignited them, blowing up the furnace. Sohn and I were thrown forty feet into a snow bank.

First Sergeant Baker came out of the orderly room half drunk, bellowing, "JUMPIN' JESUS, what the hell is going on?" He staggered through the snow staring at the giant black hole engulfed in black smoke that was barrack thirteen.

Then he spotted me sprawled out amidst the debris.

"You." Cough. Cough. "What the hell did you do Naud?" he demanded in between coughing on the dense sooty smoke. "I'm gonna kill you, ya city son-a bitch."

Then it became like a zany scene from the Keystone Cops, Baker was chasing me around the compound, firing shots left and right as I crawled behind anything I could find. The men who came out to see what was happening, quickly retreated into their barracks, for safety from the bullets.

When Baker finally had me in his sights, at point blank range, he slipped on the ice, fell back onto the frozen payment and was knocked unconscious. An ambulance took him away to the base hospital. The last thing I heard, he was being held for observation.

Now, as I watched him standing there, I couldn't resist another chance to harass him. I took my wedge and quickly lined up several pebbles the size of golf balls. I adjusted my stance and took three quick swings, lofting the stone missiles towards a large industrial size window on the second floor above where Baker was standing. CRASSH........ CRASH. .... CRASSSH. They shattered the glass in the window. The pieces tumbled down the white stone wall, breaking into smaller pieces that showered onto Baker.

I didn't wait for his reaction. I grabbed my clubs and duffel bag and jumped onto the back of the truck, squeezing between the cramped GI's along the side, just as Baker stormed up.

He was livid. "What the hell's going on here, Corporal," he demanded.

Langdon was clueless, too busy loading the truck to notice what had happened. Baker was still brushing the glass from his hair and uniform as Langdon closed the back panel and secured it with a chain. Langdon hurried to the cab to join the driver, who was juggling a cup of coffee while revving up the engine, obviously ready to go.

"Ahh!" Baker yelled as a sliver cut and bloodied his finger. He marched to the back of the truck and stared in like a fire breathing dragon. "Which one of you wise-asses threw those stones," he barked.

Then he spotted me, sitting there with my golf clubs between my legs, and knew immediately who had shattered the window.

The driver gunned the engine and the truck started to move.

"You' outta come along with us to Korea Sergeant. I'll give you a golf lesson," I quipped, smiling like a Cheshire cat, as the truck pulled away.

Baker just stood there shaking his head. "Naud, those clubs won't do you much good when the gooks start lobbing grenades at you," he yelled.

My moment of fun was extinguished, I was afraid he might be right.

The truck slid to a sharp stop at the main gate, causing the scalding coffee the driver was juggling to splash onto Corporal Langdon's lap.

"Ahh!" Langdon screeched as he leapt from the truck's cab, frantically patting and shaking his pants, trying to cool the burning in his crotch.

The gate guard grabbed the clipboard from him, ignoring his antics. He proceeded to stand at the back of the truck, checking the bodies on board against the names on the travel orders.

"Adams, James?" the guard called out.

"HERE," Adams answered.

"Aldermen?"

"YOOOOOO," rang out.

"Bachelly?"

"Present," someone answered.

The phone in the guard booth rang. Corporal Damion stuck his head out of the guard booth and called out, "Is there a Private Naud on board?"

"Here," I answered.

Damion ducked back in. "Yes, Sir!" he crisply said into the phone, and hung up. He came marching out of the booth calling, "Naud, take your gear and get off. They want you up on the hill."

I tossed my duffel bag off the truck and jumped down. Callahan handed me my golf clubs. "It's probably about Jessie," Callahan whispered grimly.

I slung my duffel bag over one shoulder and my golf clubs over the other, and started off up the hill. I hadn't gone fifty feet when I heard the truck leaving. I turned around to wave to Callahan, but the truck was gone. I kept walking towards the austere stone building. I was sure I was being called in to be reprimanded for what happened with Jessie at the Flaming Pisspot.

'But so what?' I thought. 'What could they do to me, now? Send me off to fight in Korea.'

At the front of the building were two oversized carved wooden doors, bound to the walls by thick black iron strap hinges, the kind fit for the entrance of a medieval castle. As I stood there trying to find a knocker or buzzer, one of the doors creaked open. A sharp looking security guard, with a white helmet, stepped out to block my way. He was in full military dress, wearing a white silk ascot, clean white gloves, fatigues that were neatly bloused and tucked into glistening black boots. And he wore a forty five on his hip.

"What's your name soldier?" he interrogated.

"Naud," I answered.

"OK," he responded, backing up and pushing open the door.

As I started in, the other guard was annoyed at being forced to open the left door to allow my golf clubs to fit through.

"Up that staircase to the left, all the way to the end," he ordered shaking his head.

I headed up the winding marble staircase adjusting the bags on my shoulders. The clinking rattling of my golf clubs reverberated loudly through the darkened halls.

I reached the top and another guard, in full dress, motioned with his gun for me to proceed down the eerie hallway. I continued on. Staring down at me from the vaulted ceiling above were more gold plaster dragons. Some were chipped and damaged, probably from bombings during WWII.

I passed another guard, with gun at the ready, blocking a small staircase. His demeanor signaled that it must have led to some secret area.

Corporal Plummer, whose head was throbbing from a terrific hangover, was at his oversized desk, just outside the Colonel's office, typing as fast as he could. He wished the aspirin he had taken would work faster.

The clinking clanking sounds of my clubs, echoing through the building, like Marley's ghost from Dickens *Christmas Carol*, only made his headache worse He was frantically trying to finish the daily war report so he just ignored the noise.

He stopped to proofread the pages, looking for any typos. The Colonel hated typos.

```
TOP SECRET/ASA   OJI Decrypted Communi-
que page 1 of 2
Date: 25 July 1950
To:MACARTHUR
From: JOINT CHIEFS OF STAFF
Subject: TACTICAL SUMMARY
```

President Truman supports your plan
to land a large armed force behind
enemy lines at the Coastal City of
Inchon even though he agrees with us
that it will be risky.

President also requests you apologize for statement to the press that
became the headline on the front page
of the Washington Post.
"The South Koreans can't fight thir
way out of a paper bag."

Signed
JOINT CHIEFS

TOP SECRET/ASA   OJI Decrypted Communi-
que page 2 of 2
Date: 25 July 1950
To: JOINT CHIEFS OF STAFF
From: MACARTHUR
Subject: TACTICAL SUMMARY

Have cut 7th devision to reinforce
25th and 1st Cavalry.

Now using 3.5 rocket launches
against T34 tanks.Proving effective.

Desperately need more troops.Enemy
has crossed Kum River surrounding
Taejon.Heavy casualties.We are getting our butts kicked pure and simple.

General Walker retreating to line
around Pusan Harbor in eveny we must
evacuate Korea.

Decoded Enemy transmissions indicate no knowledge of Incheon Plan.

Signed
MAC

As Plummer reread the communiqué, he proudly reminded himself it was his buddies on the third floor who had deciphered the enemies codes and revealed the weaknesses in the North's supply lines, allowing MacArthur to put his Incheon plan together. He dropped his head and resumed his typing.

I stood in front of his desk juggling my gear. "I'm Private Naud."

He just ignored me and kept typing.

"Bang!" I let my duffel bag drop to the floor like a bag of wet wash, right in front of his desk, tired of feeling like an unwanted orphan.

"How's your back?" I asked.

Plummer suddenly stopped his work and looked up at me quizzically.

"The softball game," I explained. "You slammed into the backstop, remember?" The day before Plummer had been playing catcher, at the base softball game, trying to tag out a runner who deliberately slammed him into the backstop.

"Oh, I'm a little bruised, but OK," he said, his demeanor becoming a bit more friendly.

"I'll tell the Colonel you're here, Naud," he said rising, then vanishing through the giant oak doors into the Colonel's office.

Plummer quickly returned. "You can go in now," he said.

I entered the Colonel's office. The place was the size a tennis court, with an ornately decorated ceiling, fifteen feet high. Three of the four walls were lined with empty oak library shelves. The fourth wall was all windows, overlooking the base's main gate and the village of Oji. I had been told these rooms were once used as offices for the high level echelons of the Emporer's Imperial officials of the ammunition factory, which was housed in the other buildings on the compound.

Colonel Macmillan sat at his large oak desk, reading some papers clipped in a manila folder. I stopped in front of the desk and came to attention, snapping a salute. "Private Naud reporting, Sir."

The Colonel didn't look up. He went on reading, just managing an indifferent three fingered salute in return.

'This guy's a prick,' I thought. I held the salute and looked around. Two, eight by ten framed photos sat on the bookshelf behind the Colonel's desk. The girl in one photo looked like Betty Grable, blonde, in her twenties, wearing a one-piece white-latex bathing suit. The other photo was of a very attractive dark-haired lady, about the same age, in a smartly tailored woman's suit. It was obvious the Colonel liked beautiful women.

Finally, he looked up. "At-ease," he said.

I stood at-ease.

The Colonel rose from his desk and walked to the window. I noticed he had a forty-five strapped to his hip. Plummer had a forty five strapped to his hip. Hell everyone I met in the building had a forty five strapped to them.

"Naud," the Colonel said, looking out the window. "That was a dangerous stunt you pulled last night at the Pisspot. You could have gotten yourself killed."

The Colonel wasn't telling me anything I didn't know.

"Why'd you stick your neck out?" he inquired.

"Jessie's the only real friend I've got, Sir," I answered.

The Colonel turned to look at me, to see if I meant what I had said. Yes, he believed me. "Well, according to the Mamasan at the Flaming Pisspot, your buddy did ten thousand dollars worth of damage."

I scoffed. "The whole building isn't worth ten thousand dollars, Sir."

"You're probably right Naud," the Colonel said, crossing back to the front of the desk.

"Sir? May I ask where Private Bonato is now?" I asked.

"NO," the Colonel responded militantly. He placed his hand on the manila folder on his desk. "I've been looking over your record Naud. You've been in the army 14 months and 12 days. You've spent a lot of that time in the hospital."

"I didn't get bronchitis on purpose Sir," I answered defensively.

"According to a nurse you used a Zippo lighter to raise the temperature of your thermometer, keeping you there long enough to avoid basic training. When you reached Fort Devins you spent your time playing golf, except for the one day a week when you delivered the official DOD lecture on how to survive an atomic bomb attack by hiding under your desk and sticking your head up your ass. I'll bet your ass joke got a big laugh." He glared at me.

"Not as big as hiding under the desk, Sir," I quipped.

"You went from golf, to a brief stint as a fireman where you blew up a barracks. And just before coming here, you destroyed a Morse Code training center by rewiring the electronics. He shook his head in disgust. "SOME RECORD."

"It's not easy listening to diddetda diddet for eight hours a day, Sir." 'Being on permanent golf duty at Fort Devon was Colonel Arrowsmith's idea, not mine,' I thought with irritation. I started to get angry. 'Get off my back,' I almost said out loud.

"Sir? May I ask why I'm here?" I said in a civil tone.

"NO," the Colonel said, abruptly.

I remembered what my genius code-breaking buddy, Private Sohn told me. Under military law if you were summoned before a superior, he was required to tell you why.

"Sir. I believe I have a RIGHT ..."

"You'll know what I want to tell you. Understand?" the Colonel snapped.

I was mad. If this guy was going to shit on me, I had a right to know why. "Sir, under military law, you're required to inform me WHY I was brought here."

The next thing I saw was the Colonel's Forty-five leaving its holster. "If you know something about Military law, soldier, you know there's a fine line between insubordination and mutiny. And you're right on that line, mister."

Then I felt the tip of the gun barrel press against my temple. I froze in fear as I heard the safety catch coming off.

"The penalty in a combat zone is summary execution," the Colonel warned.

'This guy is nuts, ' I thought. 'He's gonna kill me.' I started to sweat like a pig.

"Now you're gonna stand there, at attention, with your mouth shut, and listen. Understand, Private?" the Colonel said in a cold steely tone.

I was too afraid to answer, for fear any movement would nudge the gun and cause it to fire. I kept my eyes focused out the window

"Does winning this war hold any interest for you, Naud? "

He took my silence as defiance.

"ANSWER ME," the Colonel demanded, pressing the muzzle harder into my temple to evoke a response.

"Ah... Yes, Sir. Ah... No, Sir," I stammered out. My sweat was trickling around the barrel of the gun.

"Naud, we're going to walk over to those windows and I want you to tell me what you see."

I walked obediently to one of the large windows. I was more interested in finding a way to escape, than with what I could see outside. But I quickly realized it was hopeless. Even if I managed to crash through the six foot heavy glass windows, the pieces would probably slash me to ribbons, and if I didn't bleed to death, the forty-foot fall to the concrete steps below would break my neck. 'Not a very good escape plan,' I thought. I was sure I was about to die and that ugly village out there would be the last thing I would ever see.

"What do you see?" the Colonel demanded.

I rattled off, "Sir, I see an MP gate, a stone wall, a couple of guards, five girls ..."

"Do any of those girls appeal to you, Naud?" the Colonel asked.

"Yes, Sir," I murmured.

"It's virtually impossible for a man to resist a naked woman especially when she beautiful. At military school I studied every tactical war plan, but you know what I've found? Hell, son, ten beautiful women could probably conquer the world."

"I wouldn't know sir," I said. "I haven't had that much experience," I babbled.

A tense moment later I heard another click.

From the corner of my eye, I saw the Colonel return the Forty-Five's hammer to the safe position and re-holster it.

I was still frozen with fear. . "If we don't stop 'em, they're going to bury us. The trouble is, they have an unlimited supply," the Colonel said.

"Yes, Sir," I said, pandering. I had no idea what the Colonel was talking about.

He picked up a stack of photos from his desk and shoved them in my face.

"Take a look."

The grisly pictures made me sick. They clearly showed a young GI had been horribly tortured before being killed. Nestled next to his shoulder, lying in the mud, was an oriental girl's head that had been hacked off.

"Some kids found him in a drainage ditch near Haneda," the Colonel said as he sat at his desk. "He was one of my best codebreakers, Corporal Hauld-ing." He took a deep breath to suppress the fury he was feeling. As a handsome well-built forty-year-old career soldier from Atlanta, Georgia, he looked more like a tennis player than the brilliant head of the Army Security Agency-Far-East. The most important question that haunted him now was did Haulding break? He knew if they discovered MacArthur's plans the war would be lost. He also knew some jealous bastard from headquarters was certain to dump the failure on his back. Maybe it was a deeply selfish thought in the midst of war but it would mean the end of his own brilliant career.

"They're horrible," I said as I handed the pictures back.

"That girl was one of the joy girls from outside the gate. Some of them are commie spies. The word was she wanted to defect and marry Haulding, so they killed her too. The Commies know something big is coming, so they've planted their best Joy-girls outside the ASA base. They're luring the code-break-ers into sexual encounters and pumping them for every scrap of information they can glean." Frustra-tion was evident on the Colonels face.

"Look, Naud, despite your record, I'm told you're bright and resourceful and I know you have guts," he started.

I wasn't really paying attention. I couldn't shake the effects of the photos.

"We've got to keep the code-breakers away from those girls, especially for the next few months. I've got a job for you. A very important job. We've got an Em club. I want it jazzed up to keep those men on base," he said.

Suddenly the wacko Colonel seemed grimly sane. I was being offered a job, a reprieve from Korea, but I had no qualifications to run a club.

"Can you do it Naud?" the Colonel demanded.

"No sweat sir," I answered emphatically, thinking a smoky noisy EM Club in Tokyo was better than a cold wet fox-hole in Korea.

"You'd better make it work. If those commies fig-ure out Mac's plans, the whole thing will blow up in his face, and a lot of innocent GIs will die. "

He started scribbling on a pad.

"Now I'll be gone for a few days. When I return I expect a plan of action at the Board of Governors meeting. If I like it, you get the job. If not, you'll be joining you're friend Bonato in Korea. See Corporal Plummer outside. He'll cut your orders. You're dismissed, Naud."

"Yes, Sir," I responded. On my way out I caught a glimpse of a bag of golf clubs standing in the corner. "I see you're a golfer, Sir. Perhaps we can play some time," I said fishing, hoping to make some points.

"I don't play golf, Naud," the Colonel said without looking up. "Those clubs belong to a friend," he added.

Suddenly, I recognized the AAA monogram on the bag. Now I knew why I had been picked for the assignment. Colonel Arrowsmith must have put in a good word for me and had unintentionally left his calling card, like Edmund Gwen's cane in *Miracle on 34th Street*. I reminded myself how golf was much more than a game, it was a way of life. And today, it had saved my life.

Emboldened by my good fortune, I felt compelled to ask one more question. "Sir?"

What is it, Naud?" the Colonel said, flashing impatience.

"The thing you did with the gun???" I said, loosely pointing my finger at my head. "It was a joke. Right, Sir?" I said, treating it all lightly.

The Colonel stopped writing and looked up. His reaction was cold and hard. He was the consummate soldier. "I'm not a jokester, Naud. You're in a combat zone and people die here. Sometimes, from friendly fire."

"Yes, Sir," I said, trying to swallow the lump in my throat. I still wasn't certain if the Colonel was nuts or not. At that point I didn't care. I was just happy to get out of his office alive.

As I closed the big oak doors behind me, I became aware that the front of my fatigues were cold and wet, I had pissed in them.

Chapter 5

The EM Club

I stood by Corporal Plummer's desk, as he typed up the Colonels orders, making me the temporary Custodian of the EM Club. The Colonel quickly signed them and we headed out of the building. Plummer was clutching the orders like they were a weapon.

"Come on, Naud, let's go," Plummer said as he hustled me along towards a complex of three story white washed steel and concrete buildings all organized around an assembly area the size of a football field.

I still couldn't believe what was happening. An hour ago, I had been on my way to Korea. Now I was going to run a club. At least, for a while. The fact I didn't know anything about running a club didn't seem to bother the 'wacko' Colonel. I had to keep stopping to shift the weight of the heavy bags on my shoulders.

"Hurry," Plummer kept saying as he hustled along the pebbled drive past the parked jeeps.

'What's the big rush?' I thought as I awkwardly rattled along trying to catch up.

Plummer led me along various pathways around the complex of buildings, I noticed surprisingly the broken glass by the mess hall was cleaned up, and the smashed window had already been replaced.

'The army is damn efficient when it wants to be,' I thought.

"Hey, Plummer. What does a Custodian do??" I asked

"He's responsible," Plummer answered.

"For what?" I asked.

"Everything. Don't worry, the Japanese manager really runs the Club. His name is Toshiko. You're gonna meet him now," he said, opening the door of the tallest five story building and stepping in.

"If he runs the place, then what do I do?" I hollered after him, but I was talking to a door that had slammed shut in my face.

"Sorry," Plummer said as he pushed the door back open and held it for me to enter. Then he hurried up the stairs, taking them two at a time, as if he was late for something.

"I'll ask you again, what do I do if HE runs the place?" I yelled up the stairwell.

"Ohhh. Your job is to make sure Toshiko does his job," he hollered back down.

I paused for a moment to catch my breath. 'That doesn't make sense,' I thought. How could I be sure the Japanese manager guy was doing his job, if I didn't know what the job was? All I could hear were Plummer's footsteps running up the stairs.

"Does he speak English?" I called up the stairwell.

"Skoshi," Plummer answered, then translated. "A little. But enough to get by. "

I labored up the rest of the stairs staggering under the weight I was carrying, just trying to stay on my feet. I finally made it to the top of the landing on the fourth floor where Plummer was waiting for me.

He pushed through a set of swinging doors. I used my bags to push in backwards.

A Japanese chap was waiting inside. "Kunichiwa, Plummersan," he said.

Other Japanese heads peered cautiously over a low divider wall at us. There was a frosted glass door in the middle of it with a simple sign that read 'office'? I could see shadows leaning against it like someone was trying to listen in.

"Kunichiwa, Toshiko," Plummer said.

Toshiko was a serious looking man in his late twenties, with raven black hair. He looked very tired and his clothes were a rumpled mess. It was obvious the man had been up all night worrying about something.

"Is inspection over yet?" Plummer asked him anxiously.

"Hai," Toshiko answered. "Captain Mulvey is still upstairs at the Club. Any more word on Sergeant Creamersan?" he asked sympathetically.

"Creamer is very sick. He is in a hospital in the States," Plummer answered.

Toshiko had a sorrowful expression on his face.

Plummer explained to me that Creamer was the last custodian. The waiters loved him but he was drunk. The Army flew him out the night before to a detox VA Hospital in the States .

Then Captain Mulvey came marching in through the swinging doors.

I leaned the golf bag in front of my wet pants. To my surprise he was trailed by my nemesis, First Sergeant Baker.

When Baker spotted me, he became instantly annoyed. "What are you doing back here, Naud?" he asked contemptuously.

Plummer's moment had arrived. "Captain Mulvey? This is Private Naud." Here are his orders, Sir," he said smugly, handing Mulvey a sealed envelope.

I saluted and Mulvey returned it.

"At-ease, Naud. Relax," Mulvey said. He began reading as I sat down on my duffel bag.

Plummer looked at Baker with a wry smile, as he tossed a grenade of personal satisfaction in his face. "Sergeant Baker, the Colonel has made Naud here, the new club custodian," he announced.

Baker's fury was instantaneous. His face became beet red. But he said nothing.

It was obvious Plummer hated Baker too. Now it all made sense. He had rushed me over to the EM Club for just one reason: to get there in time to see the surprised look on Baker's face when he discovered, Corporal Dehler- his stooge was not getting the custodian job. He was out, and I was in. Plummer knew Baker would hit the roof when he learned that the Colonel himself had handpicked me as the new custodian.

Toshiko was visibly relieved. It appeared that even a perfect stranger was better to him than Dehler. Happy giggling sounds eminated from the other side of the wall.

"I wish you the best, Naud," Mulvey said. He was unaware of the friction between Plummer and Baker.

"Thank you, Sir," I answered back.

"Well, Sergeant Baker, we'd better keep moving," Mulvey said, as he headed off down through the doors. A fuming Baker started to follow behind. He paused long enough to glare back at Plummer and me as if to say 'the war has just begun.'

Plummer was grinning with satisfaction, watching them go. He told me that Baker was a real crook and had been counting on getting Dehler the job as club custodian. With Dehler running the EM Club, Baker could be an even bigger crook. Especially since Colonel Macmillan thought Baker 'hung the moon' and trusted him, implicitly. Baker kept on the Colonel's good side by continually proving he knew how to get things done and had the connections to do it. His methods might not always be exactly 'by-the-book', they might even be downright illegal at times, but they worked. So when Colonel Macmillan, or some other officer, needed the occasional small 'favor', they were pleased to find there was someone they could count on to get the job done, no questions asked. 'Black marketeer' had became an acknowledged but unspoken part of Baker's job description.

"Tosh? This is Private Naud," Plummer said.

I shook Toshiko's hand.

"Welcome, Custodian Naudsan," Toshiko said grinning from ear to ear. The Japanese men peaking over the wall grinned too.

"Man that was fun. Well, I gotta get back up to the hill," Plummer said. He started to the stairs chuckling in triumph the whole way.

"Hey, Plummer, where do I put my stuff?" I called after him.

"Tosh will show you," Plummer yelled back. He vanished down the staircase singing like a lark.

"Naudsan live in warehouse," Toshiko said. He led me across the office reception area, past elevators, to a pair of large gray metal doors built into a thick concrete wall that divided the fifth floor in half.

The club office area was about the size of a tennis court, the other half was a warehouse.

Toshiko unlocked the gray metal doors. The warehouse was dark.

"Naudsan, wait. I will turn on lights."

When the lights came on, I was stunned to see a mountain of liquor and beer cartons. They filled the huge room, wall to wall, up to the fifteen foot high ceiling.

"This liquor and beer supply for Club, Naudsan," Toshiko explained.

'There's enough alcohol here to get the entire American Army drunk,' I thought. I recognized some of my dad's favorite brands: Canadian Club, VO, Johnny Walker Red, and Pabst beer.

"You drink, Naudsan?" Toshiko asked.

"No," I adamantly answered. I had never taken up drinking. I still had bad memories of the ugly loud arguments my parents had gotten into when my father drank too much. Besides, to me liquor tasted like gasoline and beer looked like urine. I had other reasons, but those two worked as an excuse when people asked me to have a drink with them.

"Where do I put my stuff?" I asked.

"Come," Toshiko said.

I followed him along a five-foot wide pathway running around the mountain of liquor boxes to the place where Sergeant Creamer had lived, an eight by fifteen-foot closed off area in the far corner of the warehouse. The corner of the building itself formed the two exterior walls of Creamer's 'room'. They were almost all windows and were painted black. The two interior walls were standard, four-by-eight sheets of plywood, painted an ugly khaki- color, and set on their sides. The furnishings were all GI issue, a bunk bed, a stand up locker, and a small table and chair. The sheets on the unmade bed were filthy. Dirty clothes were heaped in the bottom of the wall locker, draped over the chair, and on one of the plywood room dividers. There were half-full bottles of stale beer stuffed with soggy cigarette butts on the floor and in the corners. Filthy whiskey glasses were everywhere. The table was piled high with moldy, food-encrusted plates, bowls, and utensils. The stench from the soggy cigarette butts, stale beer, liquor, rotting food, urine, BO, and vomit made me feel like I was back on the ship. Even with a deviated septum, I had to hold my nose.

"Sergeant Creamer get sick here, Naudsan," Toshiko said.

'Anybody would get sick here,' I thought. "Can you get me some mops and stuff, so I can clean this place up?" I said.

"Oh no, waiters clean up, Naudsan," Toshiko said. Then he disappeared back around the pile of boxes.

I heard him holler something, in Japanese, out by the office area. Several young men in white waiter's jackets appeared and looked the situation over. They scurried off, then returned a few minutes later with an arsenal of mops, rags, brushes, buckets of water and soap and began to wash and scrub everything. As they worked they kept glancing at me, smiling, seeking my approval.

I smiled back to signal my satisfaction. I was beginning to realize that, because I was now 'The Boss', people were going to defer to me. I also realized 'bossing' carried responsibilities, an experience

I had never had before. I started to feel a bit uncomfortable.

For now, I didn't want to think about being the boss. I felt dirty from seeing how Creamer lived. I just wanted to wash and change into clean clothes.

"Is there a shower up here?" I asked.

"Shower not here, Naudsan. Use bathroom on third floor," Toshiko answered. He led me to the stairwell and up to the communal shower on the third floor. I had the entire place to myself. The water was very hot and the pressure strong. I let the hot shower water blast and needle my scalp.

I returned to the warehouse to find Toshiko and his crew waiting for me to inspect their work. The living space had been transformed. The bed itself was new and neatly made up with clean sheets. My clothes had all been hung and organized in the wall locker. Even the windows in the two outside walls had been scraped clean of the black paint leaving me with a magnificent view of Mount Fuji, bathed in the afternoon sunlight.

"How do you say, 'Thank you,' in Japanese," I asked Toshiko.

"Do·ma·t·ga·toe," Toshiko said.

"Do·ma·t·ga·toe," I kept saying to the guys who had cleaned the place. They kept smiling and bowing at me.

Toshiko ordered his crew back to work in the main office and for the first time, in a long time, I was left alone. I decided to write my mom a letter, to let her know what was happening and ease her mind.

I started writing, when I noticed something odd about one of the stacks of liquor boxes visible beyond the makeshift doorway opening. There was a 'crack', an alleyway, about ten inches wide. I walked over and peered in. The opening seemed to go in about six feet and stop, which made no sense. I decided to explore and squeezed my six foot tall, one hundred and sixty-pound frame between the cartons.

Once inside, I found the boxes and cartons appeared to form the corridors of a maze two feet wide. I went forward. The boxes wobbled as I bumped them. At any time I thought they might come crashing down and bury me. Carefully, I inched along until I discovered the secret. At the heart of the mountain was a secret room about twenty feet square. Empty liquor and beer bottles cluttered four small tables. Scattered about were cigarette butts, party hats, horns, and confetti. Sergeant Creamer must have used the secret room to hold private parties. The cartons and cases of liquor and beer formed three sides of the secret room. The fourth wall was part of the building and contained an elevator. I figured the elevator was used to bring liquor and beer cases up from the street.

I made my way back out of the maze. The secret room needed cleaning but I decided I wouldn't say anything about it until the next day. I laid down on the new cot. I was tired, but I couldn't sleep. I tried to get comfortable on my side until my arm fell asleep. Then, I rolled over onto my other side until that arm went numb. I was no closer to falling asleep an hour later, so I lay there looking out the window. The light evening rain had stopped. Through the water drops clinging to the warehouse windows, I could see Mt. Fuji now bathed in moonlight, glowing hypnotically.

When I rolled back over to face the mountain of liquor boxes, my gaze came to rest on some holes in the floor by my bed. There were maybe twenty or so, all in a row, about six inches apart. Toshiko had told me the holes were for bolts to hold down milling machines, which cut shell casings for the heavy guns of the Imperial Navy. This room had once been an important part of the Judo Kaikan Arms Plant, the largest munitions factory in Japan. I followed the line of holes into the darkness half-expecting to see the ghosts of the Japanese workers still turning out the deadly missiles. I wondered what kind of person had worked at those machines and what they felt when they heard about Pearl Harbor? Did they ever hear the Emperor's voice saying: '*Attention. We have just destroyed the American fleet. So take the day off and get drunk.*' Or maybe the Emperors announcement wasn't so happy: '*We will be working six hours longer, each week, because the Yankee dog is mad and we will need many more shells.*'

I reached down and touched one of the holes. How many people were still alive who had worked in this room and where were they now?

Frustrated by not being able to fall asleep, I rolled onto my back and began some deep breathing. I soon became aware of how tired I was. Tired of worrying about Jessie, about going to Korea, about a nut with a gun to my head, and seeing Sergeant Baker again thousands of miles away from Fort Devins. Then I finally fell fast asleep.

Suddenly I was awakened by a violent shaking. The room was black and the whole the building was swaying. Then it stopped.

Toshiko appeared.

"What the hell was that?" I asked.

"Oh no worry. That skoshi earthquake. You must get up, Plummer want to see you in EM Club."

I was still dazed by the earthquake as I followed him up to the sixth floor. We entered the EM Club. It was a large L shaped room, lined with a wall of factory style windows all around. All that was visible through them was the black night sky. There were around twenty five tables with chairs, all made of steel and formica. There was a bar around to the right, lined with six or seven chrome barstools with bright red vinyl cushions. The mirrored wall of shelves behind it was fully stocked with glasses and liquor. There was a wooden dance floor spotted with screw holes and a makeshift raised stage in the corner. A few waiters were busy hanging a drape behind the stage. Others had rags and were cleaning. It was all spotless, but frankly, it all felt sterile. Just a few GIs were sitting around. Even with the small crowd there looked to be about eleven waiters on duty. All were dressed in black cotton pants and white mandarin collar jackets with their names embroidered on the front.

I saw Plummer at the bar. I climbed onto the stool next to him.

"What would Naudsan like to drink?" a Japanese bartender asked in perfect English.

I was surprised, as much by his perfect English, as his size. He was a tall man, in his twenties, built like a football player. I had the impression all Japanese people were small. Obviously, I was wrong.

"Jumbo? This is Naud, the new club custodian," Plummer said, introducing me to him.

"Hai Master," he answered.

That word hit a nerve. "No Master. Call me Bill or Naudsan," I insisted. "How about some Ginger ale?" I requested.

"Hai." Jumbo left to fill the request.

I couldn't believe how tall Jumbo was. "Do all the waiters speak English?" I asked Plummer.

"Most speak a little, but Jumbo speaks the best," Plummer said. "He played football in the states, for a year, at USC, in Los Angeles. Twenty-one Japanese men work here. And, if you don't already know all the waiters were Kamikazes."

I was stunned. "Toshiko too?"

"Yeh. He was their squadron commander," Plummer remarked.

All I knew about Kamikazes was that they had blown up American ships but not much more. "We'll, if they're Kamikaze, how come they're alive?" I asked.

Plummer leaned toward me and spoke in a whisper. "They were ready to fly their mission but the war ended before they could…," Then he made a little whistling sound and a discrete gesture, his hand diving towards the bar top, imitating a crashing airplane. "Now, they're all going to college," he added.

I tried not to stare at them. It was hard for me to believe a lethal hornet could so easily turn into a gentle butterfly.

Jumbo returned with the Ginger ale.

"Jumbo here's gonna be a banker, like his dad. The other bartender wants to be a doctor. The fellow by the door, Ota, wants to write, and Junji over there wants to be a lawyer. They're interesting guys."

I did find it all interesting but I couldn't help being distracted by my predicament, only two days to find a way to make this place appealing.

"Are there ever girls here?" I asked.

"Once a week the guys are allowed to bring a girl but only a few do. They have to have security clearances to get on the base. Hey, maybe we should go downtown tomorrow and look over some of the popular EM clubs in Tokyo to get some ideas. I'm really hoping you can make this place work," Plummer said raising his glass and toasting me.

"Sounds good to me," I said feeling like a man being offered a life preserver on a sinking ship.

Chapter 6

Downtown Tokyo, 1950

It was late afternoon when Plummer and I left for our EM Club hopping downtown. I was looking forward to seeing Tokyo for the first time.

I followed Plummer out of the gate. No sooner had our feet touched the cobblestone street, than we were surrounded by Joy-girls offering their sexual services.

Plummer plowed through them without hesitating.

One tried to block my path. She was the prettiest of all. "I bring you wonderful joy time," she said in a sultry tone. I couldn't help thinking of what the Colonel had told me about some of the girls being spies. Maybe she was one of them.

Plummer reached the waiting line of taxicabs and looked impatiently back at me. "Let's go, Naud," he hollered as he climbed into the back seat of the first red cab in line. It was nearly identical to all the other cabs in line. They looked like a row of Campbell's tomato soup cans stuck on top of three wheeled motorcycles.

I finally managed to push my way past the Joy-girls and escape into the Taxi, squeezing next to Plummer. The cabs not only looked like cans, but they were tiny with barely enough room in the back seat for two adults.

Plummer gave the driver directions in Japanese. I was impressed with how well he spoke the language. The cab bucked and lurched forward as the driver loudly grinded the gears.

The afternoon sky was gray and the air cool.

We bounced our way down the cobblestone street running through the village of Oji, then out to Avenue A, the main road that wound through the suburbs north of Tokyo and down to the center of the city.

After a few miles the landscape drastically changed to an eerie mix of old bombed out buildings, piles of rubble and an occasional new structure. It still looked like a war zone. During WWII the B-29 fire bomb raids had literally blown up most of the city. It was hard to believe five years later the reconstruction was barely underway.

Out to the east were the shattered remains of a stone stadium resembling a one-story version of the Coliseum in Rome. Plummer explained it was what was left of the Korakun Stadium, where horse races were held for the Japanese aristocracy. The betting stopped when they were forced to eat the horses during the desperate food shortages caused by the war.

As we moved down avenue A, the road improved but the traffic was getting heavier, clogged by people on bicycles, tin canned cabs and U.S. army vehicles of all sizes.

The driver was steering wildly in and out of the heavy traffic. He roared through a busy intersection, nearly colliding with a bus. Then the cab fishtailed as it skidded around a corner. I sat rigidly upright on the edge of the seat clutching the door handle tightly, trying to control my fear.

Plummer didn't seem bothered; he was busy staring ahead over the drivers left shoulder like he was looking for something. "I'll show you where General MacArthur lives," he said.

'If we don't get killed in this Campbell's soup can before we can get there,' I thought.

"This city really got clobbered in the war," I said, hoping talking might help take my mind off the crazy ride.

"Yeah, Tokyo got clobbered, but nothing compared to what we did to Berlin," Plummer said. "My dad flew thirty missions in Europe. He was a B-17 Pilot."

"I wanted to be a carrier pilot but I'm color blind," I babbled on.

"I wouldn't have the guts to fly off a carrier deck," Plummer said. "You ever heard of General Doolittle?"

My ears perked up. "Sure," I said. Doolittle was one of my heroes. He had organized and led the first American air raid on Tokyo, flying off with his group of B-25 bombers from the carrier deck of the U.S.S. Hornet. One of my favorite films, *Thirty Seconds over Tokyo* starring Spencer Tracy, told the story of the raid. In fact when I was a boy, I had spent six months building a copy of Doolittle's bomber to send to Tracy. Unfortunately he never got it, because my brother Bob sat on it by accident and crushed it into a pile of sticks.

Plummer leaned forward and said something to the driver.

"Hai," the driver nodded, turning the cab left onto a dirt road that ran parallel to a high railroad embank-

91

ment. It was filled with bombed out pot holes, but I didn't mind, at least they forced the cabby to slow down. Then we skidded to a stop.

"Come on, Naud. I'll show you something," Plummer said. We climbed out and stood before a stone train overpass.

I was just glad to be out of the cab, even if it looked like there was nothing interesting to see.

Plummer pointed to a spot twenty feet off the ground where the stones were chipped and gouged. "Guess what made those marks, Doolittle's raiders."

I focused my eyes on the scarred stones. In my mind's eye I could see it all happening: March 18th, 1942, B-25 bombers, roaring along fifty feet off the ground, spewing out a withering stream of red-hot fifty-caliber bullets at a Japanese supply train racing to escape. The bomber's slugs rake the train and the overpass, ripping out chunks of stone. The continuous spray of bullets rips holes in the boxcars, smashing into crates of live shells, and setting off a chain of violent explosions. The train blows apart erupting into a giant fireball.

I touched the gray granite stone of the overpass. It was icy cold. .

"The B-25's that attacked had to fly all the way across the Sea of Japan to China," Plummer told me. "A lot of them crashed. It was our first air raid on Japan. Interesting, huh?"

To me it was a lot more than interesting. I knew everybody on the raid was a volunteer. It took guts, real guts. It was practically a Kamikaze mission. I doubted I would have had the nerve to do it. The overpass was a shrine to a lot gutsy guys. I gave the

crumbling stones a final pat of respect before starting back to the cab.

We climbed back in. "Ee-kee-ma-show," Plummer
hollered at the driver, trying to yell over the clickety-
clack racket of a freight train as it rumbled across
the overpass above us. It sounded like the ghost of
the doomed train, trying to escape.

The cabby flicked his burning cigarette into the
street, and we roared off.

A few miles later the line of traffic ahead was
barely moving, but I didn't mind. I was enjoying a
break from the motorized madness. I glanced up at
the sun that kept trying to peek through the clouds.

The people jamming the streets were mostly on
foot or bicycle. All looked neat and well groomed.
Most wore traditional Japanese clothes. Many women
had infant children strapped to their backs.

I wondered how they all felt about Americans.
They probably resented us. Maybe even hated us. We
had taken over their country. On the other hand, what
right did they have to hate us? They had attacked us
first at Pearl harbor bringing America into the war.

Directly behind us was a three-wheeled motorcycle with storage boxes of eggs and crates of chickens mounted on the back. Plummer said most Japanese used that type of vehicle in place of a truck
because the American Air Force had wiped out their
truck manufacturing industry.

Suddenly, the impatient driver behind us gunned
his motorcycle and pulled out of line, racing to get
ahead. His boxes rocked and swayed as he sped by
us. Then he tried to rush past the army truck just
ahead of us.

Without any warning, the GI driving the truck, purposefully kicked his door open, forcing the motorcycle driver to swerve violently into oncoming traffic. The motorcycle miraculously managed to narrowly miss two vehicles coming at it, but the driver lost control, slammed into a curb and cartwheeled into a horrified crowd waiting at a bus stop. All of his cargo scattered. It became a mess of screaming people and squawking chickens.

The Corporal stuck his head out of the truck window, clucking and laughing at the havoc he had created.

I was furious.

Plummer wasn't surprised. He had seen it happen many times before. It disgusted him, too. "The GI's think its fun."

"Look," Plummer said, pointing out the window. "The Emperor lives over there."

There was nothing to see but a sixty-foot wide moat filled with greenish- brown water, a wall of large stone blocks rising fifty feet high on the far side of it, and the tops of some trees. I had read about the Emperor's Palace in the ships newspaper on the way over. The Royal family lived there on an island in the middle of Tokyo.

"The Japanese believed the Emperor was a direct descendant of God, until MacArthur made him say he wasn't," Plummer said. That was quite an ironic statement considering MacArthur expected to be treated as if he was one himself.

It looked like the moat ran for miles.

The slow moving traffic, now stopped to a halt a few cars ahead of us, like the starting line of a race line. Beyond it, the road was clear.

I got out of the cab to see what the problem was. To my surprise, a mother duck was escorting her ten tiny ducklings across the busy street. Nobody honked, made impatient noises, or screamed anything. It was hard to believe a few ducks could bring this part of the world to a standstill.

We all watched them make their way to the other side of the road. Then they hopped onto the sidewalk and waddled over to the edge of the Emperor's moat. Nothing was blocking the traffic now, but still nobody moved. People were frozen waiting to see what the ducks would do. I was perfectly content to watch along with everyone else.

The mother duck jumped first. Then the inspired ducklings leaped from the sidewalk, belly flopping into the moat water six feet below. The last few ducklings hesitated, pacing back and forth. They seemed to be gathering the courage to jump.

It didn't make sense to me. How could these people commit such horrible atrocities to fellow human beings in war, yet show such reverence and concern for some little birds?

The last baby duck waddled about in fear for a few moments, then bravely dove into the moat. In my mind, it was an act of heroism.

Suddenly a barrage of honking began. The word had filtered through the line of traffic that the ducks were safe. "Iki Masho." "Let's go!" people were screaming out. The chaotic world came to life again as the traffic started to crawl forward.

"MacArthur lives over there with his wife and son. On the top floor," Plummer said, as he pointed across the street at a five story building resembling the New York Stock Exchange, with Roman columns lining its front. At the top was a badly painted sign that read, 'Supreme Command Far-East Commander of the combined U. N. forces, General MacArthur'. It was obvious it was meant to be a temporary sign, but it was still hanging five years after the war ended. Images of MacArthur flashed in my mind: him wearing his Sunglasses, puffing on his corncob pipe, wading in the surf in the Philippines, calling out his most famous words 'I'll be back.'

"After the war the Japanese tried to write a new constitution," Plummer explained, "but they couldn't agree on anything, so they asked MacArthur to help. He wrote one like ours guaranteeing certain rights, life, liberty and the pursuit of happiness. He made men and women equal and banned discrimination based on racial, religious, political or economic grounds. Not bad for a Jeffersonian Democrat, huh?" Plummer said with pride.

"Yeah," I said, impressed with not just MacArthur's triumph but Plummer's knowledge of history. He was proving to be a fountain of information. Up to now he was tight-lipped about his personal life but during the ride he shared the fact he was a native of Boston and had gone to Boston University for a year as a History Major before enlisting, figuring he was going to be drafted anyway.

The downtown skyline came into view as we turned left down avenue Z. My stomach was beginning to grumble, reminding me I had skipped lunch.

Up ahead, standing alone in an open grassy area, was a slender eight story Yellow steel building resembling a lighthouse with metal tubes sticking up from the roof.

"That's the oldest police station in Tokyo. It was built for the Imperial police," Plummer said.

I asked him what the odd tubes sticking out on the roof were.

"Periscopes. That's how they kept watch on the Imperial Palace grounds," Plummer said. "After they caught eight of the Doolittle raiders they marched 'em down here and made 'em jump off the roof." Plummer went on, shading his eyes from the sun's glare as he looked up. "They say it was an 'honorable' way to die. "

Plummer missed the look of revulsion that came over my face. 'Honorable death. Bullshit,' I thought. 'The bastards just murdered them.'

"Come on, I'll buy you some lunch," Plummer said.

I was in no rush. I had lost my appetite.

A few minutes later Plummer announced, "There's the Nikatsu. That's where we're going to have lunch. Then he added, "MacArthur eats there sometimes,"like it was an important shrine.

The Nikatsu was the newest and finest hotel in Tokyo, a fifteen story, white marble and glass contemporary structure, looming over all the other downtown buildings. It was designed to attract western businessmen who could bring capital to Japan and hopefully help restore it to economic health.

The cab turned into the hotel's long curving driveway and came to a stop behind two other cabs and a limousine. It was a chaotic mess of uniformed doormen trying to unload and load passengers in the midst of an unruly crowd of picketers chanting angrily in Japanese. They were marching up and down the drive, dozens of ruddy faced poor laborers dressed in miners clothing, wearing hard hats, carrying baseball bats and steel pipes. A group of them surrounded the limousine parked opposite the main glass doors leading into the hotel.

"What's going on Plummer?" I said with concern.

"They're just commie miners," he explained. "They come here all the time, trying to stir up trouble. They're after the guy in the limousine. He owns a lot of the coal mines."

"What are they chanting?" I asked.

"They're saying 'MacArthur and Yamaguchi are Imperialist pigs trying to take over Japan with slave wages.' It's just propaganda."

The rest of the growing angry mob blocked the entrance to the hotel. Inside, several uniformed doorman were holding the doors closed. Some of the miners managed to climb on top of the limousine. They all began pounding it with their weapons, but there were more broken bats and bent pipes, than dents made in the western style armor plated limousine.

Hotel patrons anxiously watched from the safety of the glassed in lobby, afraid to exit the hotel.

Plummer was paying the driver with a fistful of yen notes, when the cab ahead of us decided to escape the chaos, awkwardly pulling out of line. With a gear grinding U-turn, it fled back down the drive. As the car rushed by, I could see the fear on the passengers faces.

Plummer didn't seem bothered by any of it. He was waiting for the driver to make change so we could go. With a toss of his head towards the hotel lobby he said, "It's alright. The Japanese police are inside."

It didn't seem alright. The police in the lobby seemed to be ignoring the angry club wielding mob. They were standing idly by watching it all like it was a spectator sport.

Suddenly a van screeched to a stop by the street. News cameramen jumped out and rushed up to the scene, popping giant flash bulb cameras, recording the mob's every move.

"Don't you think we should find a place that's a little safer to eat?" I said, watching the vicious crowd start to rock the limo to force Yamaguchi to come out.

"Don't worry. They don't bother GIs," Plummer said as he counted the change from the driver.

I was worrying. Especially since a group of the desperate miners were heading our way.

"Hey buddy, you owe me more money! " Plummer barked at the cabbie in Japanese.

The driver wasn't thinking about change. He was too frightened by the chanting mob encircling the cab. He panicked, shifted the vehicle in gear and hit the accelerator. The motor sputtered and roared, but the cab wasn't moving. I looked out the back window and saw three burly miners holding up the back end so the wheels couldn't touch the pavement.

"Plummer we got a problem!" I yelled.

Plummer was preoccupied searching the floor for his change. "I'm telling you their harmless."

The driver obviously didn't share his opinion, he was screaming wildly at them. But they just ignored him, picking both ends of the cab up higher in the air. Then they flipped it over and let it slam to the ground, leaving it like a stranded turtle on its back. Plummer and I wound up a tangled ball of arms and legs.

As the cab began to fill with gas fumes, the driver frantically clawed his way out through his open window, and vanished.

"We'd better get out NOW, before the cab burst into flames," I hollered as I struggled to open the back seat window. Being clubbed to death by a mob, seemed like a better idea than being burned to death. But the window was jammed.

Plummer was frantically trying to kick open his door. "You're gonna love the steaks here," he said as he finally got it open.

We crawled out expecting to be attacked by a barrage of baseball bats, but thankfully the mob was gone

Plummer tried the service door but it was locked from the inside.

We could see Yamaguchi's bodyguards, who looked more like sumo wrestlers dressed in black, battling their way out of the hotel to the limousine. They managed to form a protective tunnel by the back door. The door opened and Yamaguchi crouched out into the safety of their cocoon. The angry miners did their best to get to Yamaguchi, flailing away at the bodyguards, lashing out with fists and bats. The bodyguards kept providing a protective shield even though they were getting bloodied from the violent blows.

The hotel patrons began scurrying in every direction as the angry brawling mob began pushing its way through the main doors.

The hotel security police suddenly vanished.

The service door next to us swung open, as two frightened patrons ran out. Plummer caught it before it closed and pulled me into the lobby.

He spotted an open elevator at the back of the building and raced into it. "Come on, Naud," he called. "Believe me, the food's worth the trouble. Besides, I'm buying."

I was frozen in my tracks. I had had enough. 'Plummer's off his rocker,' I thought, 'we just escaped with our lives and he's worrying about food.' "Shit," I muttered out loud, realizing I still needed him, I had no choice, so I raced toward the elevator.

Plummer started pressing the Penthouse button but nothing was happening. He frantically pressed every other button too. The elevator wasn't moving.

"Damn it's automatic. It won't go up until another car comes down," he said in frustration.

I started to panic. I could see Yamaguchi, his bodyguard cocoon along with the angry miners, all making their way through the lobby. News cameras were snapping away. I cringed at the sight of the strikers' faces dripping with blood where they had been clawed by the bodyguards. The whole bloody, brawling mess, was headed for our open elevator, straight at us two hapless GIs.

I desperately tried to pull the elevator door closed as the battling mob began trying to push their way in.

"Hey. Guys? This elevator's taken," I said while sticking my arms out.

But they just bulldozed me and Plummer down to the floor. The best we could do was crawl to the corner to protect ourselves.

Then the door closed, and the elevator started up. The fighting raged on without so much as a pause. But the elevator was so crowded there was barely room to move or to swing, so the battle was reduced to cursing, spitting and kicking.

The one photographer who had managed to get aboard, was trying to take photos, but his camera was locked under a miners elbow.

Through the maze of arms and flesh I could see Yamaguchi in the opposite corner with a handkerchief over his nose.

It was an ugly stinking mess of sweat, flesh and blood no one could escape until the elevator came to a stop at the penthouse on the fifteenth floor. When the door finally opened the miners were met by a dozen husky Japanese police who proceeded to club, handcuff and drag them into an adjacent waiting freight elevator. They confiscated the photographers camera, throwing it to the floor and smashing it. Now I understood why the cops hadn't stopped the fighting in the hotel lobby. They didn't want the cameras to record the brutal beatings they were planning to give the miners on the top floor.

Yamaguchi and his bodyguards waited until all the miners were hauled away. Then Yamaguchi brushed himself off in an effort to restore some dignity and walked proudly into the main dining room, followed by his disheveled bodyguards.

Plummer and I went to the men's rooms to straighten ourselves up, including brushing the foot prints off our shirts.

I was still a bit stunned as we headed to the dining room.

The Maître de in the dining room greeted Plummer warmly, as if he was well- acquainted with him, and led us to a table by a large glass wall that overlooked Tokyo. It was almost dark; lights were coming on all over the city. The whole of Tokyo lay before us. The city was much larger than I thought.

The dining room was spacious and elegant, done in off-white French Provincial. It reminded me of the Plaza hotel in New York City. There was a dance floor and a small stage on which a four piece band played Japanese style lounge music. The tables were mostly occupied by well-dressed Caucasian businessmen and high ranking American military men, accompanied by fashionably dressed western woman.

Yamaguchi was seated at a large conference type table against the interior wall with two very attractive, giggly, Japanese girls in traditional dress. He was sipping his wine with a royal air, as several obsequious waiters stood by poised to serve his every need. His bodyguards were lined up along the wall behind him with folded arms and steely expressions.

Plummer handed the menu back to the waiter. "I'll have my usual," he said.

The waiter nodded his understanding.

The prices on the menu were in dollars and yen. From a glimpse I could see it was all very expensive. Since Plummer insisted on buying, I just ordered the same.

"Look out there," Plummer said, pointing out the window.

I turned so I could see. It was a magnificent view of Mount Fuji. The snow on its peak had a luminescent glow from the moonlight. I was beginning to understand why the Japanese thought of Mount Fuji as a deity. It was so striking, it looked unreal. Beautiful mountains seemed to have an inspiring effect on people all around the world. Certainly Mt Everest did, and the Matterhorn in Switzerland. The only mountains I had ever seen were in the Catskills, in New York State. All they seemed to inspire were bad comedians at adult summer camps.

The food arrived, Kobe steaks, potatoes, string beans and salad, and we dug in. I cut off a chunk of my steak and began chewing it. Plummer was right, it was the best steak I had ever tasted.

"You know, Naud, to make Kobe steaks, they have to massage the cows every night."

It was more than I wanted to know. I let Plummer babble on without hearing a word.

He managed to wolf down his steak in record time. "Great, food, huh?" he said, gulping a cup of Sake.

"Yeah, everything's great," I said.

I had eaten most of my steak and potatoes, and was saving the string beans and salad for last. I couldn't believe the size of the string beans. Each one was more than eight inches long.

I raised a forkful of beans to my mouth and started to chew them.

"Yeah, all the vegetables over here are enormous. It's from the fertilizer," Plummer said. "They grow them in human waste."

I immediately started to gag, then discreetly raised my napkin and spit the food out into it. "You mean this stuff was grown in SHIT?" I said

"Human waste is really the finest fertilizer," Plum-mer explained.

My appetite was gone. Now I had a problem. I was sure to offend Plummer if I didn't eat the plateful of food he was paying for. I put the cloth dinner napkin open on my lap. "Hey, Plummer? Is that MacArthur over there?" I asked, gesturing my head across the dining room.

Plummer turned. The moment he did, I dumped the food on my plate into my lap. I was putting the empty plate back on the table as Plummer turned back around.

"It's not MacArthur," he said, adding, "hey, I see you loved the food."

"Oh, yeah. It was great," I said, feeling relieved.

When the waiter arrived with Plummer's next cup of sake I excused myself, went off to the men's room, and dumped the food down the sink.

When I returned, I noticed Plummer was getting tipsy from all the sake. His condition was distressing to me. I wanted him alert enough to witness the diligent way I was going to study the operations of the downtown EM Clubs. It's the only way I knew I could make a good impression on him.

"Could you bring us some coffee, please?" I asked the waiter.

"Hai," he answered.

As he was serving the coffee, the band began playing plinkety, plankety Japanese music. The Maître de placed an easel on the dance floor with a sign, then went to the microphone and made an announcement. "Good evening ladies and gentlemen. Our fashion show is about to begin. For more information about purchasing the clothes, please inquire at the desk."

Moving to the music, Japanese models wearing the latest Western-style dresses entered the dining room from the kitchen. They swirled from table to table showing the clothing and answering questions about the silk and cotton day couture. My brother Bob had worked for Nat Kaplan, a famous designer in New York. I could tell the dresses were very expensive, at least a thousand dollars each.

I thought the first four girls were very attractive, but the last one to come out was stunning. All eyes were riveted on her. Suddenly Plummer was alert, sober and watching intently.

She was tall and slender, with long shapely legs. She was showing her dress to a table full of western businessmen on the other side of the room. A couple of the men made some crude remarks to her in English. She ignored them and moved on to our table.

She began swirling and flaring out the slitted skirt of the grey wool dress she was modeling. In an effort to fully display the design, she turned one way and then the other, causing her long silky black hair to swing off her naked shoulders.

I was mesmerized. She was even more beautiful close up.

Then she placed a business card on our table and said something in Japanese.

"What did she say?" I asked Plummer.

"Greetings to both of you," he translated.

"Do you speak English?" I asked her.

The girl said nothing. But I was transfixed by her eyes. I had never seen an oriental girl with eyes of cobalt blue.

"Tell her I'm sure she will be as beautiful in the fall of her life as she is now," I said.

I watched her face as Plummer said the words in Japanese.

She bowed politely and moved on to the next table.

"Naud? You're from New York, right?" Plummer asked. "So, you gotta know a lot about women and stuff. Right?"

"Kinda," I said vaguely. I was from New York, but I knew very little about women.

After a dozen more dresses, all the models swirled their way back into the kitchen. The plinkety-plankety music stopped and the fashion show was over.

The waiter took the money Plummer gave him for the check and left. As we waited for the change, I could see Plummer was still dreamy eyed.

"If I didn't have a fiancé back home, that oriental girl would be the one I would pick," Plummer said.

"You don't talk in your sleep, do you?" I asked, playfully recalling what Robert Benchley, the humorist, had said about being in love with two women at the same time. 'It's okay as long as you don't talk in your sleep.'

Plummer looked at me with an odd expression. "Why?"

The waiter arrived with Plummer's change, saving me the need to answer.

"Thanks again for the dinner," I said.

"No sweat," Plummer said.

We left the table and headed downstairs in the elevators. The hotel lobby was deserted. Yamaguchi and his lawyer were long gone. And with him went all the strikers and the police.

For the next few hours Plummer and I moved from EM Club to EM Club, walking around each of them, looking for the reasons for their success. The reasons were simple and obvious: Girls. Liquor. And gambling.

It was near midnight when we arrived at our last stop, the Army's main EM Club, a large entertainment complex with several ballrooms, bars, and three dozen gambling machines. It was packed with GI's, wall to wall.

I had been analyzing everything I saw at the clubs, out loud, just to impress Plummer with all the useful information I was absorbing. Plummer was getting bored listening to my constant chatter, so he headed to the bar for some drinks while I nosed around the club. It was getting to be one in the morning and I felt it was time for us to go home. By now Plummer was stumbling down drunk. He was still trying to order another CC-and-Water by the jam- packed bar when I told him we should be going.

"One more drink Bill," Plummer pleaded. He kept calling out his drink order and trying to catch the bartenders eye by reaching over the crowd jammed in front of the bar.

"Hey, buddy, watch who you're shoving," a husky, well built Sergeant barked.

"My apologies, kind Sir," Plummer said in flamboyant slurred speech as he leaned in again.

"And stay off my back. Creep," the Sergeants buddy complained.

"Least of all would I desire to be on your back, Sir," Plummer quipped.

The bartender had heard Plummer's order, and arrived at the bar with his drink. Plummer reached in to get it.

The Sergeant deliberately bumped Plummer's arm causing the drink to spill on the floor.

"OOOOH. Too bad, Creep," the Sergeant said, mocking him.

The Sergeant's buddies laughed along with him.

"I presume you did that on purpose," Plummer said, in a half-drunken slur.

"Get outta here, weasel," the Sergeant ordered.

"Where would you suggest I go, kind, Sir?" Plummer asked mockingly.

"Go find yourself some gook broad and catch the clap," the Sergeant responded.

Plummer became mad. "Oriental women are not 'Gooks', Sergeant," he said as he shoved in closer to him.

"No. They're whores and sluts," the Sergeant said, shoving Plummer away.

Sensing a fight was about to erupt, the bar crowd opened to form a ring.

"Asian women have nine thousand years of culture, Sergeant. About nine thousand more than you've got," Plummer lectured, trying hard not to slur his speech.

The Sergeant grabbed Plummer by his shirt collar and spun him around, cocking his fist, getting ready to hit him. "I'm gonna bust your head, you wimpy creep," he threatened.

I almost panicked. I tried to push through to get to Plummer, hoping to stop the fight before it began. Then I heard a thud and a hard crash. The crowd crushed in, I couldn't see anything.

"Let me through!" I called out, pushing between the sea of onlookers.

When I finally got through, I was surprised to find Plummer was pinned to a wall by two MP's, and the arrogant Sergeant was face down on the floor, apparently unconscious.

"What'd you do to him?" the tall MP asked Plummer.

Plummer was too drunk to explain anything or even try.

"He hit the Sergeant and the Sergeant went down," a voice from the crowd explained.

The MP was skeptical, especially considering the difference in the size of the two men. The husky Sergeant on the floor must have out weighed Plummer by a hundred pounds.

But other people in the crowd confirmed what the first guy had said.

The MP's still weren't buying the story. From what they could see, it was obvious; Plummer was no match for the big Sergeant.

"Let me see your ID," the MP demanded.

"I can't show you that," Plummer said.

"You're going to the stockade, fellow. Cuff him," the MP told his partner.

"Wait a minute, Sergeant," I yelled out.

"Who are you?" the MP asked gruffly.

"The Corporal and I are in the same outfit," I said, handing over my ID.

The MP took a look at my ID, and then showed it to his partner. He leaned in towards me. "Both you guys out at Oji?" he asked in a confidential manner.

"Yeah," I said, matching his hush-hush tone.

"You guys are sure it was the Sergeant's fault, right?" the MP's asked the crowd.

The crowd confirmed it again. The unconscious Sergeant was the guilty party.

The MP gave me back my ID card. "Come on, we'll give you guys a ride home," he said.

"What about him?" the other MP asked, gesturing to the Sergeant laying out cold on the floor.

"Leave him. He'll eventually wake up," he said.

The MP's picked Plummer up by the arms and helped him out to their jeep. I followed along. Ten minutes later, we were driving along avenue A on our way back to Oji. Plummer was lying on the back seat slumped over on me.

The MP was still curious. "I'd sure like to know what your buddy hit that Sergeant with? Brass knuckles, maybe?"

Plummer semi awoke. "With this," he said, in a garbled stupor and held up his right hand.

The MP smiled. He didn't believe him.

I didn't care what Plummer had hit the guy with. The important thing was, we weren't going to jail and Plummer still was my best and only asset.

Chapter 7

Open for Business

The EM was club open for business and it was my first night in charge. I felt I HAD to be doing something, an inescapable consequence of my middle class upbringing, so I worked behind the bar helping Jumbo and Nakijima fill the drink orders.

I was handing over a tray loaded with three bottles of beer to one of the waiters, when Plummer arrived at the bar holding a letter and looking at a snapshot. I figured it was a photo was of his girl. I was curious to see what she looked like.

"CC and Water, Plummersan?" Jumbo inquired.

"No," Plummer said with a glum look, "ginger ale." He was still hung over from the night before. Pollazzo, one of the other members of the club's Board of Governors, had told me Plummer was a devote catholic, and was saving himself for his fiancé. Celibacy was turning him into a drunk.

Plummer leaned over to show me the photo. The picture showed his girl, Anne, standing with a group of young men on a beach. There was a middle- aged guy with his arm around her. He had gray hair and looked to be in his fifties.

"It's a birthday party," Plummer explained.

Jumbo returned and put a full glass of ginger ale on the bar in front of him. Plummer pointed at an older gentleman. "That's my dad. He owns a fish market in Boston. He's expecting me to take it over when I get back home. "At that thought, Plummer's expression saddened even more.

"Anne wrote to ask for my permission to go to skiing with Al Gifman, my father's lawyer. He's the one on the left," Plummer said glumly. His tone made it clear he didn't like the idea. I had a feeling Plummer was worried his girl might be interested in more than skiing.

"Hey, I almost forgot," Plummer said, raising his glass to toast me. "Here's to you, Naud, for saving my butt last night."

"No sweat," I said, toasting myself. We drank our ginger ales. .

"By the way, where'd you learn Judo?" I asked, making a chopping motion with my hands.

"It isn't Judo, it's Gung Fu," Plummer corrected.

"It's all the same isn't it? Karate. Gung Fu?" I commented.

"No. It's a lot different," Plummer said. "A priest in high school taught it to me. He had learned Gung Fu as a missionary in China."

I had been to Catholic School and knew priests could be very strict. I smiled, imagining Plummer's priest had learned Gung Fu to protect himself from his parishioners, who felt he gave them too many 'Hail Mary's' as penance.

"What's so funny?" Plummer asked.

"The word Gung Fu. It sounds funny," I lied. It was easier than trying to explain my anti-Catholic joke. Now I understood why Plummer hadn't been worried about the brutal mob at the Nikatsu hotel. He could have chopped his way through them like Paul Bunyon.

"You don't have a plan for the Colonel yet, do you?" Plummer asked me bluntly.

"No," I admitted.

"Better hurry up. The Board of Governors Meeting is tomorrow," he reminded me.

"Without girls, any plan's a waste of time," I said glumly.

Plummer knew my precarious situation and had been contemplating a solution. "Look, I read your 201. You got an Information and Education M.O.S. right?"

"Yeah. I did some lecture stuff at Fort Devins," I said.

"If the Club thing doesn't work, maybe I can get the Colonel to let you do some lecture stuff here," Plummer said.

"I'd appreciate it. Thanks," I said. I had no idea if Plummer could save my butt, but at least I knew that he would try.

A band arrived and began setting up on-stage, getting ready to play. They looked like five Japanese penguins in their dinner jackets. The name on the drum was 'Little Joe'. They started to play. I already had no great love for drums but Little Joe was the worst I had ever heard. His banging sounded like a train wreck. The only positive thing about Little Joe was the ear to ear happy smile he sported while playing. Most of the bands repertoire consisted of a two second intro with all the musicians, then Little Joe just banged away on his drums oblivious to how bad he was.

Toshiko appeared by the bar. "Naudsan? Misa Manissa want talk to you, in office. She best talent agent in Japan. Bring talent list for you to look at," he said.

I didn't expect the Club job to work out, so why bother? On the other hand, it was a good excuse to get away from the noise. I just hoped her acts would be better than this band.

As I arrived in the office the talent broker, Misa Manissa, stopped looking through the antique telescope by the window. Misa looked like a Japanese version of Alfred E. Newman, the freckle-faced, big-eared, gap-toothed character with buckteeth out of Mad Magazine. But any thought that she might resemble the cartoon idiot in other ways vanished, when I noticed her dress and shoes. They were exquisite and very expensive. She might not be very attractive, but she had great taste, and the money to back it up.

"Koo-ni-chi-wah," I said, trying out my latest Japanese word.

"Good evening you too, Naudsan," Misa said, smiling and bowing. She laid a large, loose-leaf binder filled with eight-by-ten photos on my desk.

"I bring talent photos," she said.

I sat down to look through them. The first photo was of "Watanabe and His Stardusters", a well-known orchestra. Plummer and I had seen them at the Army's main EM Club the night before. The music they played was exactly like Glen Miller's, note for note, and they were darn good.

"You want Watanabe for New Year's Eve like Sergeant Creamersan. Must book much ahead. Very popular," she warned.

"No thanks," I said.

I turned the pages of photos, trying to look like I was interested, when I really wasn't. Then, to my surprise, something caught my interest. "Who is this?" I asked Misa.

"Lucinda and her All Girl Band. Seventeen pieces. Ichi bon."

That act gave me an idea. "Do you have any hostesses or dancers to hire?"

"Ooohh, no, Naudsan. No dancing girls. Only singers and bands," Misa said shaking her head.

I studied the photo of Lucinda and her all girl band, again. The girls were all young and attractive.

Misa could see my intent interest in them. "You like Lucinda band? Wanna book?"

"I might. But the problem is, no women are allowed on base without a security clearance."

"This true, Naudsan. Oji, very much security," Misa said.

"So I couldn't hire 'em if I wanted to," I complained.

"No, Naudsan CAN hire. Lucinda's All Girl Band has security clearance," Misa said proudly.

I thought I was hearing things. "Are you saying these girls DO have security clearances and CAN come on the base?" I asked.

"Hai, Naudsan." Misa answered.

I felt like I had just found gold. I looked happily at the photo again. Seventeen attractive girls in the Club was a pretty good idea. If they could play music, it was reasonable to expect they could dance, so why couldn't they dance with the code-breakers?

"If I hire them would they be willing to dance?"

"Oh, girls no Hoochie-Koo, Naudsan. Just play instruments."

"I just want them to dance? Fox trot? Jitterbug?" I begged.

"Not possible, Naudsan. Girls no can dance and play at same time," she said. She didn't understand my question.

"Can some of the girls dance, while some girls play instruments?" I asked.

"Oooh, too much hard work, Naudsan," Misa answered, shaking her head no. "Lucinda band just play. They very good, very cheap, Naudsan," Misa said, making another pitch.

"Let me ask you this, would some of Lucinda's girls dance with the guys up in the Club if I paid them extra for the dancing?" I asked. "No play instruments, just dance."

"Oohh, soo. Maybe," Misa paused to reflect. "How much more you pay for dancing?" she asked, sounding businesslike.

"Well, I don't know," I said. I was at a loss as to what to offer.

"How about, you pay Lucinda Band same as Little Joe?" Misa asked.

"Well, okay. Why not?" I said, sounding a bit reluctant.

"When you want Lucinda band?"

"Soon. I'll let you know. Dijob? Okay?"

"Dijob," Misa said.

I made Misa promise she wouldn't say anything about our deal until I said she could.

She agreed and we shook hands.

I was smiling from ear to ear. I had done the impossible. I had found a way to get girls on the base. Not sleazy joy girls, but attractive, educated girls who would appeal to the code guys. Now all I had to do was present the plan to the Colonel.

Chapter 8

No Hot Water

I woke around nine on Thursday morning, the day of the big board meeting with Colonel Macmillan. I was heading off get washed and found a note taped on the warehouse door. It was from Plummer. Naud, I came by to tell you the Colonel has to be downtown for a conference with MacArthur at seventeen hundred hours, but you were asleep. So you have to keep today's meeting short. Good luck, and remember, the Colonel is impressed by charts and graphs. See you later, Plummer

That meant I would only have thirty minutes to make my presentation to him. I headed down to the latrine and stepped into the shower. I turned the handle to the hottest water position, and jumped back to avoid being scalded, but to my surprise the water was only lukewarm, and it wasn't getting any hotter.

Disgusted, I wrapped my towel around my body and walked down the third floor hall with my arms folded across my chest trying to ward off the chill. The doors to the rooms along the hallway were all closed.

"Hey. Anybody? Where's the hot water?" I hollered out.

"Hey stupid," a voice rang out from one of the rooms. "There's a damn coal strike."

119

I had the feeling the coal miners who had failed to kill me at the Nikatsu hotel were now trying to freeze me to death. But I wasn't going to give up. Not yet. I pulled the towel tighter around my body and headed up the stairs to the office.

Several of the waiters were in doing inventory and were surprised to see their Master clothed only in a bath towel, chattering away.

"Where can I find hot water?" I asked Toshiko.

"No hot water, Naudsan. Coal strike. Neh?" he said.

"There's gotta be hot water, somewhere," I chattered insistently.

Junji said something in Japanese to Toshiko, who wrote it down and handed me a piece of paper.

"Find hot water here, Naudsan," he said.

"Thanks," I said.

I put on my fatigues, threw on a poncho, grabbed a change of clothes and headed to the main gate to find a cab. It was too early in the day for any Joy-girls to have gathered. I jumped in a cab and gave the driver the paper with the address of the bathhouse.

"Ginza, Dozo," I said.

"Hai," the driver said. We were off.

I was determined to look sharp for the meeting at four o'clock, confident that a victory celebration would be in order when I tell the Colonel my solution to the girl problem. To my delight the driver went along smoothly, nothing jerky or crazy, so I relaxed, looking out the window at the scenery. The sky above was gray; it was starting to drizzle. It reminded me of a summer rain in New York. As we passed the Imperial Palace I could see the raindrops rippling the Emperor's moat. I wondered how the little ducks were doing.

Thunder crackled and rolled overhead as we reached the Ginza area. It reminded me of Manhattan's Times Square. There were lots of colorful shops and streets crowded with odd-looking characters mixed in with the regular people, all shuffling along. I always found Times Square depressing. Everything about it was tacky. The Ginza didn't have quite the same effect on me and I wasn't sure why. Maybe it was because I didn't understand the writing on the signs or the fact that nothing I saw seemed quite real. The whole area looked like a big movie set from one of my favorite Japanese series, the *Mr. Motto* films. Oddly enough, a Hungarian actor, Peter Lorre, played the Japanese detective *Mr. Motto*. When the war started, Hollywood stopped making the *Mr. Motto* series obviously for political reasons.

The rain broke into a heavy downpour making it hard to see out the cab's windows. The cab driver slowed to a crawl while searching for the address on the slip of paper. The crowds in the streets scurried about seeking shelter from the sudden deluge. Some people had umbrellas, while others used newspapers to keep the rain off. The traditionally dressed women held their kimono hems up to keep them from dragging while carefully stepping through the puddles of water, trying to keep their white socks and wooden shower type clogs from getting splashed.

The driver finally stopped in front of a row of souvenir shops cluttered with colorful neon signs.

"Bath house," he said pointing through the rain-spattered windshield at a covered staircase, sandwiched between two of the shops, jammed with people seeking refuge from the rain. To me nothing visible suggested a bathhouse.

"You ichi bon, driver," I said. I rewarded the cabby by paying the fare in American dollars instead of Yen.

"Oo-oo-h-h-h.   Do-ma-te-ga-toe,"   the   driver beamed.

The rain was still coming down in buckets. I covered my head with my change of clothes, and started running toward the covered staircase. It was as crowded as a New York subway car at rush hour. I fought my way through the crowd, up the steps, toward a door with a frosted glass panel with a sign written in Japanese on it. I opened the door and stepped in, brushing the rainwater off my hair. 'Bath house, I presume,' I mused to myself, imagining I was *Stanley* searching the jungle for *Livingstone*.

The first thing I saw was a cloud of steam, rising from a swimming pool. Steam meant hot water. What I saw next made me wonder if the place was a house of prostitution. Attractive young women, dressed in colorful Kimonos and carrying stacks of bath towels, were going in and out of wooden doors which opened to the rooms surrounding the pool.

Then I heard children laughing. A lady, a man, and two children were in the pool; playing in the steamy mist; splashing each other with water. Once they noticed me, they stopped playing and stared, surprised to see an American soldier.

I thought they were naked, but I couldn't be sure. In any event, I didn't care. All I wanted was hot water.

An old woman in a pink Kimono with sparkling eyes and a weather-lined face emerged from one of the rooms and spotted me. She shuffled across the white tile floor in her clogs, bowing to greet me.

"Ohio-go-zi-mus," she said, with a smile full of gold teeth.

"You speak English?" I said.

"Skoshi," Mamasan said, apologetically. I knew that meant a little.

"Want hot shower," I said, wiggling my fingers over my head to indicate water coming down. The old woman understood and became sad.

"Ooh, nooo. Sooo sorry. No shower," she said. She pointed at the pool. "Pool ichi bon," she said, offering it as her best alternative. She spoke to the family in the pool. They all smiled at me.

"Come join us," the man said.

I was surprised he spoke English, but I wasn't interested in being in a pool full of naked strangers. Then one of the wooden doors on the other side of the pool opened. Out came a Japanese man in his fifties, wearing a western style business suit. He headed for Mamasan, gave her some money, bowed politely, then left.

She saw I was focused on the man who came out of the private room.

"How much is private bath, Mamasan?" I asked, pointing at one of the mahogany doors.

"Oooh, much expensive," she said, swaying her head like an elephant. "One thousand Yen," she said, apologetically.

To me it was cheap. The current rate was three hundred and sixty yen to one American dollar. The private room only cost about three dollars. I gave Mamasan an American five-dollar bill and told her to keep the change.

Mamasan, smiled her gratitude, and kept bowing as she led me around the pool, toward one of the mahogany doors.

The children kept watching me and giggling, and then the little girl hid behind her mother and the embarrassed boy ducked beneath the water.

I smiled and went into the private bath. It was an intimate room with white tile and an oversized sunken ceramic tub filled with steaming hot water in the center. Just inside the door, on the left, was a bench stacked high with white towels. To my right was a massage table partitioned off by a white curtain.

I hung my clean clothes on one of the wall hooks and dropped my fatigues and underwear on the floor. I took one of the bath towels and stepped down into the water, testing the temperature. It was hot, but not too hot. I sat down in the shallow end, I soaked the bath towel in the hot water and draped it over my head, pressing down on the towel to force the water to stream down my hair and face. It wasn't exactly a hot shower but it was certainly the next best thing.

I was lost in enjoying my makeshift shower when I felt a draft and heard giggling girls. I peeked out from under the towel and discovered three, kimono-clad girls, with scrub brushes and wash rags, kneeling by the edge of the tub. My ghost like appearance was amusing them. From the gestures they made with the brushes and rags, I realized, they had come to wash me.

"No washo. No wash-o. Go away. Sayonara," I said. I kept up my protests until the girls finally understood, and disappointedly left the room.

I resumed soaking the towel in the hot water and dumping it on my head. There was a knock on the door. I ignored it. Then the old woman came in, bringing with her a chilling draft. I ducked low in the water to avoid the rush of cold air.

Mamasan obviously had a problem. I gathered from her gestures, and her skoshi English, that the girls would lose face if they were not allowed to wash me.

"Me wash self-o. No girl-o's," I kept insisting.

The three evicted girls stood in the open door, waiting to hear their fate. Mamasan finally offered me a concession.

"Girls will sit there," she said, pointing at the curtained off area.

I accepted the compromise, anything to get the door shut, I was freezing.

As the disappointed girls shuffled in to their area. I held my fingers to my lips in a 'shhhhh' position. Mamasan figured out what I meant.

"Hai, No talk-talk," Mamasan explained to the three giggly girls. They just sat on the massage table looking like *See no evil, Speak no evil, and Hear no evil'*.

Mamasan walked away. Finally, the chilling draft ended as she shut the mahogany door behind her.

Occasionally, the girls would sneak a peek through the curtain.

I was in heaven, soaking in the steamy hot water.

I left the bathhouse an hour later, dressed in a fresh uniform, carrying my fatigues wrapped in a towel. The rain had gone, replaced by a sunny sky filled with billowing white clouds.

I got in a cab. "Imperial Hotel," I said. The driver took off, making his way through the morning traffic. I was off to get my haircut, or maybe there was something more I was hoping for.

The Imperial hotel was world famous. I had seen pictures of it in a *Popular Science Magazine*. It had been designed by the famous American architect, Frank Lloyd Wright built to be earthquake proof. As we approached the structure I felt it looked more like a cold abstract piece of art than a grand hotel. It resembled a layer cake made of concrete slabs with each successive layer set further back from the one below.

I paid the cab driver and strolled toward the main entrance to the hotel's lobby, studying the people coming out. They were well dressed, with purposeful, determined expressions. They all seemed to be hurrying to get somewhere. Most of them were Americans. They were on a mission, to help Japan rise from the ashes of the war. And, in the process, make a pot full of money for themselves. Why not? It was the American way.

As I entered the lobby, I immediately spotted a group of Air Force officers registering at the front desk. There were several older Japanese clerks attending them. I wondered if those clerks had been there during the WW II air raids and how they must feel now having to serve American Air Force Officers.

There were nine large clocks mounted high up on the lobby wall above the front desk. They showed the time and day in major cities around the world. It was noon, Thursday, in Tokyo. It was last night, Wednesday, nine o'clock, in New York.

I drifted around the lobby and discovered a three-dimensional model showing the Frank Lloyd Wright design of the hotel. The entire structure was floating in a pool of oil, designed to absorb all the shaking in the event of an earthquake. It was a demonstration model. I pushed the button and watched the thing shake. It didn't fall apart, so I kept pushing the button in the hope that eventually it would. Alas, it never did.

Then I spotted her. She was coming out of the restaurant by the barbershop. The girl with the cobalt blue eyes.

I strolled across her path hoping she would notice me, but she kept on going, with no sign of recognition. I followed her down the arcade hall and discovered where she worked, the *Sun Dress and Fur Trading Company*. I looked in the window until I was sure she saw me. When I entered the shop, she vanished to the back. It was obvious she didn't want to talk to me.

I told myself she was a cold fish, and that I didn't care. But I did.

I went to the barbershop. I could see through the window there were two barbers and two chairs. Both chairs were empty. I strolled in and decided I would try the barber who was smiling, by the first chair.

"Ichi bon haircut, dijob?" I said, settling in the chair.

"Hai," the barber said, nodding. He threw an apron around my neck and began snipping away. I closed my eyes and figured I would daydream until he was finished. Unfortunately another patron, an obnoxious guy with a New York accent, sat down in the other chair.

"Hey, buddy, what the hell's going on in Korea?" he complained at me. "You're letting us get our asses kicked."

I looked at him. He was glaring at me from over his newspaper.

True, I wasn't helping win the war. But I damn sure wasn't responsible for losing it either, at least, not yet. This guy was a smart-ass, I liked to deal with smart asses. "Don't worry, Sir," I said. "I'm MacArthur's aide," I confided, shoving my ID card stamped TOP SECRET in his face. "At exactly sixteen-hundred hours, this afternoon, we're gonna nuke the North Koreans and the Chinks to hell with a load of fifteen megaton atom bombs. North Korea and half of China will be gone by seventeen-hundred hours."

Obviously I was convincing. Horror struck the guy. He rushed out the barbershop. I wondered where he was going, but it really didn't matter.

The barber held a mirror up for me to see the back of my head. As he did I could see the beautiful girl with the cobalt eyes walking by. I jumped up from the chair, ripped off the apron, threw a couple yen at him and ran out of the barbershop after her.

It was easy to spot her; her glistening black hair was unbound and hung down to the waist of her wool jersey dress. I pushed through the crowd and finally caught up with her. But I was a bit dumbstruck by her beauty and started to ramble on in slow stammering English. "Remember me ...at the Nikatsu Hotel...the fashion show..." I made gestures imitating the punching and rioting of the miners, hoping my animation would make up for my lack of speaking Japanese.

"Yes, I remember you," she said gently.

"You speak perfect English," I said. I wanted to say more, but the words didn't come. Her beauty left me speechless.

"I have someplace I must go," she said.

"Well, maybe I can go along," I offered.

"I don't think you will like it where I'm going," she said with her head bowed.

"Well, I like to go places I don't like," I said.

She smiled at my joke. "I am sorry. Goodbye," she said.

I was still somewhat dumbstruck as I watched her go. Finally I snapped out of my trance, just before she was completely out of sight.

"Wait, there's something I have tell you," I yelled over the bustle of the crowd, "you're the most beautiful girl I've ever seen."

My words boomed around the lobby. People looked at me like I was crazy.

"You should tell my parents, they are responsible, not I," she called back.

The doorman helped her into one of the cabs lined up in front of the hotel.

I realized this was my only chance, I had nothing to lose. I wanted to talk to her and had the feeling she felt the same way. I ran out of the hotel, towards the line of cabs, and stuck my head in the passenger window of the first one I reached.

"You speak English?" I asked the driver.

"Hai. Speak good English," the cabby responded.

"Just follow that cab," I said, getting in.

The driver floored the gas pedal, bowling me over in the back seat before I had a chance to settle in.

Three times in less than three miles we narrowly avoided head-on collisions. But for once, I was more focused on my goal, than on how I got there. For a few moments, we lost sight of her taxi, then we spotted it again. At least, I thought it was her cab. We needed to get closer. As the driver sped up and we got closer, I was sure it was her cab. Then it disappeared in the mix of the vehicles ahead. But instead of following it, the taxi driver dropped further back, and turned down a series of alleyways, all in different directions.

"I think you lost her, buddy," I complained.

"No lose. Know where girl went," the driver said.

I was stunned. "Yeah. Where?"

"I take you," he said.

We circled around the Imperial Palace grounds. The driver came to a stop and pointed across the street. The girl's cab was just pulling up in front of a large red pagoda style building with a giant wooden goal post, marking the entrance. She was still inside the car.

"This Yasukuni," The driver said. "Very famous Shrine where dead soldiers live. Many Japanese people come here to pay respects to soldiers who die in war."

"Like Arlington Cemetery?" I said, hoping the driver would understand. He didn't. "What's the goal post thing over the entrance?" I asked.

"This is Tori gate. Is mark of Shrine," the driver answered.

Crowds of people were moving in and out under the gate. Many of them were Japanese soldiers in uniforms.

I watched as the girl paid the driver and got out of the cab.

"Girl go to Yasukuni to talk to spirit of dead warriors. They give guidance," the driver said. "Take girl here often."

I reached in my pocket for money to pay the driver. I could see the girl was going in the Shrine. "I'm gonna follow her," I told the driver.

"Ooohhh, not so good idea," the driver moaned, adding, "American here alone not good."

"Why? Is it against the law?"

"No. No law," the driver said.

"Okay, then you come with me," I said.

"No. No go," the driver said.

"I'll give you a five hundred extra yen," I offered.

The driver thought it over. He was a man with four young children.

I could see he still wasn't convinced to come along. "Okay, a thousand Yen," I said, upping the fee.

"You pay thousand yen now?" the driver asked.

I didn't hesitate. I gave him a thousand Yen note. "Now, let's go."

The driver and I had just started into the Yasu-kuni Shrine Tori Gate, when my path was suddenly blocked by a couple of young Japanese tough guys. Their angry looks made it clear, I wasn't welcome.

The driver made it clear that I was with him and he was big enough to deter them from doing any-thing worse, so they let us pass.

Beyond the Tori gate was a walkway about twenty feet wide made of pebbles. It ran for a hundred yards or so and ended at the steps of the Shrine. While we walked up it the driver kept looking over his shoulder, expecting at any moment we would be attacked by the toughs.

The older people seemed friendly, or maybe they didn't care. I didn't care either away. I was busy look-ing for the girl.

On either side of the pebbled pathway were concession stands adorned with large white cloth banners with Japanese characters painted in bright red and yellow colors. They announced each stall's specialty: souvenirs, fruit baskets, picture books, candy, incense, etc., etc. Yasukuni had the same feeling as a church bazaar.

Sitting at the end of the line of stalls was a large windowless Japanese pagoda.

"Is that the Shrine?" I asked, pointing.

"Hai," the driver said.

Four tread-worn steps led up to a highly polished, wooden porch. Beyond, were two massive mahogany doors, sculpted elaborately with horses and dragons. They were open, like huge welcoming arms. A large oriental tapestry, hung down from the edge of the pagoda's gracefully curving eave. It shaded the sculpted doors and the Shrine's interior from the harsh rays of the afternoon sun. The tapestry draped down so far, it occasionally brushed the tops of taller Japanese heads passing underneath. Heavy, red-painted wood beams held up a roof covered in shiny red enameled ceramic tile.

As I stood staring up at the structure, two old men, in weathered Japanese Army uniforms, one of them on crutches, hobbled past me. They gave me a nasty look, filled with loathing and contempt.

I was beginning to feel very unpopular.

The driver saw the girl. "Girl at concession stand," he said, pointing at her.

I spotted her picking out an apple, an orange, and some candy, along with several sticks of incense. I watched as she wrapped the fruit in red paper, then put everything in her purse.

"Is part of an offering for an honored soul," the driver explained, having seen my questioning look. The cab diver told me, he himself had made many offerings.

Near the steps leading up to the Shrine was a large brass basin filled with water. The girl stopped to purify herself by washing her face and hands. Then, she went up the stairs and entered the Shrine.

The cabby and I followed.

Two Shinto priests, in saffron colored togas, were on the porch talking with three older Japanese war veterans wearing Army uniforms. One soldier wore an eye patch. Another was missing a leg and had to lean heavily on a homemade crutch. The third looked like a dried up old stick, but he was animated and fairly spry. When they saw us coming up the stairs to enter the Shrine, the aging veterans began grumbling. The crippled veteran voiced the harshest objections directly at me, waving and yelling loudly in Japanese. The Shinto priests tried to subdue him.

"They want you to leave," the cabby translated.

I decided to ignore them, hoping they would stop.

We ducked into the sheltering arms of the large, sculpted, mahogany doors, which thankfully blocked us from the irate group.

When my eyes adjusted to the subdued light, I could clearly see the inside the Shrine. It was a room filled with historical war stuff, uniforms, photos, mementos from past Japanese conflicts, even, according to the driver, a centuries old poem penned by Japan's greatest warrior, the Emperor Meijis. The walls were lined with sandalwood and rice paper panels alternating with solid white plaster. The high ceiling was a dark tangle of carved wood beams.

I wanted to go in and look around but the driver advised against it. He assured me that I could not miss the girl coming out, because the only way in or out of the Shrine was through those great Mahogany Doors. I stood there straining to see her inside.

At the back of the Shrine I spotted her sliding open one of the rice panel doors. She stepped into the small room leaving the door partially open. On her hands and knees, she approached the altar. Quietly, she laid her purse down on the polished wood floor, clapped her hands twice, then bowed her head.

A Shinto Priest appeared at her side carrying one of the Sacred Books of the Honored Dead which contained the names of all who had died in Japan's many wars. The priest already knew which book to bring, the one with her fathers name in it, but the asking was still part of the ritual.

He handed the old black leather volume to the girl, then bowed and backed out through the door.

She placed the Sacred Book on the small black lacquered altar. She opened the book to the page where her father's name was inscribed. With the lightest brush of her fingernails, she gently traced the graceful brushstrokes, which formed the characters of her his name. Then she pulled out the photograph of her father in uniform from her purse, the one she took during his last leave from the Navy. She leaned the photo against the incense burner. For the first time she could see the likeness between her father and her brother. Then she removed the red paper from the fruit she had purchased and laid it out smooth on the altar, forming a slightly crinkled place mat. The apple and pear she placed on either side of the impromptu mat. She loosened the wrapping from a piece of candy, shaping it around the sweet to create a stylized flower. Lovingly she put it near the center of the red tissue mat, just below the column in the book. She lit the sticks of incense and waved them until the flames were replaced by a fragrant, smoldering glow. One at a time, she planted them in the sparkling white sand of the incense burner on the left side of the altar prayer, taking care that all the sticks were arranged just so, while intoning the proper prayer.

She removed a piece of white silk from her bag and began to carefully unfold it. Inside were the cherry blossom petals she had collected last spring, from the tree her grandfather had planted in honor of her father's birth. Her delicate fingers gathered the petals and let them fall, like fragrant snow, on her father's photograph. The aromatic blend of incense and cherry blossoms drifted about.

She clapped twice, as she had done many times before, and bowed her head to announce her presence to his spirit, then she began to pray. I could only guess she was telling him about her fears and the loneliness of her life.

After a few moments, as she seemed to feel her father's spirit filling the room, her eyes welled over with tears. They flowed slowly down her cheeks dropping on the bed of petals.

Suddenly the aging veterans and young toughs marched up the front steps onto the porch. They glared at me like snarling dogs as they grumbled loudly in Japanese. A large crowd began to form.

"What are they saying now?" I asked the driver.

"They say your uniform was the mark of our nation's enemy. We were sworn to kill you. Now you come to mock us with it," the driver explained with a look of fear in his eyes. "You violate the sacred spirits of the war dead."

Their words made the cab driver feel like a traitor, especially since he too lost loved ones during WWII, among them a brother at Iwo Jima.

"Go-mend-da-sigh, I must leave," the driver said, then ran off.

I could only watch him go.

The crowd continued spewing verbal venom, as well as spit, at me. One of the alarmed priests came out. "This is a Shrine for their war dead....You do not belong," he said.

"Tell them I'm sorry. I'm not trying to defile anyone," I said. "I'm only waiting for a friend. She's inside praying. I'll be leaving very soon."

The Priest translated my words but the men were not satisfied and kept yelling at me, the toughs were ready to fight

"You would be safer waiting outside the gate. Go Please," the Priest pleaded. "I will tell your friend you're waiting outside."

I didn't need any more trouble, so I started back down the pebbled pathway. No one followed me.

I decided to kill time by browsing the various things for sale in the stalls that lined the path. I bought an apple, then waited by the entrance gate, keeping an eye on the Shrine's main doors.

I felt a tug at my pants leg. I looked down into the face of a little Japanese girl. She was smiling at the apple. I held it out to her. But her mother yanked her away before she could grab it, angrily scolding the girl in Japanese. I could only imagine she was muttering, "He's one of the American demons who destroyed us."

I decided to pass the time by counting the cherry trees within eyes view. I was up to around fifty, when I heard a familiar voice.

"Why did you come here?" It was the girl with the cobalt blue eyes.

I knew what I wanted to say but the words didn't come easily.

"You were right. They don't like Americans here. Some of these guys would kill me if they could," I said.

"Why didn't you just leave?" she asked.

"I guess because hanging around to talk to you seemed more important," I said sincerely.

The thought embarrassed her. We were both uncertain of what to say next.

"I must get back to my work, now," she said, walking away towards the line of cabs at the curb.

"Wait a minute," I said, hurrying to catch up. "Every time I talk to you I wind up in a track meet."

She smiled slightly, but kept walking.

"I don't even know your name," I said shuffling to keep up with her.

"It is better that way," she said.

"Besides, what's in a name? Right?" I said.

"Shakespeare," she answered simply.

"I'll bet he's the one who taught you to speak English," I said.

She couldn't help smiling again.

"I see you have a sense of humor," I said.

"Look. Now that we know each other, we should get together," I said, undaunted. "And right away, 'cause I'm going to be shipped to Korea soon," I added.

"No. It would be wrong. For both of us," she said as she hurriedly climbed into the back seat of the first cab in the line.

"Why?" I persisted.

She didn't answer. She tried to pull the door closed but I blocked it.

"Why? Tell me. Go ahead. I'll give you an hour," I begged.

This time she ignored my humor.

"Ee-kee-ma-show," she told the driver. He started pulling away. I was forced to back up or get my feet run over.

"I still think you're the most beautiful girl I've ever seen," I hollered after the cab as it disappeared into the traffic.

Suddenly something rock hard smashed into my gut. Then, a fist slammed into my chest. Another fist hit into my jaw. I sagged to the sidewalk in pain, gasping for air. Other figures began punching and kicking me, hard. I caught a brief glimpse of the guy with the scar across his forehead. His eyes were boiling with rage.

I was starting to black out when the sound of police whistles filled the air. The next thing I knew, two Japanese policemen were hauling me to my feet, while two other officers rounded up and subdued my attackers. To my surprise the four young toughs including the guy with the scar were loaded into one of the police vans.

The girl was right, this was a place I did not like. Not at all. Luckily I was well enough to get into a cab to get back to base The driver who took me back to Oji was another Kamikaze race car driver type, so I braced my feet against the driver's seat partition and distracted my self by thinking about the big meeting. I started to worry. Now aching and dirty I had to face Colonel Macmillan.

Chapter 9

Board Of Governors Meeting

I checked my appearance in the mirror on the wall locker door, deciding it was the best I could do. I practiced my speech, but I couldn't shake the feeling that it sounded too simple, almost stupid. If that's all I say I might come off sounding like a smart-ass or like I wasn't taking the problem seriously.

"Hey, Naud," Plummer called out as he came around the mountain of liquor boxes. "Just be sure you get the Colonel out of the meeting in time for him to get downtown to that conference with MacArthur at seventeen-hundred hours. That's five o'clock to you." He knew I had trouble figuring out military time. "So you got a half an hour to get him out of there," he warned, politely.

I could get the Colonel out of there in five seconds, if I had the guts.

"See ya upstairs and good luck," Plummer said, vanishing back around the giant mountain of liquor boxes.

I ran up the stairs with stacks of poster cards and four easels. Then rushed into the club unaware that the floor had just been waxed. My feet zipped out from under me. Luckily, I barely averted breaking my neck by catching hold of one of the door handles. I hoped it wasn't an omen.

Toshiko and Tadashi had put together three of the Club's small tables to make one long conference table in the middle of the dance floor. Name cards, ashtrays, and paper with pencils sat in front of each.

Sergeant Baker and the other board members, Corporals Dehler, Pollazzo, Mula, PFCs Hartung and Zinger, were sitting at the bar, talking, smoking, and drinking. Dehler kept asking the waiters for a beer, but I had given instructions not to serve the board members anything but soft drinks and water.

Corporal Pollazzo came over to watch me line the easels up. I placed a stack of poster cards on each. The cover cards were printed in large, red, block letters, with a title explaining that stack's topic.

Dehler, who had managed to wrangle himself a Tuborg beer, started mocking the card's titles by reading them aloud. 1. DEVELOPING CUSTOMER APPEAL 2. SELECTING ASA ENTERTAINMENT 3. GAMBLING ACTIVITY 4. INCOME PROJECTIONS 5. CUSTOMER GROWTH

"Hot damn, Naud. You're gonna give us all brain fever," he said.

Sergeant Baker arrived at the conference table. "I sure hope you ain't done all this work for nothing," he said cynically.

"I sure hope so too, Sergeant," I said, mimicking Baker's 'shit-kicker' accent.

At precisely sixteen hundred hours, Sergeant Baker stood up and barked, "ATTENJHUT."

Colonel Macmillan came striding into the EM Club as I and the other board members snapped to attention.

'The Colonel might be a wacko, but he sure as hell looks and moves like a spit and polish soldier,' I thought.

"At-ease, men," he said, placing his briefcase on the table. "Light em if you got em." He began removing papers from his case while he read the titles on my cover cards. I could see he was impressed.

Plummer came rushing into the club carrying a shorthand notebook and took a seat next to the Colonel. He didn't notice the easels or the stacks of cards on them.

"The ASA EM Club Board of Governors monthly meeting will come to order," the Colonel announced as he glanced over at Plummer to be sure he was ready. "Mister Secretary, please record all members are present. In the interest of brevity I make a motion we waive the reading of last month's minutes. Any second?"

"I second," Sergeant Baker said, casually, as he kept biting off a hangnail.

"All in favor, say, 'Aye'," said the Colonel.

The response was a chorus of empty, Aye's.

"Motion carried," the Colonel said. "Any old business?" There was no answer. "Okay new business?" the Colonel snapped, moving things along like it was a track meet.

Corporal Pollazzo produced a letter from his jacket. It was from Sergeant Creamer, who was now at a VA rehabilitation clinic back in Washington. It was a 'thank you' note. Pollazzo wanted to read it out loud.

I thought reading it aloud sounded like a nice thing to do.

Baker coldly cut Pollazzo off. "Sir? We can save time by posting the letter on the Club's bulletin board, so anybody who wants can read it?"

"Yeah," Dehler chimed in, doing what a stooge does.

The Colonel responded more compassionately to Pollazzo and the letter, but made it clear that he was in a hurry to get on with the meeting.

"Any other new business?" the Colonel pressed on.

Dehler had another letter in his hand. "Sir? This letter was also written by Sergeant Creamer and was witnessed by Sergeant Baker and Toshiko."

"What are we talking about, Corporal?" the Colonel inquired.

"Sir, this letter assures board members that they will receive free drinks during the full term of their service."

I didn't know anything about such a letter.

"Sir? I'd like to know why Naud isn't continuing Sergeant Creamer's free drink policy for board members according to this signed letter," Dehler protested.

"The free drink policy is always up to the current custodian," the Colonel said, adding, "the matter is up to Private Naud."

Corporal Dehler was going to argue until Sergeant Baker glared at him to keep his mouth shut.

"Any more new business," the Colonel inquired.

"No, Sir," Baker said, helping the Colonel move things along.

"Alright," the Colonel said. He checked Plummer to make sure he had gotten every thing, so far, and was ready to go on.

Plummer was ready, so the Colonel turned to me. "Private Naud here is our interim custodian. Right now, it's very important for the EM Club to be popular, especially with the code guys. So let's hear what he has come up with."

"Yes, Sir," I said, sounding like I was ready to go. I rose and moved with unhurried ease toward the presentation easels, as I gathered my wits. Other than the fact that I had solved the problem of getting a handful of girls on the base, I had absolutely nothing else to say.

"This looks like an impressive presentation, Naud," the Colonel said.

"Thank you, Sir. I hope it is," I said. I caught the Colonel checking his watch.

Plummer looked up from his notes and was pleased to see the elaborate presentation I had come up with. To him it looked like just the Colonel's kind of thing.

Corporal Dehler and Pfc. Zinger swung their chairs around in order to be able to read the cards easily.

Baker was indifferent, keeping his back to the presentation as he lit a cigar.

"Sir, first of all," I began, very slowly and deliberately. "I'd like to thank you, Sir, and the Board for allowing me the opportunity to present my plan. I'm aware of the contribution the Club can make to the ASA's mission. And let me state, my first objective was to identify, and verify, the kinds of experiences, club experiences, the members of the code section will enjoy."

I caught the Colonel checking his watch again, a good sign. I was getting to him already. So I kept going on in the same slow deliberate manner.

The Colonel started shifting in his seat.

Plummer gestured to me to speed it up a little.

I made believe I didn't see his cue, and slowed down even more.

"Certainly one of the first questions a customer asks himself when he gets to an EM Club is, 'What am I doing here?'" I said droning on. "Parenthetically, Sir, in gathering my research, the one thing that really surprised me was the fact that not all GI's go to Clubs to find girls. You'll see on my charts, about forty- three percent go to drink or gamble."

Every word coming from my mouth seemed to come out slower and slower.

The Colonel kept rocking from side to side. He was losing patience.

Baker had lost what little patience he had and gave vent to his feelings. "Sir? No disrespect to you, Sir," Baker interjected, cutting me off. "I don't see what any of this stuff has got to do with anything."

The board members, except for Plummer and Pollazzo, burst out laughing. But I kept my poise.

"At-ease," the Colonel said, angrily. He was in no mood to joke around.

Plummer kept writing down the minutes, painfully aware that if this kept up the Colonel wouldn't get to MacArthur's meeting before midnight, if then.

"I'm sure Naud is about to get to the point," the Colonel said, in a tone that was more like an order.

"Thank you, Sir," I said. My plan was working.

"Sir, the value of my research will soon become very clear to you." I said.

"Yes. And the sooner the better, Naud," the Colonel politely but firmly interjected.

"Yes, Sir," I said. "Sir, I've spent considerable time talking with the EM Club Managers downtown. They all say the same thing. Maintaining your customer base is a dynamic thing, an ongoing process, which must be nurtured constantly. Vigilance. Vigilance is what my research tells me is needed. And I'm sure you'll see the same thing as we go through all my data."

"Look, Naud," the Colonel interrupted. "Forget the cards and the data. I'm sure your research is impressive. Let me hear your plan in as few words as possible."

"Sir, with all due respect, a sound plan can't be reduced to just a few words," I responded.

"Well do it anyway," the Colonel insisted.

"Okay, Sir, in a FEW words," I paused briefly. "My plan is GIRLS, LIQUOR, and GAMBLING, Sir. But mostly GIRLS."

The Colonel waited, fully expecting to hear more details, but when nothing more came he gave me an incredulous look. "Is that it? Your whole plan?"

"Yes, Sir," I said, but quickly added, "In a few words."

Baker was quick to try and bury me. "Sir? This whole thing is a waste of your time."

"Naud, In case you didn't know. I have given orders that nobody can bring a girl on base without a security pass," the Colonel said curtly. He started packing his briefcase, preparing to leave.

"Yes, Sir. I know, Sir." I said. " But I've solved the problem."

The Colonel froze in mid motion. He stopped packing and looked at me. "What are you talking about?" he said with a confused look.

"How?" Now Baker challenged me too.

I just ignored Baker. My shining moment had arrived.

"Well, Sir, I'm gonna hire a band. Lucinda and Her All Girl Band. Seventeen girls, who are all pretty and who all have something else in common. They all have security clearances. And they are all willing to take turns dancing with the guys."

The Colonel was obviously impressed. He looked over at Baker. "Do the bands that come here have security clearances?" he asked.

"Yes, Sir. It's Standard Operating Procedure," Baker conceded, reluctantly.

The Colonel smiled broadly.

"Well, now. Good thinking, Naud," he said.

My hopes began to soar. "Thank you, Sir."

"Get going on it right away. This afternoon," the Colonel ordered.

"Yes Sir." I said enthusiastically.

"If there's no more business, I move the meeting be adjourned," the Colonel said as he packed up the rest of his papers.

"Sir? Naud's plan is good, but it has a problem," Baker interjected, happy to put the kybosh on it all. "Money, Sir, We don't have the money to pay for Lucinda's band."

The Colonel turned to Plummer who was also the Club treasurer. "Does the Club have the money?"

Plummer squirmed, hesitating to say anything.

"Yes, or No, Plummer?" the Colonel demanded.

Baker re-lit his cigar with a sly smile on his face, waiting. He knew the answer.

"No, Sir," Plummer conceded.

To their surprise, I was ready with the solution. "Sir? If we cut the Little Joes back to two nights a week we'll have the money."

Baker blew cigar smoke at his stooges. Dehler, Mula, Zinger, and Hartung began to protest. "The guys won't like cutting back on the Joes, Sir."

Pollazzo was disgusted. He knew damn well that they couldn't stand the Little Joes.

But any argument over the matter was cut short. The Colonel had made up his own mind.

"Naud. I like the plan. We'll cut back on the Joes and give it a try," he said.

"We can't, Sir," Baker said.

"What do you mean we can't, Sergeant?" the Colonel said defiantly.

"Last month, Creamer signed a contract guaranteeing the Little Joes three nights a week. Even if they don't play, we still have to pay them."

The Colonel looked at me for the solution to this latest stumbling block. The Colonel was obviously frustrated and annoyed with the whole matter. And he was out of time.

Plummer could see he was about to explode. "Sir? Naud's got other ideas to get girls in here," he said, sounding like the cavalry coming to the rescue.

"Not now," the Colonel barked, cutting him off. "Get your ideas on paper Naud and give 'em to Plummer," he added, rising to go. "This meeting is adjourned."

"ATTENJHUT," Sergeant Baker bellowed as he rose to his feet. Everyone stood at attention as the Colonel strode briskly out of the Club. Baker and Dehler followed, at a more leisurely pace, with smiles on their faces. The three stooges, Mula, Zinger and Hartung, tagged along.

"Too bad you had to waste all your elaborate preparations, Naud," Plummer said. He walked over to the easels and thumbed through the cards, one after another, stack after stack. Half way through, he started to laugh. He realized my 'elaborate preparations' were nothing but a pile of blank poster cards.

I wasn't laughing. I was looking out the window, watching the sun go down, to the west, toward Korea, where I knew the Colonel would send me soon unless I managed to get the money for the girls band.

Chapter 10

Bingo Night Club

It was early morning and I was still feeling defeated from the Board Meeting. After showing my pass and getting an odd look from the guard, I walked out of the main gate with my golf clubs on my shoulder.

It was too early for the joy girls to be gathered at the gate, the path to the line of tinny red cabs was unobstructed. I crawled into the back seat of the first cab, "Dozo, e-key-ma-sho, Kogene," I said practicing my Japanese.

"Hai," the driver said, and fired up the engine.

I was pleased when he understood. .

Kogene was about twenty miles north of Tokyo. Once we left the city we were in farm country. The roads became dirt but they were smooth. The fields we passed were newly furrowed and gave off the smell of spring, like things were starting over. But it wasn't spring, it was summer. Still, in a way I was starting over.

After about a half an hour we passed a sign nailed to a tree that read: KOGENE GOLF COURSE, 1 MILE.

When we got to the course, I went into the western style pro shop located in a trailer park type building. There was no hint of anything oriental, except for the row of large framed photos hanging on the wall showing photos of people right out of the history books, who had played the course: Emperor Hirohito, Admiral Yamagushi, Tojo, Herman Goering and even Charles Lindbergh. There were many others but those were the figures I recognized. I spotted a photo showing the Emperor and Admiral Yamaguchi standing at the practice tee. I imagined Yamaguchi, the Admiral who had planned and led the attack at Pearl harbor, giving the Emperor golf lessons while discussing his strategy to bomb America. I could see Tojo, the head of Japanese military and Goering slic-ing up the world as easily as they sliced the divots in the turf.

The Sergeant who ran the pro shop also told me how Tojo drove his staff car right out onto the golf course to inform Hirohito about the Americans dropping the Atom bomb, destroying the city of Hiroshima. That must have been the moment the Emperor realized Japan had lost the war.

I recalled where I was when I heard about the Atom Bomb being dropped. I was at home, in upper Manhattan, sitting on the living room floor, listening to the radio with my family. I recalled thinking how the world was changed forever. If there were ever another world war, it would be the last.

Kogene had been an exclusive, world famous golf course. And still was, except it was currently also open to both American officers and enlisted men for the ridiculously low greens fee of three dollars. All the caddies were girls and they cost three dollars, plus tip. A bucket of practice balls was fifty cents.

I dumped my golf bag and the bucket of balls on the practice tee. The sun was still low, creating long shadows. The dew glistened on the grass and the air was sparkling clean. Everything seemed peaceful and unspoiled. To me this time of day on a golf course was as spiritually uplifting as being in church.

I took my five-iron from the bag, took my stance, and swung, catching the ball flush and hard. It flew dead straight. I did it a few more times with the same result.

"Your swing looks good," someone called out behind me.

"Thanks," I said, turning around to find a guy in his twenties who resembled Robert Stack, the movie actor. He was setting up to hit some balls. It was obvious he had money, or came from it. His golf slacks, golf shirt, and black and white Footjoys were all very expensive. He dumped his bucket of balls and started hacking away. His swing looked more like a controlled lunge. The first ball he hit flew two hundred and twenty-five yards, dead straight.

"If I could do that all the time, I'd beat Ben Hogan," he called over, delighted with the results.

"If you could do it every time you'd BE Ben Hogan," I said.

"How come I've never seen you around?" he asked.

"I've never been around," I said, launching a four-iron like an arrow.

"What's your handicap?" he asked.

"Right now, getting up in the morning," I quipped.

He chuckled, "You're funny." He teed up a line of six balls and proceeded to slash at them like a raging windmill. He hit one after the other: a slice, a hook, a top, and a shank, all while he grunted and groaned in frustration. Then he paused for a moment. "Got any suggestions?" he asked.

"Take up tennis," I said, then relented. "Sure. I'll give you some tips. "

"Okay," the stranger said, grateful to have the help. He followed what I told him and managed to hit a few of the balls straight and far.

"Hey, thanks," he said. "Where are you from?"

"New York," I said. "You in the service?" I asked.

"I was but now I make a living selling liquor to the EM clubs. Pretty soon I'll have enough money saved to go home and buy my own distributorship then I can pay for law school.

"Ever hear of Sergeant Creamer at the ASA EM Club?" I asked.

"Sure. I know him very well. He's a good friend. I'm going to his club on Thursday," he said.

"Don't bother. Creamer is at a hospital in the States," I said. "He got the DT's, a week ago, so they shipped him out. "

"That's too bad. Who's running the EM Club now?" he asked.

"I am," I said, wiping the mud off my four-iron with the towel hanging from my golf bag.

"How 'bout that?" he said, mimicking Mel Allen, the Yankee sportscaster and offering his hand. "Greg Surrel."

I shook it. "Bill Naud," I said, introducing himself.

"Baker must be slipping. I thought Dehler would take over the EM Club. If you don't already know, Naud, Baker runs ASA OJI. How are things going out there?"

"Not too good. I've been ordered to get girls out there to keep the code-breakers on base, it's a matter of security." My tone made it sound like it was crucial to the war effort.

Surrel looked at his watch. "It's time for me to tee off," he said, "but I might be able to help you. The company I work for is sponsoring the Miss Tokyo contest, in about a month. I'll see what I can do to get them to hold it out at your EM Club in OJI. I'll call you," he hollered back as he headed towards the first tee.

"Sounds Great!" I called after him. Things were looking up. I hit a few more practice shots, then the golf course starter found me a match with a mousy Captain and a Sergeant with a chest full of medals, who was in on R&R from Korea.

Our girl caddies were dressed identically in baggy white linen pants and shirts with a white cloth band around their foreheads. They were very attractive.

The Sergeant was taking slugs from a bottle of whiskey he had stashed in his golf bag. Between the hot sun and the straight booze he got smash-ass drunk. By the sixth hole he started trying to kiss his caddie.

She wasn't interested. "Baka, Baka," she kept screaming as she struggled to escape him.

"Hey come on Sergeant, let her go, huh?" I urged, trying to help the girl escape his grip. She finally broke free and ran off with the clubs. The Sergeant took off in pursuit. Two hundred yards down the fairway, he caught up to her. She threw his clubs at him, dove into the pond, and swam away. He waded in after her, but fell on his face in the water. Two MP's arrived in a jeep and pulled the soggy drunk Sergeant from the pond and took him away in handcuffs.

I decided this wasn't anything resembling golf and finished the round on my own, then hopped in a cab to go back to the base. The cab driver wasn't familiar with the area and had trouble finding his way to OJI, with all the war damage there were few road signs left. So I was late getting back to the base and when I arrived the EM club was already open for business.

I changed into a fresh uniform, buoyed by the prospect of Surrel holding the Miss Tokyo contest at our Club. The ceiling was vibrating from the noise of the crowd above. Toshiko had told me a large group of ASA guys were expected in from Korea for R&R, (Rest and Relaxation).

I started up the stairs to the Club. Little Joe was banging and slamming away as I entered through the swinging doors. Tonight he sounded like a train wreck having a nervous breakdown. But the crowd was cheering, they seemed to love it. Or maybe after being in a foxhole in Korea, any music sounded great.

I worked my way through the crush of bodies as the bone jarring noise continued to assault my nervous system. As I crawled behind the bar to help Jumbo and Nakijima fill the orders of the GI's crowding in, reaching for their drinks, I noticed Plummer sitting at the end of the bar looking glum.

After serving six or seven Tuborg beers and tossing their payment chits in the fish bowl sitting against the mirror on the back wall of the bar, I eased my way to Plummer, excited to tell him my promising news.

"Hey Listen, I've got some good news about getting girls here. I ran into a guy I think you know, Greg Surrel."

"Oh yeah. He's a good guy," Plummer interjected.

"He thinks he can get his company to agree to hold a Miss Tokyo contest here."

Plummer's expression soured. "I wouldn't get my hopes up. He tried that in the spring when I first got here. We lost out to one of the big clubs downtown. Good try, Naud. Give me a beer will yah," he said as he folded a letter and put it in his pocket.

I slipped from happiness to misery in the matter of a sentence. The Little Joes banging away on stage just adding to my misery.

Now I was back to thinking I was going be sent over to Korea for my failure to get the girls to the club. The only consoling thought was that at least I would be seeing Jessie there.

At the moment, I was safe. Colonel Macmillan had flown over to Pusan with MacArthur for some top-secret reason, according to Plummer. And he was the only one who could sign my transfer orders.

A clap of thunder and lightening drew my attention to the windows. Sheets of rain were pouring down making it almost impossible to see out.

Corporal Pollazzo came through the clubs swinging doors, his poncho dripping water from the storm outside. He tried to shake it dry. Then he spotted Plummer at the bar.

I was back serving drinks as he came through the crowd, coughing from the dense cloud of cigarette smoke that filled the room. I didn't really know much about Pollazzo except that he was a codebreaker and on the Club's board of governors. Plummer trusted him. He said he was an orphan from a Catholic boy's home in Chicago who had taught himself to speak and read five languages. I found that hard to believe. He sounded like an uneducated kid from the streets.

When Pollazzo finally reached Plummer he leaned in to his ear and spoke in a low tone. "His discharge just came through."

"When's the Inspection?", Plummer asked.

"Tomorrow morning after Reveille, " Pollazzo replied.

"Want a drink?" I asked Pollazzo.

"No, I gotta get back up on the hill," he answered then quickly worked his way back out of the room.

Finally Little Joe finished slamming his drums around, stood up and started milking the loud applause.

Sergeant Baker jumped onto the stage and took the mike away from him. He was wearing a gaudy Hawaiian shirt and had an unlit cigar in his mouth. His butch haircut and stocky build made him resemble William Bendix in *Life of Riley*. He stuck the mike in his armpit so he could light his cigar, took a big puff, put the mike to his mouth, "Testing. Testing, Testing" he said, blowing out the smoke into the mike. Then he announced, "Okay, folks It's, Bingo time. Are you all ready to win some dough?"

The raucous crowd answered with a resounding, "Yes!"

Joe and his band members shoved their stuff to the back of the stage, to clear a space for the waiters who brought up a chair and a table.

Toshiko appeared with a wire cage filled with bingo balls. He put it on the Table, and next to it he placed a board with numbered holes for the chosen balls.

"If you don't have a bingo card yet get one now from one of the waiters. " I announced.

"How much are they?" A GI called out.

"A mere twenty bucks, *my chickadees*," Baker answered in a bad *W.C Fields* imitation.

The waiters moved through the sea of GIs, who were waving their money and chits, exchanging the payments for a bingo card.

"Remember, tonight's super Bingo could be worth as much as $1400," Baker announced with a forced smile.

The jovial crowd got ready, grabbing a handful of little discs to cover up the numbers on their boards when they're called out.

"Okay, here we go," Baker said as he adjusted his chair next to the table. He began cranking the wire cage full of balls, spinning it around and around, then brought it to a stop. A few balls fell through the shoot and were sitting in a line on the metal chute. He averted his eyes in a phony exaggerated manner as he picked up the first ball. Then he leaned into the mike and read the number. "Our first number is G-26."

"BINGO!" somebody screamed out.

The well-lubricated crowd roared with laughter.

Baker forced a patronizing grin, playing along with the wisecrack.

"Remember, this game is worth one hundred dollars," he reminded the crowd. He grabbed another ball puffing his dying cigar back to life. "O-16," he called out.

There was a mix of grumbles, and surprised 'got its .

"Hey, Sarge, how about calling B-4," a voice bellowed out.

"N-42, please," some other GI requested.

Baker was holding the next ball in his hand. "I think it's B-6. Or is it B- 9?" he said playfully rolling it around, teasing the crowd. "IT IS, B-6."

Grumbles and cheers rippled through the men.

Baker called six more numbers while the happy crowd played along.

As their boards started to fill up, the men became quieter hoping the next number called might be the winning one for them. Baker reached for another ball as he worked the cigar to the side of his mouth. "I got a feeling we're gonna have a winner here. How about, N-41? N-41."

A booming voice bellowed out loud and clear, "Son of a Bitch! BINGO!"

The crowd reacted with a mix of disappointed moans and half-hearted cheers.

"Bring it up here. I gotta check the numbers," Baker called out.

The winning Staff Sergeant staggered his way through the fog of cigarette smoke and GIs, waving his bingo card above his head all the way to the stage. "I got it. I got it," he insisted.

Baker checked the numbers and declared, "We have a winner!" He took a handful of money from the cigar box in his lap, and made a show of paying the Sergeant in a magnanimous manner, slapping five twenty-dollar bills on the table, one at a time. "You got yourself one hundred greenbacks, Sergeant," he said.

The Staff Sergeant took his money and staggered back to his seat, waving his winnings in the air in triumph.

Baker called four more one-hundred-dollar bingo games, pausing on occasion to puff his expensive cigar back to life. "Okay, everybody. It's time for SUPER-BINGO. Are you ready?" Baker asked.

The well-oiled crowd whistled and cheered, they were ready.

"Tonight's Super-bingo game is worth one thousand American greenbacks. If you need extra cards, raise your hand. Remember the more cards you have, the better your chances of winning *my little chickadees*." Baker's greedy grin was spotted with bits of tobacco.

Hands went up all around the room. The waiters, holding stacks of cards, scurried about delivering them to GIs who were anxiously holding out there money and chits.

Plummer scoffed, mumbling to himself, "You've got a snowball's chance in hell of winning, *my little chickadees*." He nursed his beer while scanning the room. "Hey, Naud, see the beady eyed guy sitting by the window behind Dehler? He's from Hardy Barracks, downtown."

I looked over at the guy. "What about him?"

Plummer moved his lips without speaking, "he's the Super Bingo Winner."

"Why do you think it's him?" I asked.

Plummer didn't have a chance to answer.

"Okay, here we go," Baker said.

The waiters had sold out all the cards and handed the money to Baker. He stuffed the money into the cigar box sitting on his lap. It was full.

The cage of balls chattered round and round as Baker turned the handle. Then he reached down, averted his eyes, and came out with a ball. "Our first Super-bingo number is, B-10, B-10," Baker called out.

"Got it," someone yelled.

"Like lambs to slaughter," Plummer mumbled.

"N-23, N-23," Baker called out.

Another chorus of Ah's and Ooh's of near misses rippled through the room. After five more numbers the crowd started screaming out the numbers that they wanted Baker to call.

"Hold it down," he bellowed with a growl. It took a few moments for the room to quiet down, as Baker sat back picking bits of tobacco from his teeth.

"That's better. Now we'll see who's gonna get rich," he said with a laugh. He reached down, averted his gaze, and grabbed another ball. "How about, N-foor-rtty......4? N-44?"

"BINGO," somebody screamed.

It WAS the beady eyed Pfc. sitting by the window. The crowd erupted in a massive groan of disappointment. The Pfc made his way through the packed room towards the stage.

Junji was making his way through the crowd to deliver the drinks to Dehler's table. Dehler was there, along with Baker's three other stooges, Corporal Mula, Pfc. Hartung, and Pfc. Zinger. Dehler was a loud angry drunk. Tonight, he was even louder and angrier. I had given strict orders to the waiters that there would be no more free drinks for the Board of Governors members. So when Dehler refused to pay, Junji put the bottles of beer back on his tray and started walking away.

Then Dehler tripped him.

The tray loaded with beer bottles went crashing to the floor, splashing beer and broken glass all over.

Junji knelt down and frantically began cleaning up. He crawled under the table, picking up bits of glass, and soaking up the sticky liquid with a serving towel.

I was making my way through the crowd to deal with the matter.

Dehler found a half-full bottle of beer on the floor and dribbled it on Junji's back. The shock of the cold beer made Junji jerk and bang his head on the underside of the table, hard enough to lose his balance. He fell to the floor cutting his hand on the broken glass.

Mula, Hartung, and Zinger found the whole thing very amusing. Until I yanked the beer bottle from Dehler's hand.

"Get outta here, Dehler," I ordered angrily.

"City boy, I'm gonna bust your damn head," Dehler said, as he stood up. Dehler was a big guy, but he was dead drunk, which was probably why I managed to duck his first blow.

In a fury, Dehler grabbed my shirt and twisted it tight, setting himself to swing again. His rock like fist was already roaring towards my head when a blurred something struck the back of his neck. He dropped to the floor like a sack of cement. He was out like a light.

"What do you want me to do with him?" Langdon asked, rubbing his stinging hand.

"Take him down to his bunk," I said.

Junji wrapped his bleeding hand with a bar towel while he kept bowing to me in gratitude.

Baker finally finished making a show of double checking the numbers on the beady-eyed Pfc's card. With a final flourish he paid him off slapping one hundred dollar bills on the table.

The Pfc went back to his table.

Baker turned the stage over to the waiters and they started clearing off the Bingo stuff to make room for the Little Joe's.

We all headed back to the bar. Plummer told me how Baker managed to fix the Super Bingo games. Dehler would go downtown to find some GI to play the winning card for one hundred bucks. Dehler got his cut of fifty bucks to find the guy. Baker actually pocketed all the prize money.

'Baker was still Baker,' I thought, 'a crook'. I vowed I would somehow manage to run the Bingo games from that night on.

Chapter 11

Drums And Laughter

Captain Harry Mulvey knew he was in trouble. He was sitting at his desk in the dark, gazing blankly at the raindrops meandering down the window panes. He took another good slug from the half empty bottle of CC whiskey, hoping the liquor would numb him more than it had. He choked and coughed as the fiery stuff went down the wrong side.

He rarely ever drank.

He couldn't believe his former Supply Sergeant, Valkovitch, who was now in Korea, would steal. But he must have. Or, at least, turned a blind eye as someone else siphoned off Company equipment. Sergeant Calvin, the new Supply Sergeant, was adamant, there were all kinds of things missing, from generators to paper clips to furniture. In all, more than twenty-four thousand four- hundred and fifty dollars' worth of Company property was unaccounted for.

Tomorrow morning, as the last real order of business before formally turning over command to Captain Cross, they would take inventory of all the Company property, together. And according to Army law, Mulvey, the standing officer, would be held responsible for any shortages found. There was no way he could raise the twenty thousand four hun- dred and fifty dollars to pay for what was missing, which meant he would be court-martialed. He knew the sentence by heart:

In accordance with the provisions of the Uniform Code of Military Justice, it is the decision of this court that you be reduced to the rank of private, with forfeiture of all accrued or future pay, rights, privileges, and benefits, and shall be confined at Fort Leavenworth for a period not to exceed ten years, after which time you shall be dishonorably discharged.

The consequences scared Mulvey so much he had started drinking. Not just to escape, but to calm himself down enough to think. He clung to the belief that the shortages were really the result of a previous clerical mistake.

He crossed the room and sat at his standard army-issued desk and turned on the OD-green gooseneck lamp. He reached over to tune the Bakelite radio to music of the armed forces station, anything to get his mind off his problems.

"Hey, guys. It's twenty-one past midnight here at Armed Forces Radio, Tokyo," the voice said. "And now here's a song that has probably waltzed its way into your heart, *Tennessee Waltz* by the inimitable Peggy Lee."

Mulvey hummed along feeling the effects of the whiskey. Barbara his wife loved to waltz, at least before the accident. He again relived the painful incident in his mind, as he had so many times before. It was a cold rainy night ten years ago, when he and his wife were driving the fifty miles to Barbara's parents' fiftieth wedding anniversary party. They knew the news that Barbara was pregnant would thrill her folks. But it was dark and Mulvey couldn't see well. Their car was struck by a truck backing out of a driveway. The crash paralyzed Barbara's legs and she lost the baby. Mulvey had always felt guilty he walked away unhurt.

Now, he wanted to call Barbara and hear her voice but he knew he would wind up telling her he was going to jail for a crime he didn't really commit. It would devastate her and probably destroy any desire she had to recover the use of her legs. The VA was sure to strip him of all medical benefits including those that he had planned to use for her operation. If convicted, the army would cut off his pay, leaving them with nothing. They would be forced to live on the charity of her parents.

Mulvey rested his aching forehead in his hands. He wanted to cry but refused.

He wondered how he was going to feel when it finally came time to say goodbye to his men. Most of the guys in the company were codebreakers, egg-heads, the army's intellectual elite. Men who naturally fought his authority. Men who had discovered the army needed their minds and took advantage of that need.

A year ago, when he had taken over the company, they were unruly. They talked in formation and were often disrespectful. They rarely washed or shaved and were usually late for work.

He had pulled their passes, given them extra duty, put people on report, anything to force them into line. But everything he tried, failed. Then he decided to follow some advice from his school teacher mother. She knew how to deal with bright undisciplined kids. *'They need some freedom to use their mental abilities,'* she had told him. So he assembled his men, and promised to be flexible, to give them some breathing room, and help them with their problems, if they would meet him half way, cooperate and do their job.

The proof it worked came months later when the head of the agency, Colonel Macmillan, told him he had the *'worst soldiers in the Army, but the world's best damn code-breakers.'* His mother would never know how much she contributed to the war effort.

When Mulvey took command he also made a pact with the Doctors and Medics at the base dispensary, making sure the unofficial word got out to all the troops: "No VD records will ever be kept." He had seen the sad devastating effects of those who sought treatments off base at some quack doctor, for fear of retaliation by the army. The men soon learned they could trust Mulvey's word, and before long, any one who needed help came to the dispensary. His policy was in direct violation of Army policy, he could get three years in Leavenworth for it, but it saved lives. Someone once said, *'The road to hell is paved with good intentions.'* Harry Mulvey was certainly proof of that.

Mulvey stared at the three important photos on his desk. A wooden frame, which held his wife's picture with an unopened letter leaning against it, a black wood frame, that held a picture of his mom, and the white bamboo frame with his own photo shaking hands with General Patton. His memories of World War II were never far away.

He had been a young Lieutenant in Graves Registration in Sicily. It was April Fool's day, 1944. He had been working in one of the Morgue tents in the midst of a raging thunderstorm. The smell of death was all around him as he emerged from the tent for a breath of fresh air. General George Patton pulled up in a jeep. He had come to pay a surprise visit to the field morgue. An army of photographers were along to record the event.

"Are you in charge here, Lieutenant?" Patton asked Mulvey.

"Yes, General," Mulvey said.

Patton returned Mulvey's salute, tucked his helmet neatly under his arm, and entered the leaking tent, alone.

It was a ghoulish scene.

Mulvey watched him walk slowly up and down the rows of lifeless bodies. At each slain man, in turn, against the background noise of wind whipped canvas and thunder and lightening, Patton murmured something, then ended with a salute.

Two hours later, the storm had subsided. Patton emerged from the dripping tent. Mulvey snapped to attention.

"At-ease, Lieutenant. How long you been in Sicily?" Patton asked.

"Four months, Sir," Mulvey answered.

"Do you believe in God?" Patton asked.

"Yes, Sir," Mulvey said, without hesitation.

"Good," Patton responded, climbing aboard his jeep.

"General?" Mulvey blurted out before Patton could leave, "I keep applying for combat, Sir, but they keep turning me down."

"You're doing valuable work here, son."

"Yes, Sir," Mulvey said, feeling rebuked.

"God bless you," Patton said, with his steely blue eyes still riveted on Mulvey.

They shook hands and exchanged a final salute while flashbulbs went off.

Patton, with his white helmet and entourage of jeeps, bounced and splashed away down the muddy Sicilian road.

A week later, Mulvey was reassigned to a combat unit. He fought with Patton's eighth army in Europe and he was part of the spearhead to free Bastogne, in the *Battle of the Bulge*. After that he was wounded in a mortar barrage and won the Bronze Star.

It was time for Mulvey to do something he had been looking forward to, reading one of his wife's letters. It was full of small stuff, about family and neighbors, but it always comforted him. 'Guess who the largest contributor to the school's building fund is/ Mr. Loganspur,' his wife wrote.

Mulvey had to smile. Mr. Loganspar was his close neighbor, a man who had been like a surrogate father to him. His real dad had died in France, during World War I, while Mulvey was just an infant. When he needed money for college, Mr. Longanspar, offered to let him work in his funeral parlor. It was honest and dignified work. It bothered some, especially the girls in town who wanted nothing to do with him when the word got out he was an undertaker. But Mulvey worked proudly, remembering what his mother always said, '*Nobody ever dies, Harry. The real person goes on to a better place.* '

The GI Disk Jockey was introducing Nat King Cole, singing, *Unforgettable*.

Mulvey smiled to himself. *Unforgettable* was the song he and his wife first danced to when they met at a church social. From then on, they considered it 'their song'. She didn't care he was employed as an undertaker. Reverend Boche married them a year later and Mulvey opened his own funeral parlor with

Barbara's full support and a no-interest GI loan. The business was doing well, but then came the accident.

Years later, on Barbara's thirty-first birthday, Mulvey wheeled her into a restaurant for a surprise party. But she had her own surprise. The doctors told her that, with an operation and a lot of physical therapy, she might walk again. They were singing *Happy Birthday* when a State Trooper, who was a Sergeant in Mulvey's reserve unit, informed him that their outfit had just been activated. They were headed to Germany for duty in connection with the Berlin blockade.

Mulvey tried to resign his commission citing a need to care for his wife. His resignation was denied, twice. He dutifully shut down his funeral parlor business and took Barbara to live with her parents.

The day before he was to leave, the Berlin crisis ended and he was re-routed to Tokyo, Japan.

Now after a year of being away from his wife, he had the chance to go home to be with her, and his heart ached for that moment. He looked out the window. It would be morning in just a few hours, and the inspection with Captain Cross that would reveal the missing property, and probably delay his home coming for many many years to come.

Chapter 12

Secret Mission

I was in a deep sleep, when I was awakened by a noise at the warehouse door. Was someone knocking to come in, or trying to break in? Toshiko had told me of several attempts to rob the Club's safe, which was located just inside the warehouse doors.

I sat up quietly on the edge of my bunk and listened. The clock on top of my locker showed it was almost two in the morning. For protection, I kept a bayonet hidden under the bed. I reached down and grabbed it, then tiptoed around the mountain of boxes to see who was there. I stood by the door waiting in silence, with the bayonet poised.

Suddenly there was more banging.

"Hey, Naud. It's me," a voice called out.

I recognized the 'me', and opened the door.

Corporal Plummer and Sergeant Dollin, the guy in charge of the motor pool, slipped in. I saw a third person out in the reception area, a shadowy figure half hidden by the darkness, it was Pollazzo.

"I need your help, Naud," Plummer said.

I was just relieved someone hadn't been breaking in after the safe. "Sure. Whatta ya want?" I said.

"Trucks," He said, quick and to the point.

"Those I don't got," I said, sounding flip.

"Oh, but you do, Naud," Plummer said.

Sergeant Dollin kept looking around nervously, like he didn't want to be caught there.

"The Club custodian is authorized to sign for trucks," Plummer said. He took a clipboard and pen from Dollin, and handed them to me.

I looked at Dollin. He shook his head in confirmation.

"Just put your signature on the bottom line," Plummer continued.

I started to sign when Dollin interrupted.

"Hey wait, WAIT," Dollin said, anxiously, adding, "What about the deal??? You gotta promise to book the Coca-Cola lady for me."

I looked at Plummer in confusion. He shook his head, yes.

"Okay, I'll book the Coca-Cola lady," I said, taking my cue from Plummer.

"You gotta swear to do it, or it's no deal," Dollin demanded.

"Okay, I swear," I said, signing the sheet. I handed the pen and the clipboard with the sheet back to Dollin.

"All right. Now, you got it, Dollin," Plummer said, doggedly, knowing he had delivered on his part of the deal. "So let's go," he added.

Dollin was being deliberately slow and methodical. He handed me a copy of the trip ticket he had just signed. "It's your receipt and authorization," he said. Then he turned to Plummer. "Okay, you got two deuce-and-a-halfs for two hours."

"We agreed on THREE," Plummer protested.

"Oh, no. NO WAY," Dollin said.

"THREE or NO deal," Plummer insisted.

Dollin could tell Plummer wouldn't go for anything less. And I guess seeing a private act by the Coca-Cola lady was worth more than three lousy trucks.

"Okay. Three," Dollin said, reluctantly, to save face. "But who's gonna drive the third one?" he inquired.

"YOU, Dollin. Like YOU said YOU would," Plummer said, instantly angry.

"No way, GI. I'm not sticking my neck out that far. My wife just had a baby, and I'm not gonna raise him from a jail cell! Forget it," Dollin said, backing out.

Plummer's response was equally firm. "No drive, No Coca-Cola lady," he said.

Dollin wasn't changing his mind. "If Baker finds out I helped you, I'll be drivin' a mine sweeper in Korea," Dollin said.

It was a standoff.

I knew I wasn't going to get to sleep any time soon so I decided to volunteer.

"I can drive a truck," I said.

"You can't handle a deuce-and-a-half," Dollin said, challenging me.

"Are you kidding? I love trucks. Specially deuce-and-a-halfs. I used to drive 'em all the time at Fort Devins," I bluffed.

Dollin was skeptical.

Plummer knew I was bullshitting, but he had no other option. It was me or nobody. "Alright, Naud, get dressed," Plummer said.

"Can I ask where we're going?" I inquired.

"We're just gonna pick up some stuff," Plummer said, lightly.

'Just pickin' up stuff, huh? At two in the morning?' I thought. The mystery and intrigue appealed to me.

I jumped into my fatigues. As I did, I caught my foot on one of the pants leg openings and lost my balance, falling onto my bunk. Embarrassed, I tried to recover my balance and fell again. This time I landed face down on the floor. It was a classic display of physical ineptitude.

"I hope you drive better than you dress," Plummer said wryly.

'So do I,' I thought, getting up.

We left the warehouse and headed for the stairs.

The shadowy figure I had seen waiting in the darkness joined us. Pollazzo was trying to keep a low profile.

Pollazzo gave me quick lesson on driving a truck at the motor pool. We piled into the three deuce-and-a-halfs. To my surprise, Langdon had the main gates open. With only the blackout lights turned on, we drove out and turned west.

Plummer insisted we drive in close formation. He drove the lead truck.

Pollazzo the second.

I drove the last.

The blackout lights were so dim, they were practically useless. My speedometer said I was only doing thirty-five. But when you're driving in tandem, in the dark, as close as we were, it felt more like eighty. I had no idea where I was going or why, but driving a truck to nowhere in the middle of a sleepless night on a mystery mission, was a whole lot better than lying in bed staring at a pile of booze boxes.

Driving last in line gave me the best chance of avoiding the deep potholes. I kept my eyes riveted on Pollazzo's brake lights ahead. If they suddenly came on, I knew a pothole was coming up and I would slam on my brakes.

Every time I shifted gears, I heard a loud grinding noise. But I just kept doing it the way Pollazzo had showed him. 'Keep the lever with the red knob up, and shift it like a car,' he said.

I reassured myself that the gear grinding wasn't a problem. Unless I ran out of gears to grind.

I followed along as a blast of cold night air rushed in. Pollazzo had opened the plastic window when he gave me my driving lesson, and now I couldn't get it closed. There were lots of knobs on the dashboard, but none labeled 'HEATER' and I was afraid to start pulling or pushing things. So I put up with the cold air. I was freezing.

We turned onto a dirt road and slowed to a crawl. I was so focused on steering carefully through a maze of mounds and deep potholes, that I discovered I had lost sight of Plummer and Pollazzo's trucks. After a few anxious moments, I swung around a sharp turn and almost crashed into them. They had been waiting ahead for me to catch up. We drove on, finally hitting a stretch of level asphalt road. It was pitch-black all around us.

'Where the hell are we?' I thought.

Pollazzo's brake lights flared as he came to an abrupt stop.

I slammed my brakes, just in time to skid to a stop and avoid slamming into Pollazzo's rear end. I couldn't see anything, no buildings, no people, no cars, no lights, only a few disconnected amorphous shapes out there in the silent darkness. It felt like the dark side of the moon.

I opened the canvas door with the floppy plastic window, and jumped down onto the concrete.

Plummer came back carrying a large Army flash-light, "You okay, Naud?" he asked.

"I'm freezing my nuts off," I said, pumping my shoulders and flapping his arms.

Plummer faced into the darkness, then turned the flashlight on and off, ONE, TWO, THREE times. He was signaling to somebody, but no one was signaling back. He did it again, in a slightly different direction. Again no response.

"What do you think?" Surrel asked.

"He's out there," Plummer replied with a creepy kind of certainty. "We'll wait."

Plummer and I sat on the running board of my truck, smoking. Pollazzo sat on the ground. Every few minutes Plummer would walk out into the darkness and flash the signal, ONE... TWO... THREE. When nothing came back he would sit back down on the concrete.

"Where are we?" I inquired. "The North side of Tokyo sitting on a runway," Pollazzo said. "A runway?" I said, with obvious concern.

"Yeah. It's called Shingu. They used to build Zeros all around this area and then fly 'em off to the war," Pollazzo said. "Here's a souvenir," he added, picking up and tossing me a small piece of asphalt. "This piece of runway could be valuable someday. The most famous Kamikaze mission of World War II, took off from right here."

He proceeded to tell me what had happened. It was on Sunday, September 2, 1945. MacArthur and the Japanese were to sign the surrender documents on the deck of the Missouri, the American battleship anchored in Tokyo Bay. Admiral Onisha, the founder of the Kamikazes, ordered thirteen of his finest Kamikaze pilots to uncover their hidden planes and follow him into the air on a suicide mission, to dive into and destroy the Missouri. It was a last prideful attempt to save face for the Japanese people. As they were approaching the Missouri, the Emperor reached Onishi on his radio, and urged him to abandon the mission, believing it would only bring shame to the Japanese nation. Japanese fisherman reported seeing Zeros dive into the sea south of the city that day. One after another they exploded on impact. Those men's flying skills were unmatched, but above all else, so was their devotion to the Emperor.

I studied the chunk of asphalt runway. It was hard for me to understand how those Kamikaze pilots could believe in something so strongly, they would die for it. It all seemed senseless to me.

Pollazzo lit a cigarette and scanned the darkness. "Hey, Plummer? I don't think he's coming," he said, getting up.

Plummer ignored him, continuing to flash the signal into the darkness.

"We gotta get these trucks back, remember?" Pollazzo warned.

I agreed with Pollazzo, but Plummer said nothing.

Then Plummer finally gave up. "Okay. Come on, let's go."

"FREEZE," a commanding voice cried out from somewhere close behind us. We were caught like animals in a blinding searchlight. I froze in fear. My heart almost jumped out of my mouth.

Another foreign voice barked out, "Put your hands behind your head, SLOWLY! And lock your fingers. Make any quick moves and you're dead," he threatened.

Plummer, Pollazzo and I complied, as out of the beam of light came three rugged MPs with their carbines leveled at us. The tallest MP, a Sergeant, was the leader. He kept us covered, while his partners frisked us for weapons.

"They're clean," the small bullish MP announced.

The Sergeant started to chide us. "What have we got going here, guys? A little black market action, huh? This'll get ya twenty years," he snidely said with a smirk.

"For what?" Plummer asked.

"To start with, being in a restricted area," the tall MP said, gesturing to his partners. The other two started checking the cabs and cargo bays of the trucks.

I could feel my heart pounding even harder. I glanced at Plummer. He didn't look the least bit worried. Pollazzo didn't either. 'They must have nerves of steel,' I thought.

"Sergeant," the bullish MP surprisingly reported back, "there's nothing there."

The Sergeant MP leader looked directly at me. He decided I was the weakest link. "What are you doing here, soldier?" he demanded.

"The truth?" I asked.

"Don't smart ass me," the MP warned.

"The truth is, I have no idea, Sergeant," I said with a straight face.

Pollazzo smiled.

"Okay, let me see your ID," the Sergeant demanded.

"We don't have any," Plummer announced, cutting in, abruptly.

Plummer's statement annoyed me. We were only supposed to show our ID's if it was 'absolutely necessary'. If ever there was a NECESSARY time, THIS was it. But I had an idea.

"Hey, Sergeant. Those trucks are legal," I volunteered.

"Yeah, I'll bet," he answered, skeptically.

"It's true. I got a trip ticket here," I said, reaching nice and slowly into my pocket.

Plummer and Pollazzo looked at each other, wondering what the hell I was doing.

I handed the Sergeant the trip ticket Dollin had given me. It was folded over something. When the Sergeant opened it, my ID fell out. Plummer glared at me realizing what I had done. Pollazzo smiled.

The Sergeant picked it up and looked it over. "Keep 'em covered," he said to his buddies as he walked over to his jeep.

"Don't get restless, boys," the MPs taunted, while we were waiting.

The Sergeant got on his field phone. After a few moments, as he walked around the jeep with the phone to his ear, it was obvious somebody on the other end was harassing him. "Yes, Sir. Yes, Sir," he kept apologizing.

When the call ended the chagrined Sergeant returned. He gave me my trip ticket and ID. "Sorry to inconvenience you, gentlemen. Carry on," he said.

The other MP's were shocked and disappointed.

"What's going on here, Sarge?" the bullish MP whispered gruffly.

"Yeah. We got 'em hands down," the other MP bitched.

"We got NOTHING," the Sergeant barked, cutting them off. "Shut up and let's get outta here."

The three of them got back in their jeeps and drove away without a word of explanation.

Plummer didn't say anything to me about showing my ASA ID. We just wanted to get out of there so we climbed into the trucks and brought the motors to life. As we swung the vehicles around and were starting to go, I saw something.

"Stop," I screamed.

Plummer and Pollazzo pulled over as I pointed at a light off in the distance. It was blinking on and off, ONE...TWO...THREE blinks.

"There he is," Plummer hollered.

"Yeah," Pollazzo agreed.

My heart was racing. I didn't know who was out there, or what this whole thing was about, but I was even more curious now after we almost got arrested by the MPs.

"Hey, Naud?" Plummer called, "You don't have to come with us if you don't want to."

"I'm coming," I said. My heart was still going a mile a minute.

"You got the dough?" Pollazzo shouted at Plummer.

"Yeah," Plummer said, patting his fatigue jacket pocket. He added a "thumbs up" sign just to make sure there was no misunderstanding. He blinked the flashlight into the darkness and pulled away,

I followed as we drove along the edge of the runway, watching for the blinking light, but the weeds had grown up making the edge hard to see. I was afraid we might drive off the runway and get stuck, or turn the truck over. Fifty yards later, Plummer made a left hand turn onto another concrete strip. Pollazzo followed, and I kept right behind him. I was forced to lean way out of his window to see where we were going. The beacon light they were heading for was straight ahead, about two hundred yards.

"Hi·ho. Hi·ho. It's off to work we go," I sang, humming the tune from *Snow White*. It was my way of staying calm.

Two minutes later Plummer and Pollazzo stopped in front of the beacon. It was a collection of army flashlights taped together and mounted on top of a three-wheeled Japanese motorcycle. Nobody was in sight.

It felt like a set-up to me.

A harsh voice suddenly screamed something in Japanese.

Instantly, fifteen bandits wearing handkerchief masks, and carrying American M1's, rose up out of the weeds lining the runway and ran out to surround our trucks.

One of the Japanese pirates rushed at me, frantically gesturing with his rifle for me to get down from my truck.

As I climbed down, he screamed "Hi·ya·koo," and jabbed his gun in my side. The kerchief covering his face fell off, revealing a horribly scarred face and an almost toothless mouth. It was one thing to be shot by a sharp looking American MP, but another to be killed by an unmasked, oriental version of Lon Chaney's character from *Phantom of the Opera*.

Two other bandits jabbed me in the sides with their rifles, prodding me to move toward the empty motorcycle.

Pollazzo and Plummer were already there, surrounded by the rest of the bandits.

"Relax, Naud. You're safe. It's over," Plummer said, trying to put me at ease.

It was hard to believe him.

"Welcome Plummer-san," a happy booming voice exclaimed from behind the motorcycle.

I recognized the voice; it was Black Market Sam, the laundry owner from Oji.

The bandits backed up to clear a path for him. The chunky overweight Oriental figure with a pony-tail and a handle bar mustache came forward. Sam reminded me of *Fat-Stuff* from the *Smilin' Jack* cartoon, only Sam was real and so were the other guys with the guns.

"You understand my caution, Plummer-san," Sam said in English, bowing to Plummer.

"Hai, Samsan. I find wisdom in it. MP's are every-where now," Plummer said, bowing back.

"Is true," Sam said. "Who do you bring me?"

"Here is the new EM club custodian. His name is Naud," I bowed the same way Plummer did.

"May I wish you great prosperity in your new work, Naud-san," Sam said.

"Do-ma-t-ga-toe," I replied. All of a sudden I was starting to feel comfortable in this den of thieves. Black Market Sam was further impressed by my attempt to speak Japanese.

"Hai. Sometime we have tea and talk, Naud-san. Not to speak about business but about life and other things," he offered, then added, "but this is the Japa-nese way. You are Americans. Our way is not your way. Now we do it your way. Have you money?" Sam asked Plummer.

"First, where's the stuff?" Plummer said trying to take control of the transaction.

Sam nodded to his right, at a large mound in the darkness fifty-feet away. It was an Army tent covering a huge pile of stuff.

The bandits turned the bank of lights on it.

I couldn't help wondering what was under the tent: cigarettes, liquor, food, guns, ammunition. I doubted there were any joy girls there, they probably didn't store well beneath an army tent in the middle of a deserted runway on a cold night.

"Corporal Dollan-san come earlier," Sam started. "He check everything. All there. Now money, Dozo," he said firmly.

"That guy over there just took it," Plummer said, gesturing towards the bandit with the badly scarred face.

Sam glared at the scarred man, who scurried forward to give him a wad of American money, with several apologetic bows.

Sam counted the money as we watched. He seemed surprised. "Only five hundred dollar here, Plummer-san, am I wrong?" he asked.

"No, Samsan. You are right," Plummer acknowledged.

"We make deal. You pay three thousand dollar," Sam said, averting his eyes from Plummer's so as not to embarrass him, it was the Japanese way.

"True, Samsan. Dollin gave you fifteen hundred dollars. Now I give you five hundred. You'll get the last thousand dollars at the end of this week."

"You give two-thirds of money. You take two-thirds of stuff," Sam said adamantly.

"We gotta have it all, Sam," Plummer pleaded.

"Then you must change laws of mathematics so money counts up to three thousand, Plummer-san," Sam answered back.

"That's not possible," Plummer begged.

"Then you must get more money," Sam said, keeping his eyes lowered so as not to appear hostile. Sam would never argue. It was not the Japanese way.

"Look Sam," Plummer said, offering a solution. "I'll get you a case of CC as collateral against the other thousand, okay?" Then he added, "in a bar, it's worth at least a thousand dollars."

"Sam-san doesn't own bar," Sam said, without looking up.

I had come this far and wanted to see what was under the tent and to get the heck out of there. "I've got a case of CC I'll give you, too, Sam," I said.

Sam considered the offer, rocking his head slowly from side to side, making guttural birdlike noises. "Two case of CC against a thousand dollar for a week?" he computed out loud. Then he looked up, straight at Plummer. "With one condition. Everything be back in my warehouse by tomorrow night at midnight. If not, you owe me three thousand American dollar and I keep all the CC."

Plummer and Pollazzo stared at each other. That would be an almost impossible task.

"Sam, you just wished Naudsan prosperity," Plummer reminded him, adding, "how can he become prosperous with such an unfair deal?"

"Things which are not fair often bring the best test to character, "Sam said, lowering his eyes again to let us decide in private. After a moment, he asked, "You speak. Yes or no?"

Pollazzo and Plummer knew they had no choice.

"Okay, it's a deal," Plummer said. "We'll have it all back tomorrow night, by midnight."

Sam screamed commands at the bandits, who became like locusts. They swarmed around the pile of things beneath the tent, sorting it all out and loading it onto the trucks.

I watched in surprise as they worked. I wondered what anyone would want with this pile of junk: beds, cabinets, dressers desks, chairs, heating units, bedding, foot lockers, carbines, portable field ovens, generators, toilet paper, eating utensils, towels sheets, duffel bags, and who knows what else. I had spent the whole night risking my life for a load of junk from an army surplus store.

In less than thirty minutes, everything was on the trucks and we were on our way back to Oji. For some reason, the road back seemed smoother. I did manage, with some help from Pollazzo, to get my window zipped back up and the heater on. Now I was boiling hot and couldn't turn the thing off. And I still didn't know what they were going to do with all the junk.

I followed Surrel and Plummer though the front gate. At the motor pool, Plummer told me a little about Sam. He had been in his forties and running his father's laundry, when WW II started. He had avoided the army, first by committing petty crimes and going to jail, then when he got out, he stayed out by stealing stuff for members of the dreaded Tokko, the Emperor's version of the Gestapo. Sam had become an important man in the black market. When WWII ended he found a new lucrative partner, our own Sergeant Baker.

That didn't seem to surprise me.

Once back in my bed, I fell instantly asleep, until the bugle blew Reveille, only sixty minutes later.

Chapter 13

Change Of Command

It was 10a.m. the next morning and the final inventory of the company equipment was well underway.
Plummer was lying on the stage in the Em Club with
his eyes shut, trying to rest, while Pollazzo kept his
eye on the company supply room below with a pair
of army field glasses.

"Cross knows what's happening. I'm telling you,"
Pollazzo insisted. "We're in deep shit, Plummer," he
added. .

"Pollazzo? If Cross knew...," Plummer responded,
"the inspection would be over by now. So just shut up
and relax." Plummer and Pollazzo were exhausted
and edgy. They had helped unload the trucks and
neither one had been to sleep.

Mel Beamer, a code breaker, and Langdon, the
gate guard, had joined the vigil, and like us were anxiously awaiting the outcome of the inspection.

I had only slept an hour. I could barely keep my .
eyes open. I was busy chipping golf balls into a
bucket ten feet away on the dance floor, trying to
stay awake. Most of the balls were slamming into
the side of the bucket. Plummer's head would flinch
at every clunk. "How long does an inspection usually
take?" I asked.

"It's already taken long enough," Plummer answered, adding to the heightened anxiety.

I hit another ball towards the pail, it went right over. Then I hit a second and a third. They all missed, rolling and clanking somewhere in the back of the club. I found it hard to believe Plummer could be so relaxed.

"You keep hogging the glasses," Beamer barked at Pollazzo.

"If you wanna look, LOOK," Pollazzo said, holding the glasses out to him.

"What for? There's nothing to see," Beamer bitched. "Where's Mulvey anyway?"

Pollazzo swung his glasses to the left, directing them at Mulvey's office window. "He's standing in his window, staring at the supply warehouse door across the compound, waiting too," he said.

"How does he look?" Beamer asked.

"Worried. What else?" Pollazzo said.

"What does that tell you?" Beamer asked.

"It tells me he knows as much as we do. Nothing," Pollazzo answered. annoyingly.

Pollazzo and Beamer reminded me of *The Bickersons*, a radio show I liked. It was about a couple who did nothing but argue. They almost seemed to enjoy it.

Plummer sat up, put his feet on the floor, and stood up. Using the backs of the chairs around the dance floor to maintain his balance, he made his way to the bar. He crawled behind it, put a towel over his head, leaned over the sink and puked his guts out. When there was nothing more to throw up, he wiped his face clean and headed back to the stage.

I watched him walk back across the dance floor with the towel over his head. His face was white.

I sat on the edge of the stage as he lay back down and blotted at the heavy perspiration running down his face with the towel. The tension had obviously gotten to him. 'He was falling apart like a cheap suit' I thought. For what, I had to know.

"Look, Plummer, I haven't said a word up 'til now. Would you mind telling me what's going on?"

"Captain Mulvey is responsible for all the company property," he started, then took a deep breath. "When a new commanding officer takes over, he does an inventory to make sure all the property is there. If it's not, the government will charge the standing commander for what's missing. If he can't pay for it, they court martial him, and sentence him to jail time. There was $24,000 worth of property missing, but we replaced it all last night."

"Who took all the stuff in the first place?" I asked.

"A couple of previous supply Sergeants, but Baker took most of it and sold it on the Black Market.

I was floored. "You mean we rented our own stolen stuff back from Black Market Sam! That's Nuts!"

"Some people call it free enterprise," Plummer quipped.

"Where did all the money come from?" I asked.

"The troops chipped in," he answered.

"Why?" I asked.

Plummer took a few seconds to answer. Maybe he was afraid his words might sound trivial or unimportant. "When I got here in January, I was assigned as Mulvey's clerk. There were all kinds of personnel problems, the biggest with the codebreakers. They knew the agency needed them and they took advantage of it. Mulvey tried to 'hard discipline' them. But it didn't work. Then he took another tack. He tried to become their friend, their brother, their father, and their confessor. It worked. And that's all that really matters to the higher-ups, especially Colonel Mac-millan. "

"What are you worrying about, you got the stuff back," I said

"The new commander Cross is a hard ass. If he spots the phony serial numbers we're dead in the water," Plummer explained.

Pollazzo added, "That means ALL of us. He's bound to spot some of them phony numbers and start digging further. "

"Damn it, Pollazzo. Shut up," Beamer exploded.

"They've been at it, now ... three hours," Pollazzo complained, checking his watch.

"Don't remind me," Plummer said.

"Hey, something's happening," Pollazzo yelled, as he adjusted the field glasses and squinted harder.

Plummer and I rushed to join him at the window.

Captain Cross and Sergeant Calvin, the supply officer, were coming out of the warehouse door. We couldn't tell a thing from their expressions.

Mulvey was watching from his window. His face filled with apprehension as he watched them cross the Parade Ground, heading right towards his office.

"How will you know if it's worked?" I asked.

"When Cross signs the sheet on Sergeant Calvin's clip board," Plummer said. "Then Cross becomes responsible for all the company property and Mul-vey's off the hook."

Mulvey left his office and went outside to face the music, joining Cross and Sergeant Calvin in the com-pound.

Pollazzo followed him with the glasses. "Mulvey's walking up. It looks like Sergeant Calvin is explaining something on the clipboard to Mulvey."

"What are they saying?" Beamer asked Pollazzo.

"I can't tell," Pollazzo answered.

"You said you could read lips," Beamer demanded.

"I can't see their 'damn lips'," Pollazzo countered.

I was trying to interpret what was going on, when I noticed something odd, men were gathering on the rooftops and in the windows of the buildings, all around the Parade Ground.

"Is he signing it?" Plummer asked, anxiously.

"I can't tell. He has his back to me," Pollazzo said. Then Pollazzo started beaming. "Yeah, Cross IS signing," Pollazzo said.

"Gimme those," Plummer said, grabbing the field glasses out of Pollazzo's hands. He had to see for himself.

"YEH, HE IS," Plummer announced. "Now Mulvey's signing it too," he added.

"You son of bitch, Plummer. You did it," Pollazzo said with a giant smile.

"Yeah, we did it. We did it," Plummer said lowering the glasses. Tears were welling up in his eyes.

Next I saw Sergeant Calvin take possession of the clipboard and the signed documents. Then Captain Cross walked off, a smiling Sergeant Baker held the mess door open for him.

Mulvey took the clipboard back from Sergeant Calvin. He just stood there with his eyes fixed on the signatures. Cross was now the de facto Company Commander with all its attendant responsibilities. Mulvey had prayed and gotten his miracle, but he had no idea how.

Sergeant Calvin knew what had happened but he had sworn not to say anything.

Then a deep, resonant voice bellowed out. "COMPANY, ATTEN-HUT,"over the loud speakers.

Calvin motioned Captain Mulvey to look up at the rooftops.

Mulvey followed Calvin's gaze up to the buildings surrounding them. Troops were everywhere, jammed together in windows and along the rooftop ledges. They had been intently watching the events taking place in the Parade Ground below.

The same resonant voice issued a second command, "PRESENT, ARMS."

In one single motion, the men of ASA Headquarters Company saluted.

Plummer, Pollazzo and Beamer were at attention too, saluting proudly. I could see tears in their eyes.

Captain Mulvey returned the men's salute. Tears were running down his cheeks.

My eyes began welling up, too. I couldn't help it.

The only problem now was getting the stuff back to Black Market Sam without anyone, especially Baker, finding out.

Later that night I was behind the bar, making believe I was reading a Letter, but I was really keeping an eye on Baker, waiting for him to leave so we could return the stuff. He should have been out of there more than an hour earlier. He was supposed to have gone to a labor conference downtown at General Head Quarters, right after dinner. Yet, there he was, still sitting in the Club, drinking with two of his stooges, Corporal Mula and Dehler.

The clock behind the bar showed ten p.m. We only had about two hours left to get all the stuff back to Sam.

Plummer and Pollazzo were down in the warehouse with the loaded trucks standing by.

As soon as Baker left, I was supposed to let them know that the coast was clear. But Baker wasn't going anywhere.

Pollazzo came in the Club, spotted Baker, and made a beeline for me.

"How come he's still here?" Pollazzo asked anxiously. We both knew we were running out of time.

"You tell me," I said, adding, "are the trucks ready?"

"Yeah. The stuff's loaded and ready to go. Dollin is Sergeant-of-the-Guard, so he's keeping an eye on the motor pool," Pollazzo said, adding, "I gotta get back to work on the hill."

Baker grinned like he was enjoying some private joke as he watched Pollazzo leave.

'Something's wrong,' I thought, 'Baker must know what's going on.'

Plummer came marching anxiously into the club.

"Plummer? You said Baker had to go downtown after chow," I reminded him.

"He'll go soon. He has to. The Colonel ordered him to be a guest speaker at the GHQ labor conference," Plummer said. "Soon as he's gone, we're outta here."

"Yeh, well, what if they canceled the conference?" Pollazzo suggested.

"GHQ never cancels anything. Will ya stop worrying?" Plummer insisted.

"You better check to be sure," I said.

Plummer was reluctant to call downtown, but we were running out of time, and the pressure was getting to him, too.

"Okay. If it will make you guys feel better," he agreed.

We went down to my office. Plummer called the GHQ Exchange. The phone operator switched him upstairs.

"Hello, is this the West Conference Room?" Plummer asked. "This is Colonel Macmillan's office. We just wanted to confirm that the Labor Conference is still on and that Sergeant Leroy Baker is scheduled as the guest speaker. Is that information still correct?" He listened for a moment. "The conference IS still on. I see. But ...," Plummer said, parroting the voice on the phone. His face went white. "But you say Sergeant Baker had to cancel?"

Pollazzo's jaw dropped.

Plummer thanked the guy and hung up.

We were sure now Baker was on to us. He was waiting to catch us trying to move the stuff off the base.

"Now what, Plummer?" I said.

Junji appeared at the office door. He was out of breath from running down the stairs, but managed a quick bow as he spoke. "Naudsan? You ask me tell when Bakersan leave club."

"Where did he go?" I asked.

"Not know," Junji said.

"Thanks. You can go back up to the Club, "I said.

"Hai." Junji punctuated his reply with a staccato bow then quickly left.

"What if Baker starts looking around? He'll find those loaded trucks," Pollazzo said.

"Maybe he's just going home," Pollazzo said, trying to quiet the panic.

"What home?" I asked, out of curiosity.

"He's got a civilian home near here," Pollazzo said.

Plummer had moved to the window and was looking down at the company assembly area through the antique telescope. "Nope he didn't go home. There he is," Plummer said.

Baker was walking across the Parade Ground, heading for the orderly room.

My phone began to ring.

"Hello?" I answered, cautiously.

"Naud, it's me, Dollin. Baker's coming over and wants to check the motor pool with me. As Sergeant of the guard, I gotta do it." I could hear in the background, Baker knocking on the orderly room door.

Dollin abruptly hung up.

"Baker wants to look around the motor pool," I told Plummer and Pollazzo.

Plummer could see Dollin and Baker through the telescope talking in the orderly room.

"What are they saying?" Pollazzo asked.

Plummer gave Pollazzo a disgusted look, picked up my phone, and dialed the Orderly Room. Dollin answered.

"This is Plummer. We can see you and Baker, so be careful what you say," he whispered into the phone.

"I understand," Dollin said cryptically.

"You tell Baker you gotta take a dump, and make it a long one."

"Why?" Dollin asked.

"Just do it, Dollin, or we'll all be room-mates at Leavenworth!" Plummer answered through gritted teeth.

"Okay," Dollin said and hung up.

Plummer watched through the telescope as Dollin went into the orderly room bathroom. Then Plummer rushed to the desk and started crushing a piece of paper in a ball. "Maybe, we're not dead yet," he said. He was acting really weird, unfolding the paper, then wadding it up again, slowly listening to the sound.

He gave some fresh paper to Pollazzo and some more to me.

"What are we doing?" I asked thinking he was really coming unglued.

"Just do what I'm doing. Crumple it like this," Plummer said.

"Why?" Pollazzo asked.

"Do it, damn it, and don't stop," Plummer barked.

Plummer picked up the phone and dialed with one hand, while he continued to crumple paper with the other.

Baker was still in the orderly room waiting for Dollin to come out of the crapper. Pollazzo and I were crumpling paper with no idea of why.

I heard a Japanese voice come on the phone line. Plummer screamed out something in Japanese, then started twisting and breaking pencils from the desk. He motioned us to crumple the paper closer to the phone.

I was lost, but I went on crumpling.

Plummer gave out a series of anguished cries and then hung up the phone, motioning for everyone to be quiet.

"Ssshhhhh!!! LISTEN," Surrel said.

"Nothing's happening," Pollazzo said.

"Come on, damn it, Come on," Surrel said tensely, urging something to happen.

Suddenly the air was filled with the wailing of a distant air raid siren.

"They're coming out," Pollazzo said. Dollin and Baker emerged from the orderly room. "They're heading for the motor pool."

The noise got louder as others sirens picked up the coded signal and joined in. One long blast then two short.

"YES! Hot damn. There it is," Plummer said, beaming.

Baker was hurrying to his motorbike.

"He's getting on his bike," Pollazzo said.

Baker started the motor and revved the engine as the sirens kept sounding. One long, two short...... One long, two short. Baker's bike roared down the Company Street towards the main gate.

"It worked," Plummer yelled out." He's going home to save his house."

"From what?" I said perplexed.

"Fire. He thinks his house is burning down," Plummer said triumphantly.

I finally understood. Plummer's ploy on the phone convinced the local fire department that Baker's house was burning down.

"Come on, let go," Plummer yelled.

The three of us raced down the stairs, across the Parade Ground to the motor pool, and climbed aboard the trucks.

The motor pool dispatcher stuck his head out of the booth window.

"Baker just went out the gate, GO!" he hollered, giving us the 'thumbs up'.

Plummer waved and pulled away. Pollazzo followed. My truck was last to move, bucking and lurching until I got it under control. A minute later our three trucks, loaded with the stuff we had rented from Sam, roared out of the main gate headed for Sam's warehouse.

When we finally got back to Oji hours later, I was totally spent.

Plummer and Pollazzo seemed to enjoy living on the edge.

Oddly enough I thought, 'A fox hole in Korea might even be a vacation. '

Plummer ran back to the office to type up an important communiqué that had just come in:

....

TOP SECRET/ASA Copy I of 2 Decrypted
Communique
Date: 1 SEPT 1950
To: JOINTS CHIEFS OF STAFF
From: MACARTHUR
Subject: TACTICAL SUMMARY

TOP SECRET

Synopsis:
   Incheon landing plan set for 15
Sept. General Walker can't hold
Pusan perimeter beyond end of month,
unless we end run Incheon. Extreme
tides and high sea walls during the
invasion are dangerous, but acceptable, risks. I am reviewing problems, including security, and recognize serious consequences if we fail.
Inform Truman, I am proceeding.

   Signed
   Mac

....

Chapter 14

Gift of Love

Around midnight my office phone rang. I tried to ignore the ringing, but finally gave in and went out to answer it. I was surprised to hear Greg Surrel's voice.

"Listen Naud, the liquor company has agreed to hold the Miss Tokyo contest out by you. You'll have all the girls you want. I'll be out around four o'clock to go over it all and get your liquor order." Then he hung up.

I put the phone down and just looked at it. What he had just said so casually, could mean the difference between life and death for me.

I made my way back to bed and fell asleep like a baby.

No sooner had I fallen asleep than I was awakened by the scratchy sound of a bugle playing reveille over the compound loud speakers. Thankfully my duties at the club allowed me the luxury of not being a part of the morning ritual.

I grabbed a towel and some soap and headed downstairs to shower. As I passed the office window I could see the men filing out of the barracks, meandering towards the assembly area.

A disgruntled crowd was closing in around the company bulletin board where Private Holchum was posting a notice. I swung Toshiko's antique telescope around and focused on the bulletin board. All I could see clearly were the words *'Change in VD Policy'*. The rumor had been circulating that Cross was considering revoking Mulvey's liberal VD policy and reinstating the army's stricter regulations. So anyone who turned themselves in with venereal disease was subject to disciplinary action, including loss of pay and promotion.

Sergeant Baker came storming out of the Company Headquarters door, barking like a guard dog, "Alright, At Ease, men. Let's form up."

The men gathered in loose formation, seven crooked lines of ten across. They were still grumbling to each other while Sergeant Baker was making a few announcements, which most of the men didn't seem to care about.

A moment later, Captain Cross strode out of the orderly room door and took a position at the front of the formation. He had the look of a bulldog.

"Company, ATTENJHUT," Sergeant Baker commanded, then turned to salute the captain.

The codebreakers made a feeble effort to comply.

Cross glared at their version of attention with contempt.

To me, it was instantly apparent there was going to be a contest of wills: the bulldogs against the eggheads.

"Sergeant, this company is not at proper attention," Cross complained.

Sergeant Baker at once turned to address the formation. Hoping louder would produce a better result, he bellowed, "Company, ATTENJHUT!"

The formation came to a slovenly attention, with not much improvement.

"Sergeant," Cross ordered," we're going to keep on doing this until we've got something resembling a military formation."

"YES, SIR," Baker responded.

The eggheads knew now Cross was after them. He walked down the line glaring at each man with con-tempt, as he addressed the group. "Men, whatever else you do in in this army, you are SOLDIERS first. As long as you are under my command, you WILL act like soldiers." Cross studied their faces to assure himself they understood the message.

'The guy's a chicken-shit asshole,' I thought. But then I reminded myself, 'the chicken-shit Captain down there is up for the Congressional Medal of Honor."

Two hundred yards away Colonel McMillan was standing in the window of his second-story office watching the proceedings. He looked mad as hell.

Again Cross hollered, "Company, ATTENJHUT." The formation came to something slightly above a slovenly attention, but it was obvious nothing the group did, or was going to do, would satisfy Cross.

I was fascinated wondering who would the next bout.

"Sergeant, KEEP them at attention, if you can call it that, until I decide to release them for work."

"Yes, Sir," Sergeant Baker responded.

Cross disappeared into the building just as a phone began ringing loudly from the orderly room.

Plummer complained from the ranks, "Sergeant the codebreakers are late for work. That's going to make Colonel Macmillan very unhappy."

Before Baker could react, Captain Cross emerged from the orderly room.

"Sergeant, why haven't you dismissed the formation? They're late for work!"

I looked up and Colonel McMillan was gone from the window.

"Yes, Sir," Baker said as he and Cross exchanged salutes. Then Cross started back to the orderly room with an annoyed look on his face.

"Headquarters Company, DISS-M-IS-SED," Sergeant Baker barked.

A chorus of clicking boots sounded as the codebreakers snapped rigidly to attention. They looked like wooden soldiers, all sharp and stiff, with a slight smile on their face.

Cross paused at the door, pondering what was happening.

"Headquarters Company, DISS-M-IS-SED," Sergeant Baker repeated with more gusto.

Still nothing happened. It was obvious the codebreakers intended to stay just as they were.

"Sergeant, is there a problem?" Cross called to him.

"No, Sir," Baker shouted back red faced.

Cross took him at his word and entered the orderly room.

No sooner had the door closed behind Cross, than the eggheads broke formation and began laughing. They had proved to Sergeant Baker and Captain Cross they were somewhat beyond their control. They could take whatever was dished out to them, and more.

I felt the eggheads had won this battle, but I knew a Captain who was about to receive a Medal of Honor, would not give up his authority easily.

Baker barked, "Come on, move it! You're late for work." The men casually wandered off to work like they were going to an Easter parade. They knew they had the only job in the army, where the tail wagged the dog.

I continued down stairs to shower.

Right at four o'clock Greg Surrel arrived at the Club office with several hundred photos of Japanese girls who wanted to be *Miss Tokyo*. He and I began laying out the girl's photos and applications on the warehouse floor.

"How should we pick 'em'?" Surrel asked.

"Why don't we each pick thirty or so and see how they stack up. Then we can hang their pictures in the club and let the guys vote. From that we'll get the final forty contestants.

"Okay, but remember talent counts, it's not just a beauty contest," Surrel said.

I flipped through the photos and picked thirty of the prettiest girls I could find in ten minutes. I didn't bother to look at their applications to find out anything about them, it wouldn't have done me any good. They were all written in Japanese.

Surrel started reading the girl's applications to me. Most of the talents listed were for singing or dancing. Some played musical instruments. One girl did a magic act. Not only were the girls pretty and talented, but most were also well educated. They seemed to be the Japanese equivalent of girls who entered the *Miss America* contest. Over the next hour we whittled it down to sixty girls. I was confident that the guys in the code section would respond much more strongly to brains and beauty, rather than to just beauty.

"How long will it take to get the security clearances?" I asked.

"I already had all the girls cleared. We just need their gate passes for competition night. I'll stop at Sergeant Baker's office on the way out, to put in for them. My company wants the contest held no later than two weeks from now.

"That's fine," I said. I knew hanging the pictures in the club, and allowing the guys to vote on their favorites, would bring more GI's in until the night of the contest. .

Surrel was packing up the applications when Toshiko came into the warehouse. He had a serious look on his face. "Naudsan, we have problem. Junji's work pass has been revoked."

"What do you mean?" I asked in disbelief.

"Baker fired him. Say he is stealing," Toshiko explained.

I instantly became annoyed. "He's just getting back at me for what I did to Dehler in the club."

Surrel had been listening. "Hey Naud, maybe I can help." He picked up the phone and started to dial. A few minutes later, after greeting and chatting with someone on the other end, he held the phone out to me with his hand over the mouthpiece. "This is Mel Rorshack, a lawyer in charge of the Domestic Military Labor Commission. I told him about the incident with Dehler."

I took the phone. "Naud here," I said.

"Look Naud, I've been getting a lot of cases like this, so I'll be blunt and to the point. Do you have Junji's labor application?"

Before I could ask Toshiko, he handed me a paper from a folder.

"I've got it here," I said into the phone.

"I've got three questions that have to be answered," Rorschack started.

I held the phone out so Toshiko could hear too.

"Number one. Does he have a criminal record?" Rorschack asked.

Toshiko shook his head NO.

"NO," I said into the phone.

"Was he hired and employed under Military Occupation labor Laws?"

Toshiko shook his head.

"Yes," I said scanning the papers Toshiko handed me.

"Last question. Are his parents alive?"

Toshiko whispered the answer to me. "No," I repeated into the phone, "both were killed during WWII." The thought made me cringe.

"What's your name again?" Rorshack asked.

"Naud." I answered.

"Alright, Naud. I do this twenty times a day, so listen hard and don't ask questions. Okay?'

"Okay," I answered.

"The labor commission is legally bound to give your friend Junji a hearing. When they do, they'll have to fire him because the American Sergeant who is accusing him will make the evidence irrefutable. But, firing an indigenous waiter from a high security base like Oji, is just what the commies want. Best excuse in the world for them to call a sympathy strike. "

I was lost.

He went on without even taking a breath, "The labor commission's job is to maintain peace. Which means we will probably not be holding a hearing for your waiter friend next month, six months, or even a year from now. Maybe not not ever. Especially, since I schedule the meetings. Clear?"

"I think so, "I said.

"In plain language Naud, in the interest of labor peace, the labor commission will ignore the incident and let it die. I'll call this Sergeant Baker now and have him restore Junji's work pass now. Clear? Good-bye. " He hung up.

I put down the phone.

"What did he say?" Surrel asked.

"I'm not sure. But Toshiko, find Junji. Tell him he's rehired," I said.

One of the waiters went down and tacked a notice on the bulletin board in front of the mess hall announcing the Miss Tokyo contest and the voting for contestants that will take place in the club. Before the Club doors opened, Toshiko finished nailing a large new bulletin board on the wall near the entrance. I tacked up the announcement and rules for voting. We set up a box, on the bar, so the men could write down the name of their favorite contestant and drop it in. Photos of the sixty girls were hung all around the club walls.

Word spread quickly. There was an immediate crowd that evening. They were all codebreakers.

To make sure word got around, every couple of hours or so, as more faces joined the crowd, I turned on the mike and announced the contest from the stage.

I figured some "well endowed" women would attract even bigger crowds, so I cut out pictures of buxom girls from Japanese girlie magazines. The next afternoon, I was hanging them up in the club as the waiters were cleaning. They took a peek at the new photos and began to snicker.

Toshiko and Junji entered the club. There was a sudden hush in the room. I turned around and was happy to see Junji was back. But he was oddly dressed in a ceremonial Shinto outfit with a pinkish robe and carrying a large framed photo with a fabric curtain draped at its edges.

"Excuse Naudsan, important Junji talk to you," Toshiko said.

"Sure, what about?" I asked,

Junji bowed, and showed me the photo proudly. It was a snapshot of himself in his school jacket, standing next to a girl in a Japanese costume. She wore an elaborate black kimono. Her face was painted chalk white. Her hair was piled neatly on her head, held there by large white combs.

I thought she might be a Geisha. "Who's the girl?" I said.

"Girl Junji sister," Toshiko explained.

Junji confirmed it with pride. "Hai," he said.

"She looks very nice," I said, just for something to say.

"Sister very beautiful, Naudsan. Take picture at costume party," Junji said.

"Naudsan? Junji wish to thank you for keeping his job. He say he owes you much for doing this."

"Tell Junji he's welcome. All he owes me is to do his job well," I said.

"Junji say you must 'take' sister as gift to pay this great debt," Toshiko said.

I was stunned. It was the first time anyone had ever offered to give me another human being. I found the idea both bizarre and comic and was sure that he had somehow misunderstood him. But from the expressions on their faces, I could see they were serious. I was embarrassed.

"Junji doesn't owe me anything and neither does his sister. Tell him," I firmly stated.

"Japanese custom say must repay debt for such a deed or lose face. Saving face in Japan very important, Naudsan," Toshiko said. "You must do this or Junji lose face," Toshiko persisted.

"Look, I realize it's important, but I'm an American. We don't have a custom in America where you just give people to other people." Then I corrected myself, silently thinking about the slaves before the Civil war. "At least we haven't done it since we abolished slavery a long time ago."

"Ooooh, Naudsan must do," Toshiko insisted, adding. "If Junji lose face, must leave club."

It was crazy time. I was ready to tell them both to forget it, and get out of there. But I knew how much I needed Toshiko to run the Club. I looked around at the other waiters, they had all stopped working and were listening intently waiting for my reaction. I didn't want to be disrespectful and create a rift with the other men by turning Junji down. So I decided to go along. "What do I have to do?" I asked, hedging.

Toshiko mumbled to Junji, who smiled and mumbled back.

"Naudsan go meet sister. Make love. Come back one hour," Toshiko said.

He made the whole thing sound as appealing as taking a laxative. I wasn't against sex, but I felt stupid and awkward being the winner of what amounted to a 'sexual give-away contest'. It made me feel cheap and dirty. Especially in view of the fact that I had almost no sexual experience. And what if I failed to meet

Junji's sister's standards? Did I have to keep doing it until she gave me a passing grade? My only real sexual experience consisted of one messy encounter with an aging blonde from Long Island, who put her cheap perfume on with a sponge. Just remembering the experience was depressing and degrading.

"Where is she?" I asked.

"She wait now at Flaming Pisspot," Toshiko said.

'Oh, shit,' I thought. The Mama-san who owned the place already hated me for what had happened there with Jessie.

"You go, Naudsan," Toshiko pleaded.

Practically speaking, I had no choice. "Okay, I'll go. But first, I have to change my clothes," I said.

Toshiko and Junji bowed and beamed their gratitude.

I changed into a fresh pair of pants and shirt, and left the base with Junji and Toshiko. I was striding down Oji's main street with them thinking, 'If a guy in America ever tried to tell his sister who she must have sex with... Well, let's just say, he had better be wearing an iron jock.'

We arrived at the Flaming Pisspot. Haruka, Mama-san's best Joy-girl, led Junji, Toshiko and I across the downstairs foyer to an open wall panel overlooking a garden filled with life sized statues of Japanese warriors with grotesquely fierce expressions. There were flowers and greenery lining the winding walkways. Mamasan was standing barefoot on a large mound of red clay, sculpting. She wore a dirty white apron over her Kimono and held large handfuls of mushy red clay. She pounded the clay into the thick layers of straw tied around a six-foot high post buried in the ground.

Haruka mumbled something to her. Mamasan nodded and mumbled back. "Choto-ma-tay," Haruka said to Toshiko.

"What is she doing there?" I asked.

"Mamasan make statues. She very famous," Haruka said.

'If she's so famous how come she's running a whorehouse,' I thought.

"She only make statues for Emperor," Toshiko explained.

Mamasan paused in her work and stepped nimbly into her sandals. She walked across the garden to greet us.

"E-ka-ga-des-ka?" she said, bowing her greeting to all.

Toshiko and Junji returned the bow. I bowed, too, hoping it would make amends for his previous visit.

Toshiko and Mamasan spoke briefly.

Toshiko and Junji waited downstairs while Mamasan led me to the second floor, down a darkened hall, past the room where Jessie had made his standoff, to the end of the hall. She stopped in front of the last, sliding, sandalwood panel.

"Girl wait in here," Mamasan said, bowing, then headed back downstairs.

I stood in the hall, listening. I couldn't hear any noise coming from the room. Finally, I slid the panel open to look in. Nothing was in sight but a small black-lacquered table in the center of the room.

I entered and sat at the table. I faced a window set into a rice paper paneled wall. The golden rays of the setting sun streamed in through the window. The rice paper panels around it glowed as if they were on fire. I lowered my gaze to the table. The glare from the sun made the wall hard to look at.

In one corner of the room was a futon bed. In another, a small makeshift cubicle had been created from delicately painted screens with a curtain for a door. Behind the curtain, I could see the shadow of a girl changing her clothes.

I had a plan wherein Junji could save face, the girl wouldn't feel rejected, and I wouldn't feel like some perverted ogre. My problem was I didn't speak Japanese.

The curtains on the cubicle parted. The girl walked to the opposite side of the table from where I sat. She was backlit by the sun's rays, flooding in through the panel behind her.

I looked up and gasped. Her silhouette was breath taking. The sun's golden light poured through her clothes, seeming to melt them away, revealing a perfection of the female form that seemed to belong in a dream.

I still couldn't see her face because of the glare but it didn't matter. It took a moment for me to compose himself.

"Look, I hope you understand. But, we're just gonna talk," I said, giving the words a moment to register. She didn't respond, so I repeated the message slowly. "We'll just talk for a while. And then we'll go. No lovemaking. Okay?" I said.

The sun was so intense behind her I had no way of knowing what her reactions were. But I could see she was tall and her glistening black hair hung down to her waist. She was wearing a loosely draped American style dressing gown on her slender frame, not loose enough to hide the jut of her full breasts against the material or the curve of her slender hips. Her shapely legs peeked out through slits on either side of the teal gown.

My eyes were suddenly riveted on her hands as they slid down her body and untied the sash around her waist. The gown fell open revealing her soft flesh.

"Look, I guess you didn't understand what I said," I said gulping, trying to stay calm. She let the gown fall from her shoulders, past her firm young breasts to settle in a heap at her feet. She stood there naked.

I had an instant erection. Any thought of not having sex was fast going to hell as she lowered her naked body onto the futon, out of the sun's blinding rays.

At last, I could see her face. I was stunned again. 'Oh no, Jesus,' I thought. My emotions went from anger, to frustration, to lust and back again. I was looking at the one person I had never expected to see. The girl with the cobalt blue eyes. "What are you doing here?" I asked. I was angry.

"Junji is my brother. I didn't know he worked for you," she said, lowering her eyes.

I reached across the table and recovered her dressing gown. "Here, put this back on," I said, tossing it at her.

"I'm obligated to pay his debt. It is the Japanese way," she said apologetically.

"Well I'm an American. And it's not my way," I said.

"Is it so easy for you to mock our ways?" she said embarrassed.

"Japanese women are people now, too, with new ways. Read your constitution," I said. "Besides, Junji doesn't have to 'save face'. The only reason he was accused of stealing was because a Sergeant was try-ing to get even with me. Junji's not a thief."

"Junji IS a thief. All the waiters are thieves," she said.

I was stunned again. I didn't want to believe it. But I knew there was no reason for her to lie.

"I don't believe it," I said.

"Sergeant Baker makes them steal as part of their job," she said. "Ask any of them. I have told you the truth."

I had nothing to say. Those waiters were men I had come to trust.

Do you not believe me?" she said.

"I don't know. I guess so," I said.

"You wanted to be my friend. Now you hate me," she said. Tears began flowing down her cheeks.

"Look, even if we did, uh ...make love. It wouldn't be that at all; it would be, uh ... It, uhh ...Well, I don't know what it would be, now, and I don't wanna find out." I rose from the table and opened the sliding door panel.

"I'll tell your brother his debt is paid and I'm sorry I made you cry," I said, as I closed the panel and left.

The girl lowered her face to the pillow and began to sob uncontrollably.

Chapter 15

Fortunes of War

Corporal Dehler hit a pothole, momentarily losing control of the jeep. He was driving through the dark twisted back streets of Oji with only blackout lights to show him the way.

The big handsome country boy shook his head, trying to clear the cobwebs. He was tired and angry with Sergeant Baker for not living in a place easier to find. Dehler wished he had a giant floodlight to see the whole area. He turned left and squinted his blood-shot eyes to try and see through the darkness. All he could see on his left was a drainage ditch. On his right he could barely make out a row of single story houses. They all had red tiled roofs, white plaster walls with neatly kept gardens, and were big by Japanese standards.

He crept along until he caught sight of a familiar object, Baker's motorbike. He parked the jeep in front of it, jumped out and started up the pebbled path towards the front door.

Though it was still dark an old man wearing a caped hood like a monk was busy at work in the front garden. He was trimming the edge of the walkway by the light of a Japanese lantern. When the man caught sight of Dehler, he rose, and bowed slightly, gesturing him to pass.

Dehler knew the old man's story from Baker.

Mr. Matsuka had once owned a prosperous furniture factory in Tokyo, until the American fire bomb raids destroyed most of the city, leveling his factory. Among the dead were his wife and son. Though he was badly burned, he and his twelve-year-old daughter Kumiko survived. In order to stay alive and pay their doctor bills he was forced to sell his house, and the services of himself as the gardener and his daughter as housekeeper.

Sergeant Baker had bought the house and the Matsukas, 'lock, stock, and barrel'.

Mr. Matsuka stepped back, returning to his work in the garden.

Dehler walked onto the porch and tapped lightly on one of the sandalwood panels, then pulled on the chord of the wind chime. The delicate tinkling sound didn't match the angry thoughts running through his mind. 'You're stooge is here Baker. You're stooge is here.'

Dehler knew what he was. That didn't mean he liked it. But it was a means to an end. He had been doing Baker's dirty work for months, waiting for his chance to take over the EM Club, expecting to share in the profit which would give him enough money to buy a farm in Iowa after his discharge. But so far all he had gotten from Baker were empty promises, and his payoffs have amounted to a few crummy bucks for helping to fix bingo games. Dehler was angry, fed up with Baker's bullshit. He felt like nothing but a flunky.

Now Baker had him helping smuggle art objects out of the country. Smuggling was a court-martial offense. And if they turned you over to the Japs instead... Christ. Dehler felt he had to do something.

But if he came on too strong, Baker would have his ass shipped to Korea. He'd seen it happen to others. He felt like a rat on a wheel, going around and getting nowhere. 'He'd better come through this time,' Dehler thought.

The panel door opened to reveal Matsuka's daughter, Kumiko. She was now in her late teens and lovely. She wore a pink kimono and her jet-black hair was pilled neatly on her head, held by two long white combs carved of whalebone.

"I must see Bakersan," Dehler said.

"Hai," Kumiko said, bowing and gesturing for him to enter.

Dehler kept smiling at her as he followed Japans custom and kicked his shoes off onto the porch. He couldn't help wondering if Baker was sleeping with her. Dehler was sure he was.

Dehler followed her down the hall. It was first time he had been inside Baker's house. The hallway was covered with a fine straw matting. The sandalwood panels lining the halls were decorated with hand painted scenes of nature and dragons.

Dehler could hear the sounds of Kumiko's kimono rustling as she walked and he caught the aroma of incense. She stopped by a pair of panels depicting ancient Japanese homes floating in a sea of misty mountain water. She slid one open and stepped aside gesturing for Dehler to enter.

Baker was in a small steamy pool in the center of the room. Black market Sam was lying on a massage table near the far wall.

"Finish Sam's massage," Baker ordered. The girl paused and acknowledged Baker's command with a slight bow.

"Have a seat Dehler," Baker ordered.

It bothered Dehler to see such a young attractive girl being the obedient slave of such an uncouth slob as Baker. To him, Baker was nothing but a shit- kicking thief from Bristol Tennessee who loved to make him feel like a slave.

Baker rose up out of the tub, wrapped himself in a towel, and walked over to one of his prized Japanese artifacts. "Sam? How does this look?" Baker asked as he held a scowling black ceramic mask over his face. It was from the Nara period and probably worth fifty thousand dollars.

Kumiko kept on massaging Black Market Sam's back as he lifted his head to see what Baker was talking about.

"You look... like...old man... with long...nose," Sam said in staccato grunts, as Kumiko's hands pounded their way down his spine.

Baker knelt on the floor near one of his large display cases, taking the objects out, wrapping them in thick white towels and putting them into a four- foot square wooden crate. It was now almost filled with the fluffy white bundles. Baker finished wrapping the scowling ceramic mask in a heavy white towel and placed it carefully in the crate.

"This mask reminds me of Jimmy Durante," Baker said.

"Who Jimmy Durante, Bakersan?" Kumiko asked, halting the massage while Sam moved his head and shoulders to find a more comfortable position.

"He's a movie star who's famous for his big nose," Baker said.

"Non-desk-ka 'nose'?" Kumiko asked. It was a word she hadn't heard.

Baker used his hand to pantomime a long nose on his face.

Kumiko giggled at his comic gesture and the distraction caused her to press a tender spot on Sam's neck.

"Arrgghh," Sam cried out.

"Go-men-di-sigh, Sam-san," Kumiko apologized. She continued on, being careful to use less pressure on Sam's neck muscles.

"Why you like Durante, Bakersan?" Kumiko asked.

"Probably 'cause he reminds me of my old man," Baker said.

"Father alive, Bakersan?" Sam asked, moving his head to another position.

"No," Baker answered.

"Father die in war," Sam said. "Father bring honor. Die glorious death."

Baker knew the Japanese believed there was glory in dying for the Emperor. The idea of dying for the Emperor, or the President, or the Pope, or anybody, was bullshit to Baker. He still recalled the feeling of terror he had cowering behind a dead German soldier and watching his head explode during WWII. It was back when he was twenty-four-year-old Private Leroy Baker. His company had been pinned down by a barrage of German mortar and machine gun fire and he was just trying to stay alive when the bottom half of an American soldier's body came flying at him, slamming him to the steel roadway of the Remagen Bridge. It was a horrifying sight. His face and hands were splattered with bits of skin and bloody goo from the pulverized remains of the dead soldier.

He was frozen with fear. "I said MOVE Baker or I'll blow YOUR fuckin' head off," a Sergeant screamed again as he jammed the muzzle of his rifle hard against his head. There was another explosion close by. Baker started running, half expecting the Sergeant to shoot him in the back. He found a burned-out half truck just ahead. It was the perfect refuge. He was four steps away, when another mortar barrage hit. The two soldiers just ahead of him evaporated in a blinding explosion. Baker was slammed to the ground and there, lying at his feet, with the angry look still on his face, was the Sergeant's head. Baker began to scream hysterically as he discovered the red goo oozing from the side of his body. He had been hit. None of those feelings had anything to do with glory. All they did was make him vomit.

"You no like 'smiling woman' mask, Bakersan?" Kumiko asked. Her voice brought Baker back to reality.

"Sure. I like ALL the masks. The scowling man, the warrior face, and this here Amida, too," Baker said as he secured the towel around it with a couple more wraps of electrician's tape.

When Baker discovered the fire alarm which had sent him rushing to his house in a panic was a hoax, he was ready to kill. But, when he calmed down, it also had an unintended beneficial effect. He realized he could easily have lost his entire fortune had the fire been real. It made him appreciate what his mother used to say when something frightening happened, 'It's a blessing in disguise, Leroy.' The blessing in disguise for his mother was the ribbon salesman she ran off with.

He had stuck his neck out now too far, too often, to let it go up in smoke. He was going to send the stuff to the states where it would be safe in a fire-proof vault. He put the Amida mask in the crate, carefully packing another towel around it.

"Hey, Sam? Where did ya manage to get all this art stuff?" Baker asked, as he was printing the name 'Amida' on the towel with black crayon.

"All things come from the winter mist," Sam said.

Baker smiled and shook his head. He knew when Sam didn't want to answer a question he would respond in a poetic riddle.

"You send valuable things to sister?" Sam said.

"No. My sister's useless. This stuff's going to a vault," Baker said.

"Who take?" Sam inquired.

"I found an Air Force guy," Baker answered. Baker had discovered there were people in the army who would do things, even when it wasn't exactly legal, for a price. Baker didn't mind doing *not-exactly-legal things*.

"What if Air Force guy steal?" Sam asked.

"Then, I hire you to unsteal. Wa-ka-di-mawsh-ta?" Baker answered with a sly look.

Sam smiled demonically, indicating he understood.

The one item Baker wasn't sending still lay on a small black table near his side. It was the only copy of a very old book by a man who was the Shakespeare of Japanese literature, Ihari Saikaku. It was made by Saikaku's apprentice and penned at about the time the English were landing on Plymouth Rock in America. It was a perfect reproduction of the original. Baker couldn't read Japanese, but Sam told him it was a book of erotic poems called, *Man Who Spent Life Making Love*. It was Baker's prized possession, owning it gave him a great sense of importance.

Baker knew it was illegal to send or take Japanese art out of the country, but he also knew he could get ten, maybe twenty times, the amount he paid for the treasures in the states.

He made a final check of the objects in the crate to be certain everything was there:

1 Gigaku mask, Nara period; (alias Jimmy Durante)

3 Haniwa clay warriors from the Grave mound period, including the horse's head; 1 Amida Buddha, Kamikura period;

1 Warrior head of Meikara Taisho, Nara period;

1 Koomote mask,

1 Skiami mask, both from the Momoyama period;

6 Shino ware ceramic plates, bowls, Showa period;

1 Tea bowl, called Black Raku, Edo period;

1 Clay vessel, Jomon period;

1 Lacquer box, Edo period;

1 Kimono with a Noshi design, Edo period;

1 Fan from the Heian period

Baker put the lid on the crate and began carefully nailing it shut. When he had driven in the last nail, he leaned back on his haunches and arched his back up to stretch out the kinks. Then he relaxed back to a comfortable kneeling position to admire his fortune. The things in the crate were worth at least three-quarters of a million American dollars. Leroy Baker was a rich man. Pretty soon he would have enough money to leave the army and return home to Bristol, Tennessee. He was going to build a mansion on the tiny plot of land he grew up on, and use the cold water shack as an outhouse for his guests. He had told everyone his father owned a coal mine, but in reality his father was just one of the miners working down in the shafts.

"Too bad you didn't come earlier. Kumiko woulda given you a massage," Baker said to Dehler.

'Bullshit,' Dehler thought. Baker was taunting him. He would never let him get anywhere near the girl.

Kumiko stopped massaging Sam long enough to toss her silky black hair over her shoulder and smile at Dehler. Dehler could see she liked him. He promised himself months ago, when he first saw her, he would set her up in a house of his own when he got the dough.

"All right, Dehler, let's go. We're late," Baker said.

"Look, Sergeant, I gotta talk to you," Dehler protested, determined to speak his mind.

"Okay, go ahead, talk. But make it fast," Baker said.

"Not in front of them, okay?" he said, gesturing at Sam and Kumiko.

"All right," Baker conceded. "Grab hold of the crate and we'll talk outside."

They carried the valuable cargo out and placed it on the back seat of the jeep. Baker took a roll of hemp rope from the back pocket of his uniform and cut it in half. He gave Dehler one of the pieces.

"What's on your mind, Dehler?" Baker asked. He sensed what was coming.

Dehler started tying the crate down as he realized he didn't have enough guts to confront Baker.

"I know what's bugging you, Dehler," Baker said, in a fatherly tone.

Dehler pulled the rope tighter. He gave the knot he was tying a last violent tug to set it. He glanced at Baker, defying him to read his mind.

Baker smiled slyly. "Hell, boy. I know things haven't worked out like we planned but I told you patience would pay off, didn't I?" Baker said. "About taking over the Club, like I said."

Dehler looked at him quizzically.

"Next month," Baker promised.

Dehler was leery. Baker had fed him this same bullshit story before.

"Why you think I'm sittin' on those gate passes for the girls in the Miss Tokyo contest. Think, Boy, THINK."

Dehler wasn't getting it.

"The Colonel wants the code guys at the Club right away. But it can take time to check on those girls. Lots of time. Without passes, there's no contest and no code guys coming to the Club. By the next board meeting the Colonel will be out of patience. Naud will be gone and the Club will be yours."

The plan made sense to Dehler but he still wasn't totally convinced. Baker's plans had gone bad before.

"We'll talk about it later," Baker said, checking his watch.

"You gotta get this crate to Sergeant Stauling at Haneda's main gate." Then he added, "And make sure you get the stuff there in one piece." Baker handed Dehler an envelope. "This envelope is for Stanley. " He reached into his wallet and pulled out two bills. "Here's two hundred for you."

"Don't worry. I'll make it," Dehler said, feeling a little better. It was a first step toward what Dehler still hoped was going to be a prosperous relation-ship.

Dehler climbed into the driver's seat and turned to Baker.

"Look, Sergeant, you better know who your friends are."

"What are you talking about, boy?" Baker said.

Dehler relished the fact he knew something about Sam that Baker didn't.

"Plummer didn't bail Mulvey out by borrowing supplies from other posts. He rented the stuff from Sam, who made himself three grand on the deal."

"I knew all about it, boy," Baker lied.

Dehler was disappointed. He had hoped to drive a wedge between Baker and Sam.

"But I do appreciate your looking out for me," Baker added.

Dehler drove off, feeling that at least he was back on track for the EM Club's custodian's job.

Baker watched the jeep vanish around a corner with a cynical smile on his face. "Three thousand bucks, eh?" he mused. He hadn't known a thing about Sam's rental deal with Plummer. But Baker wasn't angry. He knew Sam was a guy who would steal from his own mother, if he could get away with it. Sam was his partner. And business was business. He and Sam were fifty-fifty on everything. Baker wore a shit-eating grin on his face as he started into the house to collect his half of the money, fifteen hundred dollars.

Chapter 16

The Passes-Board of Governors Meeting

The EM Club's business was beginning to boom. Every day I posted a few new pictures of the Miss Tokyo contestants around the club and on the bulletin board. And every night, as I had hoped, bigger crowds showed up to look over the photos and hear about the contest first hand. I was beginning to wonder if all I had to do was go on putting up photos of buxom girls to keep the code guys coming.

Plummer was worried about the big-boobs pictures. He was afraid there was bound to be some backlash when those particular girls didn't show up for the contest. I assured him, it was a problem I could handle.

After morning chow I went up to the parade ground to practice hitting my wedge shots, hoping to take my mind off the latest problem. The bastard Baker was trying to kill the contest by dragging his feet on the passes for the Miss Tokyo contestants. He was hoping if he held them up long enough the code guys would lose interest and stop coming to the Club. So far he had only issued six passes. At that rate the war would be over before we could hold the contest.

As I dropped a group of balls on the grass I reminded myself of Plummer's words. ""The Colonel needs your plan to work. Let him handle the passes." My only hope was the Colonel would light a fire under Baker at the Board of Governors meeting and get him to issue the rest of the passes right away. I spent a few hours hitting balls but my heart wasn't really in it.

Two days later on September 1st, the day of the Board of Governors meeting, at 7a.m. Plummer was at his desk staring at a letter from his fiancé back home. He carefully slit it open just as the guard from the code room upstairs arrived at his desk with two top secret war communiqués. Plummer put the letter down and signed for the communiqués.

Colonel Macmillan was due back from Korea momentarily so his first order of business was to copy and summarize the decoded messages so they would be on the Colonel's desk when he arrived. The News from Anne had to wait.

He typed the following two messages:

....

Top Secret/ASA OJI Decrypted Communique

Date: August 31 1950

To: MACARTHUR

From: GENERAL WALKER

Subject: TACTICAL WAR SUMMARY

Synopsis:

   Enemy forces have Taejon.   Moving
to encircle Pusan Perimeter.
   Don't know how long I can hold them
back.   Without major troop replace-
ments we will have to evacuate.

Signed

General Walker

....

Top Secret/ASA OJI Decrypted Communique

Date: September 1 1950

To: JOINT CHIEFS OF STAFF

From: MACARTHUR

Subject: TACTICAL SUMMARY

Synopsis:

General Walker can't hold Pusan perimeter beyond the end of the month, Sept., unless we end run Incheon. Going ahead with Incheon landing set for Sept. 15. Extreme tides and sea walls during invasion are dangerous but acceptable risks. I am reviewing problems uncluding security, recognize serious consequences if we fail. Decyphered communiqués from enemy indicate they have no knowledge of the Incheon landing.

Signed
MAC

The Board of Governors meeting was at 12:00 hours and I wanted to look sharp. Plummer had promised me he would tell the Colonel about the delay in passes as soon as he arrived back on base.

"You like haircut?" the Imperial barber asked, holding the mirror up for me to see the back of my head.

"Ichi bon," I said, pleased with how I looked.

The barber removed the apron from around my neck. I paid him in American greenbacks, including a tip. Then I strolled down the arcade in the lobby hoping to find what I had really come for. Now that it looked like I was staying in Japan for awhile I was determined to get to know the beautiful girl with the cobalt blue eyes who clouded my mind.

The giant clock on the wall told him it was almost noon. My family, half way around the world, was fast asleep.

I spotted her in the arcade dress shop where she worked. She was showing a dress to a middle-aged lady. Each time I saw her she seemed more beautiful. I wandered up and down the arcade, working up the courage to walk into the shop. When I finally did, I saw her vanish into the back of the store.

The old lady who ran the store kept insisting she wasn't there. I tried to explain that I just saw her going into the back of the shop but the woman acted like she didn't understand what I was saying. I knew she was lying but it didn't matter I had to get back to the base for the meeting. I asked the woman for a piece of paper so I could write a note. That she understood.

Dear Miss,
I just came by to say "Hello". I'm sorry if I offend you so much you feel you have to run away from me. I am still hoping we can be friends.
William t. Naud

I left the note and headed back to the base just in time to pick up my laundry and change into a fresh class A uniform.

I bounded up the stairs to the Em Club for the Board of Governors meeting. I found Toshiko waiting for me on the office floor landing with an obvious look of concern.

"Plummer-san sick, Naud-san," Toshiko said, "he in Golf room."

We squeezed our way through the liquor crate maze to the secret room in the warehouse which I had turned into a golf practice range. It looked as if a hurricane had blown through, clubs and balls were strewn everywhere, even the golf net was ripped in several places.

Plummer lay face down on the straw practice matt that was shredded to pieces. He had gotten sick all over himself but was still holding an empty bottle of CC whiskey. "Fore. Fore, "he mumbled in a drunken slur. "What a stupid game," he uttered as he rolled over pulling his legs up in a fetal position.

"What happened?" I asked Toshiko in a whisper.

Toshiko shrugged ignorance. "Shi-do-ni," he responded. I knew it meant, 'I don't know'.

"Get a pillow, towels and some warm water," I said.

"Hai, Naudsan," Toshiko said and hurried out of the maze.

"Bring some hot coffee too," I called after him.

Plummer was a disgusting mess covered in dripping sweat. I took the towel off my golf bag and began cleaning him up. The stench was almost more than I could bear.

Plummer started to show some signs of cognizance as he fought to focus his eyes on me. "You know Naud," he mumbled in a barely audible tone, "when I first saw you, I thought you were a real screwup. ...But you got guts."

"Thanks," I said. I noticed a somewhat crumpled letter stuffed halfway into his shirt pocket. It was postmarked, *New Bedford, Massachusetts*. I wondered if the letter was a *Dear John* from his fiancée.

"What happened?" I asked.

Plummer answered by closing his eyes.

Toshiko appeared with a pillow, several towels, and a teapot filled with warm water. "I get coffee now, Naudsan," Toshiko whispered and left again.

I covered the pillow with a towel and slipped it under Plummer's head.

He was starting to shake with the chills. "Golf is a stupid game for old men, right?" he said.

"Right," I said.

"I don't feel so good," Plummer moaned.

I kept wiping his face with the warm towel trying to calm the shaking.

"You're a good friend, Naud," he said softly.

My motive for helping him wasn't just friendship but I was glad he said that. I really was counting on him being at the board meeting to help me handle Baker and the Colonel.

"My dad had a heart attack, Bill. He's killing himself trying to save a stupid fish factory for me. I don't want his fish factory. I want him," he mumbled with a deflated look.

Jumbo returned with the coffee. I held Plummer's head up to let him sip from the mug. Quietly I inquired, "Did you mention the passes to the Colonel?"

He barely nodded yes. "I left him a note," he uttered as his eyelids closed and he fell asleep.

I could understand Plummer's feelings. I hadn't said anything about my own father's painful condition to anybody.

I turned to Jumbo. "Bring the blankets from my bed and cover him up."

"Plummersan no go board meeting?" Jumbo asked.

"No," I said. I knew the Colonel would crucify Plummer if he showed up drunk, better he didn't show up at all.

I headed off to the meeting. Now I was on my own now. I hoped the Colonel would be in a good mood, but I wasn't counting on it.

I entered the Club and took my place at the end of the table, making note of those who were present. Seated on one side were Bakers three monkey stooges: Dehler, Hartung, and Zinger. On my side were Pollazzo, Dollin and Toshiko. Toshiko was busy putting the club records in order. Every month he struggled to type up the minutes of the meetings.

Dehler started complaining for all to hear that the water needed more ice but I could see there was plenty. He was acting like a bratty child but I didn't feel like being drawn into a childish argument. Jumbo brought him more ice.

"Hey, Naud? Where's Plummer?" Dehler asked.

"He's not coming, he's sick" I said loud enough for everyone to hear.

Before I came up, I had called Sergeant Tiff, who ran the dispensary. In case anyone inquired, I told him to tell them Plummer had gone on sick call with a fever and that he had confined him to bed.

Jumbo leaned in to me. "Dehler wants beer, Naud-san."

"No drinks for sale till the Club is open," I said loud enough for Dehler and the others to hear. My edict only angered Dehler more.

ATTENJ HUT," Sergeant Baker barked as he stopped and came to attention just inside the Club's front door.

Everyone, including me, stood at attention while we waited for the Colonel to enter. Only, it wasn't the Colonel. I was startled when I saw who came through the door. It was Captain Cross.

"Where's the Colonel?" I whispered in panic to Pollazzo.

Pollazzo shrugged. He was just as mystified as me to see Captain Cross.

"At-ease," Cross said as he and Baker taking took their places at the end of the table, adding, "Every body, sit, please."

I suddenly felt doomed. First Plummer had crashed and burned, and now I had lost my most important asset, the Colonel.

Captain Cross removed a manual from his brief-case and placed it flat on the table. The cardboard cover read, "ASA EM Club, Standard Operating Procedure (SOP)". He opened it to a place with a red bookmarker and kept it open by pressing it down flat on the table with an ashtray.

"Colonel Macmillan has not returned from Korea. He's been held up by urgent military matters. As second in command, I will stand-in under authority of the company by laws," Cross explained.

Nobody said anything.

I caught a glimpse of Baker smirking as he lit a cigar.

Cross searched the manual page and finally found the section he had been searching for.

"This meeting will come to order," he announced. Then he read on, following all the proper procedures to a tee. First he noted who was present. He asked Dehler to write down the minutes since Corporal Plummer was out sick. Then he asked for the minutes of the last meeting.

Toshiko came forward proudly clutching copies of last month's minutes. He was pleased Cross was going to have them read.

Baker offered a motion to wave the reading of the minutes. Dehler seconded, and the rest agreed, so Toshiko disappointedly sat back down.

I was preoccupied with my dilemma, whether to mention the passes to Cross or wait for the Colonel to return which could be God knows when.

Cross reached into his briefcase searching for something. "We have a wire here from Captain Mulvey," he said finally holding up a telegram.

"'To my friends at ASA, Oji,'" he read, "'I have returned home safely and wish to thank you again for all your help and consideration. Best to all, Harry Mulvey.' I'm sure we are all grateful to hear of Captain Mulvey's safe return to his family and wish him all the best in civilian life." He gave the telegram to me and asked it be tacked up on the Club's bulletin board.

I was surprised to hear the compassion in his voice. The scuttlebutt was Cross didn't give a damn about anybody. He was an army by the book, no exceptions kind of commander, a West Point graduate who had been ASA OJI's morale officer for the past four months. He knew he wasn't popular and didn't care. Being the new company commander was a job he didn't want but the ASA had stuck him with it.

"Alright, any NEW business?" Cross proceeded.

Pollazzo made a motion that the bingo prize money be divided evenly between all the games rather than having one Super Bingo game at the end of the night. I asked him to do it figuring Baker wouldn't be interested in stealing smaller pots of money, and wouldn't dare fix more than one game.

I seconded the motion.

Baker strongly objected, claiming that Bingo Night's popularity was based mainly on the very thing I wanted to change. He reminded Captain Cross that they had been doing it this way for months and it worked, so there was no need to change it. Of course Dehler and the other stooges added their voices, agreeing there was no reason for a change.

Cross called for a vote.

Without even a glance from Baker, Dehler and the stooges voted no. That made the vote five to three against.

"Motion is defeated," Cross declared.

Baker took the cigar from his mouth and leaned forward on the table, grinning snidely at me in his victory.

I decided I had to take a chance and say something about the passes, even though I knew Cross and Baker were buddy-buddy, and there wasn't a snowball's chance in hell that Cross would help me. "Sir, as you know we have the Miss Tokyo contest coming up. Unfortunately I have only gotten a few of the gate passes for the contestants from Sergeant Baker. I realize how busy the Sergeant has been with other matters, but the passes are important."

Captain Cross looked at Baker for an answer.

Baker's expression hardened defiantly. "As the Captain knows I have been swamped with other matters regarding the ninety-six members of the Japanese indigenous work force, issuing gate passes, health permits and security clearances. Hell, I barely have time to keep up with it all. I'm going as fast as I can."

"That's understandable Sergeant," Cross replied.

Cross was doing exactly what I thought he would do, nothing.

"Captain," I persisted, "If we don't get the passes right away they're liable to hold the contest at some other base. The contest is very important to the Colonel."

Baker barked back snidely, "You're *Miss Tokyo* contest ain't so important Naud. Besides I ain't got much time to write passes for a lot of JOY GIRLS so our guys can make goo-goo eyes at them. I'll do the passes when I'm damn good and ready, Private," Baker snapped, then sat back and lit a new cigar.

He had gone too far.

Cross glared at him for a moment. He could abide Baker's anger because of of a heavy workload, but he could not tolerate his blatant abuse of a subordinate, especially in a pubic forum.

"Sergeant?" Cross said with a mild rebuke in his voice. "The Colonel did mention the passes to me at lunch before he left, so I assume he did so because he felt they WERE important."

"With all due respect, they AIN'T, Sir," Baker responded in a condescending and defiant tone.

Cross took a moment to bring his anger under control and compose himself. "Sergeant, this is a direct order," he said in a cold steely tone, "You WILL make those girl's passes a priority. Am I clear?"

"Yeah," Baker mumbled as he removed the soggy cigar from his mouth and pressed it down hard in the ashtray.

"Yes, WHAT, Sergeant?" Cross said, reminding Baker of the military protocol.

"Yes, SIR," Baker said, grudgingly.

But Cross wasn't through with him yet. "Yes, Sir, WHAT? Sergeant?" Cross persisted.

"Yes, Sir, CAPTAIN," Baker responded, loud and clear.

I loved every humiliating moment of it.

"If there is no other business this meeting is adjourned," Cross announced while standing up.

I should have felt like I had won a great victory but Surrel's words echoed in my head, 'Baker runs Oji.'

There was nothing else I could do. Colonel Macmillan was still in Korea, and no one was certain when he would be coming back.

When I came down from the meeting I found Surrel waiting for me in the office. Something was up. I wasn't expecting him until later in the week.

He was looking though the antique telescope by the window as I entered. It was aimed at the Korekum Stadium and he was twisting the lens to focus it. He started to laugh. "You gotta see this Naud, it's insane," he said as he stepped back from the telescope.

I pressed my eye close to the eyepiece. "It looks like some kind of bicycle race," I said sounding less than enthusiastic.

"Just keep watching, "Surrel said.

I suddenly gasped. One of the riders had taken a bad spill and the other guys had just pedaled right over him. "Holy Shit," I exclaimed. "Those guys are gonna kill each other!" I continued to watch, amused as the bikers pedal over other bikers like they are speed bumps. It was like a *Three Stooges* comedy, until I caught the eyes of a fallen biker and saw his pain. I stopped looking. Suddenly it wasn't a silly cartoon. It was all too real and painful.

"Any luck with the passes?" Surrel asked.

I handed him the large brown envelope from my desk.

"We've got six so far," I said with frustration. " Baker is handing out the passes alright, but only one at a time."

"Six out of forty. I told ya. Baker runs this place," Surrel said ominously. "Look," he said slowly, as if he was carefully choosing his words, "it's not your fault Naud. But if I don't get the contest going, my bosses in the States feel it could really hurt Christmas sales. They want a firm date for the contest now."

The reason for Surrel's unexpected appearance was now painfully clear.

Surrel couldn't hold back his bad news any longer. "Bill I gotta move the Miss Tokyo contest."

I could see he felt badly.

"So where are ya gonna hold it?" I asked with resignation.

"Probably at the Army's main EM Club downtown," Surrel said. "I'm sorry, really sorry, Bill. Look I gotta go."

"Hey, I understand. I appreciate you even tried," I said with a defeated shrug. There was nothing more to say. Surrel vanished down the stairs.

I headed into the warehouse feeling like I had just been kicked in the head. Baker had beaten me. This time it felt bad, real bad.

I lay down thinking I might escape the whole mess by taking a nap, but I really wasn't tired so I just closed my eyes.

Someone started rapping on the warehouse door. "Naudsan? Naudsan?" It was Toshiko. A second later Toshiko was in front of me holding a bulging brown envelope.

"Naudsan? Orderly room send this," Toshiko said, handing me the envelope.

I couldn't believe my eyes. I unwound the string holding the flap closed and looked in. It was stuffed with pieces of paper. I dumped the contents onto the bed to reassure myself they were real. It was the passes- ALL of them.

I ran around the liquor mountain out to my office and grabbed the phone.

"Hello, ring the main gate, hurry!" I said. I moved to the window trying to see the guard house, as I waited anxiously for the call to go through. Then I saw a familiar figure coming out of the company orderly room. It was Colonel Macmillan. He had gotten back, and he looked mad. He must have gotten Plummer's note.

Now I understood what had just happened.

Corporal Damion came on the phone.

"Damion? Has Greg Surrel left the base yet?" I asked.

"He's here now," Damion replied.

"Put him on the phone. I gotta talk to him," I yelled.

A moment later Surrel came on.

"Guess what?" I said. Surrel didn't have to guess at anything. It was all there in my voice. I could see him giving me a thumbs up from the gate. It was show time at Oji's ASA EM Club.

Chapter 17

The Contest

It was Saturday night, the night of the contest. I joined the stream of GI's making their way up the steps to the club. From the raucous noise echoing in the stairwell, I could tell there was already a big crowd up stairs. Langon was at the entrance to the club, wearing an MP arm band acting more like a bar bouncer than a policeman.

"Is Plummer inside?" I asked him.

"No, haven't seen him. Looks like every off duty codebreaker is here though."

A couple of GI's in on R&R from Korea pushed past me and headed for the bar. As I entered the club I felt a tap on my shoulder. It was Corporal Klein, a bookish codebreaker from New Jersey, standing in his own smoke filled cloud.

With an inebriated smile, he pointed at one of the well endowed magazine pictures I had posted. "I'm waiting for that girl to come in. If she shows up I'm gonna ask her to marry me," he said. Then he planted a big kiss on the picture. Cackles of laughter sounded from the guys within earshot.

I just smiled along and headed to the bar to see if Toshiko needed anything. It had been a busy week of preparations by myself and all the waiters, and though I was tired the electric energy of excitement in the room was starting to revive me.

The waiters had done a great job decorating the club. Suspended above the makeshift stage, hung a thirty-foot long banner. It was hand-painted with large red block letters that heralded the evening's event;

WELCOME TO THE MISS TOKYO CONTEST

They had also draped multi colored crepe paper strips along the walls, and spotted Chinese lantern lights around the room. We borrowed a few gate spotlights and rigged them up to light up the stage. There were drapes covering the windows and rows of chromium chairs were set up for the contestants.

The Club was jammed wall to wall with happily inebriated codebreakers and a dozen or so guys who were in on R&R from Korea. A few impatient GIs began stomping their feet and clapping their hands, calling for the contest to begin.

The contestants had arrived by bus with Surrel, and were down in the office getting ready. Toshiko had the waiters fix up a dressing area with mirrors and lights. Right on cue, Surrel appeared by the door to the fire escape with five of the Miss Tokyo contestants trailing behind. We figured that was the most secretive way to get the girls safely into the club and to the stage. He helped them in, one by one.

The impatient shouts of the GI's turned to whistles and catcalls. Flash bulbs were popping all around the room, as the GIs with cameras recorded the event. Dehler was near the fire escape door taking pictures with his Nikon. I found out he was somewhat of a photography buff, so Surrel had asked him to take pictures for the press releases.

As Surrel led the line of girls in, he motioned for the enthusiastic men to move aside. It was like Mosses trying to part the Red Sea, a narrow pathway opened up lined with gawking clapping GIs. The twenty nervous contestants filed in. Some were in traditional kimonos, but most were wearing western style dresses. They were all pretty, and the crowd loved them. To me it felt like they might be consumed by the sex starved mob of eggheads before the contest could even begin. As the girls took their seats under Surrel's direction, the expressions on some of their faces made it clear they shared my concern.

I was still finding it hard to believe that the girls were really there, in the Club.

I approached the mike on the dance floor. "Okay, now listen up," I said waving my hand to quiet the raucous crowd and shield my eyes from the blinding flash bulbs. "AT-EASE," I screamed into the mike.

Finally the room quieted.

"Guys, here's what you've been waiting for, the twenty finalists for the Miss Tokyo Contest. And one of these lucky girls is going to win 1,000 U.S. dollars. So, let's give them a big hand."

The mob jumped up exploding with catcalls and applause. Some of the girls rose from their seats, smiling and bowing their appreciation. A few of the others were out of their seats, crowding around Surrel, it looked like trouble was brewing already. I turned off the mike and stepped back to find out what was going on.

"What's wrong?" I asked Surrel.

"They say you lied to them and they're gonna quit, "Surrel explained. "The application says Miss

Tokyo will be picked from 10 finalists. Now there are twenty, so the odds aren't the same."

A few girls looked like they were going to leave.

I had managed to get this far and I wasn't about to let it all go to hell, now. It was 'make it up as you go along' time. And make it up fast. "Tell them... We're going to have two first place winners," I babbled.

As Surrel interpreted my words the crowd started to chant loudly, "Go, Go, Go. . " They wanted to see the girls do something, anything besides what they were doing now, which was leaving.

I turned the mike back on. "We'll be right with you guys," I assured the boisterous audience. Then I covered the mike and leaned towards Surrel. I thought I had solved the problem, but the girls were still upset and were chirping angrily at him.

"They say two winners don't help, Naud. It means the thousand first prize will be divided between two girls," Surrel complained.

"Tell them they didn't understand," I said, vamping again with a phony chuckle while I figured out what to say next. "Tell them, we're going to give out two first prizes, $1000 for each winner."

Surrel went ballistic. He leaned in closer to my face. "Naud! Two thousand dollars is a thousand more than we got," he whispered angrily. Two thousand dollars was a lot more than his bosses had planned. If he upped the prize money and it wasn't paid the contest could be a public relations disaster. It might even cost him his job.

The crowd was starting to get out of hand. The floor was shaking from the angry stomping.

"I'll get the money, Surrel. Just tell 'em," I pleaded. "Please. Before we have a riot."

Surrel shook his head, knowing he was sticking his neck in a noose. "I gotta be nuts," he mumbled. He told the girls, in Japanese, that they had misunderstood. There would be two winners and two one thousand dollar prizes.

The girls seemed to be appeased and were returning to their seats.

"Okay Folks, we had a little hold up here, but it's okay now," I explained into the microphone.

The protests and complaints turned into shouts of approval. I was back from the brink of another disaster.

"Listen up. Hold it down so you can hear the rules."

The room quieted to a low murmur.

"Guys. Remember, you're gonna be the judges. We want you to rate each contestant from one to ten on three things, their looks, talent and personality."

"Who cares about talent?" Corporal Harding screamed out.

"Or Personality?" a gruff voice chimed in. Others voiced their agreement, while some guys just made hoots and wolf howls mixed with off-color remarks.

The girls didn't understand so they just ignored the rude comments.

"Between each contestant's act," I said, pausing for effect, "you're gonna judge the girl's personalities by DANCING with them."

"Whahooo!" The thought of dancing with the contestants brought a lion's roar of approval.

"What if you can't dance?" somebody screamed out.

"Then talk to 'em," I hollered into the mike. I waited until they settled down enough that so everyone was sure to hear me. "If anybody gets out of line, you'll be outta here FAST. Clear?" I warned. Langdon and a few MPs dotted around the room stood like warriors ready for trouble.

A chant to start ·· "GO, GO, GO!" ·· rippled through the crowd.

Surrel reached into the shoebox he was holding and pulled out a piece of paper which he handed to me.

"Okay, here we go with our first contestant." The chants died down. "Let's give a big hand to ... Miss Misako Umerie."

Misako Umerie rose gracefully from her chair to wild applause. She was tall and attractive. Her long black cotton print dress defined her as a young lady with money, taste, and breeding. She made her way to the side of stage carrying with her a seventy-eight record.

I noticed Baker was watching Miss Umerie like a vulture. Baker, Dehler and the other stooges were sitting at a table down front, next to the dance floor. Plummer had suggested it would be a smart idea to give the board members a good table, as a peace offering.

Jumbo was standing near the stage stairs. Next to him was a small table on which his portable record player sat. Miss Umerie bowed slightly to Jumbo and handed him her 78 record.

I looked at the back of her name slip and brought the mike close to talk. "Miss Umerie will sing, 'Tennessee Waltz'," I announced.

As she started down the stairs off the stage, I offered her my hand. Then I retreated out of the spotlight.

The room went dead silent as she stood at the mike, and composed herself.

Jumbo put on her record. It was a scratchy instru- mental version of *"Tennessee Waltz"*. She began to sing. Her voice was thin, she was no *Peggy Lee*, but she had some style and managed to stay in tune. Most importantly, she was stunning and regal. It looked like every GI in the room was happy just to look at her.

I stood next to Jumbo, feeling good about how things were going. The Colonel was getting what he asked for, a Club overflowing with distracted code- breakers.

Miss Umerie finished her song and received a standing ovation. She bowed and smiled her appre- ciation.

I took the mike. "And now Miss Umerie will to lead us off in the dancing," I said. Then I remembered I hadn't explained the rules. "Guys, listen up. They'll be five minutes of dancing between each contest- ants act. You can cut in, but only if the girl approves, and no pushing or hogging."

Jumbo put one of Glenn Miller's best-known songs on the record player, *'Tuxedo Junction'*, as the girls joined Miss Umerie down on the dance floor.

A few minutes later the floor was jammed with horny young codebreakers dancing nervously with the pretty contestants, while other guys hovered about looking for a chance to cut in. I was pleased with how well the eggheads were behaving.

Miss Umerie was teaching Pfc. Dutton to dance when Sergeant Baker cut in. Dutton tried to cut back in, but Miss Umerie politely turned him away. Baker's

Rank helped Miss Umerie decide whom she would dance with.

I went to check the bar to see how the liquor was holding up.

"Hey you're the custodian right?"

One of the guys in on R&R pressed into the bar to speak to me.

"Yeah. What'll you have to drink?"

"I got a message for you from your buddy Bonato."

"Jessie... ..is he here?"

"No... He's in a foxhole back with my outfit, the 308th. Man he's a real tiger. He saved my life. "

I couldn't believe my ears.

"It was a couple of days ago, we were in a foxhole we'd dug out along a ridge. There was a bad barrage of incoming junk from the gooks so I was keeping low just trying to stay alive when I heard some scratching and clawing on the slope. When I peered out over the top I caught the glimmer of bayonet moving up the hill. Suddenly a screaming gook rose up and dove at us, with his bayonet pointed right at me. Jessie reached out and caught the guy in midair, and hurled him down the slope. He rolled back down like a log, crashing right into the rest of the gooks creeping up the hill. They all went tumbling back down the ridge, while our guys opened fire, filling em with 50 caliber slugs." He shook his head as he relived it all in his mind. "He said if I found you I should tell you he's okay, it's not so bad. Look I gotta go to the head." Then he walked away.

I was stunned, Jessie was a hero. I felt an odd kind of pride. I was happy he was okay. I just hoped his luck held out.

As the evening progressed with more acts and dancing, the talents displayed by the contestants ranged from a couple of more renditions of *Tennessee Waltz*, to a Judy Garland version of *Somewhere Over The Rainbow*, to a fumbling magic tricks, to tap-dancing, even a Shirley temple imitator complete with red mopped hair wig and cutesy version of *On the Good Ship Lollipop*. And still Plummer hadn't showed up.

I took the stage to introduce the next act. "Okay, now, let's have a big hand for Iko Arakii and her Origami act." I had to smile. It sounded so dumb.

Miss Arakii came down from the stage carrying several large sheets of colored paper. She wore a sky blue kimono with a bulky white cummerbund, called an Obi, around her waist. She was a pretty girl with glistening eyes, an impish smile, and a slight limp.

I felt the need to explain to the audience what she was about to do. "Origami means she's going to fold paper," I said. I couldn't help adding a shrug, suggesting 'paper folding' had about as much entertainment value as watching cement dry.

Miss Arakii bowed deeply to the audience as I left the dance floor. Then she started. She turned her back to the men and began folding the colored papers on a table the waiters had placed on the dance floor. Her movements were small, quick and without any flourish.

I smiled to myself, thinking here was a girl displaying a talent where she said nothing, and nobody in the audience could see what she was doing, yet they all seemed transfixed. Especially the waiters. They had all gathered by the stage stairs, craning their necks to catch her every move. From the looks and smiles on their faces, Miss Arakii was doing something extra special.

Several minutes of muffled paper sounds had gone by when the crowd in the bar area, probably out of sheer boredom, began to sing *Tennessee Waltz*. It acted like back ground music for the Origami lady until she finally finished the paper folding and turned to the audience.

She shook the paper, hard, then hard again.

The crowd gasped in amazement at what appeared.

As if by magic, the colored sheets of paper had been transformed into a giant technicolour swan.

The room burst into applause, the kind only given to a famous symphony conductor or honored Sumo wrestler.

Even the waiters were bowing and applauding.

Miss Arakii bowed her gratitude. She left the technicolour swan on the table and went back to her chair in front of the stage without ever having said a single word.

Everybody was left smiling.

I was amazed at the effect her artistry had on the crowd. Maybe what the world needed was an army of Origami ladies to bridge all the culture gaps.

When the dancing began, Pfc. Pollazzo was the only one who had the courage to ask the Origami lady to dance. Her limp probably scared the other guys away. Miss Arakii walked with a limp, but when she danced, it vanished as if it had never existed.

The night was going along well and the time had come for the club to close. The last dance ended, and I jumped up and grabbed the mike, ready to do more of my used-car-dealer routine.

"Guys? I think we got TWENTY Miss Tokyo's here, don't you?" I said. I got the roar of approval I wanted from the crowd. "Unfortunately, it's getting late and we're not going be to able to see all of these lovely ladies perform tonight."

There was a general groan of disappointment, which didn't bother me as much as the disappointed worrisome looks on some of the girl's faces as Surrel translated to them what I had said.

"Now, it wouldn't be fair to pick our winners without giving everyone an equal chance, so don't worry. To be fair, we'll postpone the judging until we have had the chance to see all the contestants perform. That means we're going to continue the contest with the last four contestants next Saturday. So we're gonna invite all the ladies back. And girls.... You can't win if you're not here," I said finishing with a big smile.

I was half expecting another mutiny from the girls as Surrel finished translating. But it didn't occur. At least not that I could tell. I guess the allure of one thousand American dollars was strong. Just how strong it was, I would find out next week. I was trying to drag the contest out as long as I could, believing as Pavlov did with his dog, that creating a habit was the way to keep the code guys coming.

I had come to the end of a successful evening. But instead of feeling good about it, I had more things to worry about than before. 'How do I get a thousand dollars for the extra Miss Tokyo' prize? Will any of the contestants ever come back? Will the code guys come back?' "Jesus, is life just one worry after another?" I mumbled to myself.

I was sitting at the bar and spotted an ant meandering across it. I envied the ant. What did an ant have to worry about? I was beginning to wish I had been born an ant. Then some guy took aim with his beer bottle and squished it flat.

As the last of the GIs filed out, Plummer finally arrived.

"Hey, what happened?" I asked.

"I was downtown with the Colonel. We got back in time but the decoded messages were streaming down to the office," he responded.

I could see something big had gone down.

"The Colonel is really happy with the job you're doing. I can tell you now what's happening. "

Plummer drew what looked like a map in the condensation on the bar. "Five minutes ago the bombardments commenced here. "He marked an x halfway up the west side. "The US navy has leveled the landing site. " Then he wiped the bar clean and handed me a note from the Colonel. It was part of a top secret message that read, 'The enemy had no knowledge of the reconnaissance teams dropped in a week ago on the adjacent island. Their information on tides and enemy forces were crucial. Decoded enemy transmissions show the north Koreans had no knowledge we were coming. ' Hand written at the bottom was, 'Good Job, Naud, Colonel Macmillan.'

Plummer took the note, lit his Zippo and burned it.

I knew that wasn't the end of it. The days ahead would be crucial but I also knew Plummer had revealed all he could. "Here have a ginger ale," I said. I reached behind the bar and we celebrated the success of the evening.

It was 2 a.m. when my head finally hit the pillow. I was exhausted and expected to drop off to sleep, but the evenings events kept running through my mind. So far the Miss Tokyo contest was a roaring success, and to top it off was Plummer's good news, that the bombardment of the Incheon beach landing site had come as a complete surprise to the North Koreans. There had been no intelligence leaks from the Oji codebreakers. For the first time I had the feeling I was actually contributing to the war effort.

I was worried, though, about Junji. He hadn't shown up for work and none of the other waiters or Toshiko had a clue as to why.

Chapter 18

Captain Cross

As Cross walked towards his office, he smiled, recalling the stunned look he got from his buddy, Major Murphy the evening before. He had told him he might withdraw his name from consideration for the Medal of Honor. Murphy almost choked on his dinner, he found the thought inconceivable, almost treasonous.

Cross never answered Murphy's questions as to why he might withdraw, but the answer was to humiliate the man he hated, his father, the General.

But Cross now realized, he didn't have the guts to do it. It was one thing to humiliate his father. But it was quite another to thumb his nose at his country and at the brave men who died under his command that day.

Dehler handed the Captain a stack of messages as he entered.

"Thank you, Corporal," Cross said, leafing through the messages.

"What else have we got?" he inquired.

"Pfc. Hartung's requesting to be excused from projectionist duty, Saturday, to go downtown to see the dentist, Sir."

Cross didn't really care much for Pfc. Hartung or Corporal Dehler. They always had some phony excuse to get out of one duty or the other. To Hartung's credit, his excuses showed more imagination than Dehler's.

"Tell Pfc. Hartung he's excused, Dehler, but on one condition...." Cross said.

"Yes, Sir."

"YOU take his place."

"Yes, Sir," Dehler said.

'No, Sir,' Dehler thought. 'Hartung will do his own duty.' He was adamant.

The pained look on Dehler's face was just what Cross had expected. With a wry smile on his face, he kept checking the messages.

"What movie is playing this week?" he asked.

"*Sunset Boulevard* with Gloria Swanson, Sir" Dehler said.

"She's a great actress," Cross said. He noticed Baker's office door was closed.

"Is Sergeant Baker here?"

"In his office, Sir."

"Ask him to bring me the VD reports from the dispensary."

"He's already sent them downtown, Sir," Dehler said.

Baker had sent the reports down early, because Dehler had begged him to. He was afraid Cross would find out that Dehler had the clap again and would send him to Korea.

Cross found four messages in the stack from General Cross, his father. He threw them in the trash.

"If General Cross calls again tell him I've gone to Osaka," Cross said.

Dehler shuddered as Cross headed toward his office door, he had just gotten a call from the gate, a special visitor was on his way.

As Cross entered the office, he heard the crack-ling of gravel under a jeeps tires as it rolled across the Parade Ground, then parked out front of the building.

He sat down at his desk. He was back to work. He hated his job. Being a nurse maid and disciplinarian to a lot of spoiled children was not something he enjoyed. He often wished he could take every one of those egghead bastards to a battlefield in Korea and send them out to collect body parts. He was sure it would cure their damned whining.

There was a knock at his door. "Yes," Cross barked out impatiently.

"Sir," Dehler started gingerly.as he entered and closed the door. "The General, your father is here to see you.'"

"I gave you strict orders son," Cross barked.

"I told the General you weren't coming back until later but he insisted on waiting."

"Never mind, Corporal." The angry look was still on Cross's face as he opened his office door.

"Good afternoon, General," Cross said, coldly. "Come in." He closed the door behind him.

"Hello, Paul," the General said, standing near the window addressing his son. He was a distinguished looking immaculately uniformed man, in his late fif-ties, with cold gray eyes. He was a professional sol-dier, and one of the best. Custom demanded that a son must love his father, or at least, respect him. But Captain Cross could neither love nor respect General Arthur Bayliss Cross.

"I can't say I'm glad to see you, Sir," Cross said. For something to do, he sat at his desk and lit a ciga-rette.

"Since you refused to join me for dinner at GHQ, or answer my calls, I decided to come see you," the General said.

"What do you want, General?" Cross asked in an icy, matter-of-fact way.

The General noted his son's chilling manner, and addressed it immediately. "We should at least try to be civil to each other, Paul," he said.

"If you'll tell me why you've come, General, we can get this over with quickly."

The General turned back to the window, struggling not to strike back verbally. He had come seeking help. He knew it wasn't going to be easy either for himself, or his son, because he knew he hadn't been the best of fathers.

"Paul? When you come back to Washington for the medal of honor ceremony, I'd like you to consider hanging around for awhile."

"Why?" Cross asked, suspiciously. He assumed his father always had an ulterior motive.

"Because you're my son and I'm proud of you. Isn't that reason enough?"

"I'm sure you've got a better reason, Sir," Cross said, with a cynical tone.

"My God," the General exclaimed, showing the hurt he felt. "Do you really hate me that much?"

The younger man hesitated for a moment. Then, for the first time in his life, he figured he had earned the right to speak honestly with his father.

"Yes, General, I do. You AND you're Army," Cross said bluntly.

"Then, I'm sure you'll be pleased to hear I'm resigning my commission."

Cross was stunned. The General had sacrificed everything for the Army, including him and his mother.

"I'm sorry, General, I find it hard to believe," he said matter-of-factly.

"Whether you believe it or not, it's true," the General assured him.

"Paul? I don't know exactly why you hate me so much. But it doesn't matter, because there isn't anything I can do about it. Is there?"

"Just tell me why you're here, General," Cross said, cutting him off.

The General stood looking out the window letting the tension clear. Now he hoped to reach his son on another level. "We live in a dangerous world, Paul. Our nation didn't ask to be the world's leader but we're stuck with it. If we're going to survive we've got to maintain our military strength, and have the wisdom and the courage to use it."

"You sound like a politician," Cross said, cynically.

"Some people in Washington have asked me to run for the Senate."

Cross realized his father hadn't lost his ambition. He was raising his sights, Senator Cross. Then, eventually, maybe even President Cross. God forbid.

"Then I suppose I'll be calling you Senator soon," Cross observed, coldly.

"Not without your support, Paul," the General said.

"You're not here from Washington to get my permission to run for the Senate."

"Of course not. I'm here because Truman wants a first hand account of the war. The President of the United States trusts me, Paul, I wish to God you could."

"I can't help you, father."

"If I run, the election could get very rough. The Washington press has already gotten wind of your mother's suicide. If you'll let the press see you're with me, it'll help kill the gossip and speculation."

"And tell them what, father? What a great family man you were?"

"Tell them whatever you want."

"The truth?"

"Do you know the truth?" the General pressed.

"The truth is you caused my mother to commit suicide," Cross spit back.

"That's not the truth, Paul," the General said.

"Then what is?" Cross demanded.

"Your mother was an alcoholic."

"She became one because you never gave a damn about either one of us."

"You self-righteous snot," the General shot back. "I didn't kill your mother. She did it to herself."

"You didn't see the pain she went through because of you," Cross countered. "You were gone all the time, remember?" he added bitterly.

"Everything was falling apart. It was a World at War. Remember? I was doing my job. Doing it the best I knew how," the General defended, then stopped himself and sighed in resignation. "You're a lot like her, Paul. You feel too damn much."

"How would you know what I feel?" Cross said, bitterly.

The General stiffened angrily but managed to keep himself under control. He took his coat and cap and stopped on his way to the door, turning back to face his son. "With or without you, Paul. I'm gonna run for Senator. Even if they crucify me," he said.

Cross watched his father pull the office door closed behind him. He sat at the desk asking himself, why he should help him. Why? Because he loved his father, in spite of it all? Because the General was a sad, lonely man and he felt sorry for him? Because someday he might need a favor from Senator Arthur Bayliss Cross?

None of those things really mattered to Cross.

There were only two valid reasons for helping his father. The first was to keep his mother's memory from being publicly smeared. The other was a feeling that, in spite of all else, his father would make a damn good Senator. Cross believed in America, and in the best of what it stood for. He had tried, in his heart, to forgive his father, before. But, so far, it had been an impossible thing to do. Maybe, for the sake of the country, it was time for him to let his anger and resentment go, but he doubted that was possible.

Chapter 19

The Ginza

After lunch I left the main gate and climbed into a cab. "Imperial Hotel," I said to the driver as I pulled the door closed behind me. "And no crazy driving," I added. As the driver stepped on the gas, I was hoping it wasn't going to be like another E-ride on the Coney Island roller coaster.

I entered the crowded lobby of the Imperial Hotel just as the clock above the reception area chimed noon. All the way downtown I told myself I was going there to find out what had happened to Junji. None of the waiters had a clue where he was. I figured the best chance I had, was to talk to his sister. If nothing else the thought of seeing the beautiful girl with the cobalt blue eyes again would make the trip worth while. As I headed down the arcade towards the dress shop where Sunlei worked, I was surprised by the flood of emotion that warmed me. The truth was, at that moment, nothing seemed as important as seeing her again.

I hesitated at the shops door. The girl was nowhere in sight. My confidence began to wane. The old lady that owned the dress shop was busy helping a customer as I made my nervous entrance. I waited until the customer was preoccupied with examining a dress, before I gestured for the owner to come to me.

"Me talk Sunlei," I said, mimicking a mouth talking with my hand. "Ichi Bon important. Wa Kadimshta?" I asked, which meant do you understand.

"Hai. Sunlei ichi bon busy," she replied as she pantomimed holding a telephone to her ear.

I wasn't sure whether my pigeon Japanese was being understood but it felt like she was giving me a polite brush off, so I nodded my thanks, "Domigatoe," and left. She nodded back. I headed out into the lobby and wandered around. I wasn't anxious to leave.

I was feeling discouraged, so I headed over to the exit nearest a line of cabs. Then I heard my name being called, "Naudsan. Naudsan." I turned to see Sunlei rushing to catch up to me. Every time I saw her she looked more beautiful, even now when worry consumed her face.

"Junji has been hurt," she said

"Where is he?"

"He is with a friend. I will take you to him."

She started to enter the revolving door when it began to rattle. A loud earthquake warning siren echoed through the lobby. "Awhooo! Awhooo!"

I gently pulled her back in. Though our feet felt steady, and nothing seemed affected in the lobby, people outside were swaying oddly, trying to keep themselves upright, some gave up and sat on the ground. Cars were screeching to a halt. Cabs were being shaken like toys, the luggage from their rooftops flying off in every direction. The trees were swaying violently. One cab driver was clinging to the empty metal luggage rack on his car to keep from falling down.

"Don't worry Naudsan, it's just a small earth-quake," Sunlei said.

I was trying to take it lightly, but I couldn't ignore the dangers of the wildly swinging signs and rubble falling from the buildings. After a few moments the shaking stopped, and the alarm was silenced. The westerners in the hotel remained frozen, not sure of what might happen next. The Japanese people resumed their activities, like nothing had happened. I was impressed by their resilience.

"It is safe now, Naudsan," Sunlei said. We pushed our way through the revolving doors. As Sunlei and I made our way down Avenue Z, through the crowds of people, the only fear apparently left from the earth-quake appeared in the faces of the youngest children who clung to their mothers as tears rolled down their cheeks.

After a few blocks we turned down a wide crowded street that reminded me of Times Square in new York City. This, Sunlei told me, was the Ginza district. The streets were lined with gaudy novelty shops and girly stores lit up by buzzing multi-colored neon signs. The sounds of plinkety plankety Japanese music poured out of speakers over the shop doors. Everywhere I looked I saw odd, colorful characters, mixed with normal looking people, shuffling along.

A couple of run-down looking Japanese war veter-ans were loitering in a doorway, smoking. They spit on the ground as I went by, and stared at me with angry resentment. In a way, I could understand how they felt. During the great fire bomb raids of WWII eighty percent of the city was burned to the ground by America and its allies. As I glanced up at the sky for a moment I could see the ghosts of the b-29 planes reining their lethal bombs down on the city. When I first read about it seemed like such a great victory. But now, walking amongst the Japanese people, it just seemed like a very sad event.

"Is it always crowded like this?" I asked.

"Yes, I think most people come here to be part of the crowd," Sunlei said, "I think it makes them feel alive." She stopped at corner grocery store. "I will be just a few minutes, Naudsan. Please wait," she said. Then she disappeared inside behind the rows of hanging meats and Japanese cakes and hand dipped candles.

I lit a camel cigarette, and stood leaning on the building waiting for her to return. I studied the people's faces as they came across the street toward me. They had oriental features, but their expressions were the same as New Yorkers, everything ranging from happiness to depression. At that moment, I decided people had to be pretty much the same everywhere.

I snapped the burning cigarette butt onto the pavement, and crushed it with my foot, as Sunlei came out carrying a few groceries packages wrapped in paper. We started across the street.

We made our way down deeper into the Ginza area. I was surprised to see one of the store windows had a winter scene with a large animated Santa Doll sitting on a sled. He was lifting and lowering a bag of toys while he chimed, "Ho, Ho, Ho!" There was a Christmas tree too, decorated with blinking lights. Crowds of people were stopping at the window to look at the jolly fat man who made them smile and giggle. To me it seemed oddly out of place, especially since it was only the end of September, but mostly because I knew most of the Japanese were Buddhists.

I wondered if they understood who the jolly fat man was.

Sunlei had a warm smile on her face as she watched.

"Will you miss being home for Christmas, Naud-san?" Sunlei asked.

"Yeh," I said. "Christmas is a great time in America."

"I know," Sunlei said. Which surprised me. Then she told me about how her parents had met and fell in love in San Francisco, and had to apply to Tokyo for permission to get married. Her father's boss, the Japanese Consulate, was opposed to him marrying a member of a French ballet troupe. The Consulate warned her father that it would hurt his career. He did it anyway. Sunlei was born in America. Her mother had put her in Catholic School until the Japanese Consulate found out and ordered her father to take her out. Her brother was sent back to Japan to Military school when he was very young. They retuned to Japan when she was just seven.

A bullish weathered old lady pushed past us with an angry snarl on her face. She growled out something harsh in Japanese. Most of the Japanese disliked seeing their women with Americans especially soldiers.

"What did she say?" I asked with annoyance.

Sunlei lowered her eyes. "Nothing. She was just in a rush and we were in her way," she said politely.

I knew she was lying. From the bit of Japanese I had learned, I guessed the bullish old lady had called Sunlei a Joy-girl, the lowest possible form of prostitute but Sunlei didn't want to tell that to me.

"Haven't you ever heard about 'sticks and stones'?" she asked, hoping to disarm my reaction.

"Where are we going?" I asked.

"To a Kabuki theater. Junji is with the brother of an old girlfriend. He works there.

"Does your girlfriend work there to?"

"She died, right after the war," Sunlei said, as lightly as she could so as not to embarrass me.

"I'm sorry," I said.

She smiled, accepting my apology.

We had to stop to wait for another traffic light to change.

Sunlei told me the Japanese wanted the same things Americans did, peace, health, prosperity, love, etc. So I had to wonder why did the world have the problems it did? Was it because there weren't enough 'good things' to go around, so the leaders started wars to be sure that they got their 'good things' first. Maybe the problem was more complicated but I doubted it.

"There it is," Sunlei exclaimed.

We waited for traffic to go by, then hurried across the street. A block away was a three-story red brick building, which still showed damage from the World War II air raids. Hanging from the front edge of the building's roof was a thick, blood red rug. It was about as wide as the building and resembled a giant red window shade that had been pulled down almost as far as the theater's main doors. Painted on the rug in gold were eight-foot high Japanese symbols. Sunlei said they meant, 'Kabuki Theater'.

Fearlessly, she started down the alley on the side of the theater. Homeless people were sprawled out making it hard to pass. There was no way to tell if they were asleep, drunk or dead.

"We have to go in down there," she said continuing on, ignoring the bodies. Near the end of the alley were a set of stairs leading up to a door. She went up and knocked on the stage door.

An old man with sparkling eyes and a wrinkled face, opened it.

Sunlei spoke to him in Japanese. He gestured for us to enter. I followed her in the door out of the sunlight into the pitch dark theater's backstage area. The old man said something more in Japanese and then vanished through a door.

"He asks that we remain here," Sunlei explained.

It took a few moments for my eyes to adjust to the dim light before I could see my surroundings. It was a dramatic setting. The ceiling soared up four floors with cables and lights draped from a thick beam above. There was a honey combs of metal stairways and landings that led to doors on each floor. An actor in a garish costume came out of one and made his way down the steps to the stage.

We stepped into the middle of a crowd of actors who were milling about in their elaborate costumes, mumbling to themselves, apparently rehearsing their lines, waiting to go on stage. They wore exaggerated makeup, which, Sunlei explained, was done to make it clear to the audience what the character's emotional state was.

Suddenly two fierce looking warriors wielding swords leaped out and began to battle. The moment they saw Sunlei they stopped and bowed to her.

Sunlei pointed out a group of men dressed in black from head to toe. "They are in black so the audience will think they are invisible," she explained. "They're known as Kurogas which means 'black child'. Some of them work on stage with the actors helping them with their props," she added.

We moved around past the actors, the set pieces, and the glaring stage lights to see out into the theater. Every seat was full. I guessed there were a thousand people on the main floor, which was divided in half by a four-foot wide runway. Two balconies above were full also.

Sunlei took my hand and led me along the wall. Quietly we joined a group of stage hands watching the performance from the wings.

In the center of the stage actors dressed like tree branches gathered in a circle forming a seven foot high tree trunk. The clack of wooden blocks and discordant wind chimes echoed through the theatre bringing the tree branches to life. The leaves began twisting and turning, sagging every so slowly to the stage, revealing the figure of a beautiful princess dressed in multi-colored veils. Her hand shielded her eyes from the gaze of the Devil Demon who floated in the air ten feet above the audience. He swung his scaly arms and clawed fingers at her. She recoiled.

Suspended above the audience surrounding the devil demon were the Gods of rain, who began casting handfuls of raindrops down towards the princess. The Devil Demon was enraged. He flew among the raindrops swiping them away. It was like watching Japanese acrobats flying around in a Shakespearean circus, screaming nonsensical lines at each other. I had no idea what it was about, but I was impressed by how the actors above the stage moved about on wires that were nearly undetectable.

The princess kept her hands out hoping to catch the raindrops, but the Devil Demon made sure none reached her. She began to wilt. The leaves on the branches reached up and peeled the colored veils from her body. As they whisked them away her voluptuous figure was revealed.

Suddenly the Devil Demon's angry mask turned to lust. He flew to her and embraced her from head to toe, trying to consume her. As he did, the branches took hold of him, and pulled him to the ground where they fell on top of him, burying him in a tomb of leaves. He vanished into the earth, probably through a trap door in the stage, leaving the rain gods free to pour drops of water down on the princess and the garden. Fans of flowers burst from the branches as the princess rose, gratefully letting the raindrops trickle down her face.

There was a sudden wooden clap, clap. A large striped curtain closed in front of the actors. The audience broke into applause.

Sunlei asked me if I enjoyed the play.

"Yes," I said. It was very different from the Broadway Theatre I was used to in America. But then everything in Japan was different from what I was used to.

The wooden clapping sounded again as the curtain rose. The two fierce warriors we had encountered, rushed out onto the dividing runway and began battling over two old men who were cowering on stage. To the sounds of their own ear piercing screams, the warriors swung swords at each other. The acting seemed exaggerated but the swords were real.

I found it scary watching actors swing real swords at each other knowing a slip could result in somebody getting something chopped off. The audience found the battle spellbinding, like watching a couple of death defying daredevils.

Occasionally, a member of the audience would jump up in his seat and scream out something to the actors, which caused them to freeze like statues. The actors would answer the audience remarks by sticking their tongues out or crossing their eyes. It looked stupid to me, like a bad *Three Stooges* movie.

Sunlei explained that the person in the audience was complimenting the actor's on their performances and the actors facial reactions were a way of saying 'thank you'. "In Kabuki, it is customary for the audience and actors to do this," she said.

The old doorman with the wrinkled face reappeared. Quietly he led us through the backstage jungle of sets, and wires, and up a flight of steps to a green door, and then vanished again.

Sunlei hesitated. "I must explain something to you about Kiku before we go in. "When the war ended, we were told the Americans would rape all the women. The idea was so terrifying to Yoko, my friend, that she killed herself. It was her suicide which caused Kiku to hate Americans."

Now I was hesitant.

"You are an American, but you are also a good person. Junji has told him how well you have treated him," she said.

"I don't think I'm gonna change the way he feels," I said.

"Perhaps a little," she said with hope. Then she knocked lightly on the green door.

"Ee-kee-ma-show," a high thin voice answered.

Sunlei opened the door.

I followed her in. The room was dark and reeked of cigarette smoke. There was a makeup table with a large round mirror in the middle. Next to it was an electric fan pointed at the ceiling. The walls were lined with shelves, which were filled with elaborate wigs like the ones we had seen on the actors below. Most of the light was shut out by a small rug, which covered the only window.

"Gum-ba-waa, Sunleisan," the owner of the thin voice said, pushing aside the black velvet curtain which acted as a door into his bathroom. He was about my age with feminine features and wore a white cotton dressing gown. The gown had streaks of makeup across the front.

Sunlei greeted him with a bow. "Kikusan? This is my friend. I'd like you to meet Bill Naud," Sunlei said.

"Naudsan," Kiku said, responding to me with a cold nod.

Sunlei ignored the chilly greeting and I took my cues from her.

"How is your work, Kiku?" she asked.

"Ichi Bon" he said, warming a bit.

"The play about the princess was wonderful," I said.

"Sunlei is the real Princess," Kiku insisted. "Everybody loves her. Yoko did, and so do I."

Sunlei was embarrassed enough to turn the talk away from herself. "Soon, Kiku, will be an Onnagata."

"No. Not so soon," Kiku said, modestly. "But perhaps. In time."

"All Kabuki parts are played by men. The actors who play the women's parts are the best. They're known as the Onnagata," Sunlei explained.

Kiku told how men playing women's roles stemmed from blood fights the feudal lords had over the erotic women who played the parts back in the middle ages.

"Kiku's father was a translator for NHK, our national radio. He was American too."

"Sunlei told me about your sister, I'm really sorry," I said.

Talking about his sister's death to an American obviously made Kiku feel awkward, but he nodded his appreciation.

"I will visit Yoko's grave tomorrow and send her your prayers, Kiku," Sunlei said. "But now we must see Junji. How is he?"

"He is mostly sleeping. I know he will be glad to se you. I must go to work now. Please make your-selves a home."

Sunlei nodded her appreciation as Kiku left.

I didn't know if I had done any good for Japanese-American relations. But maybe it wasn't ALL Ameri-cans Kiku hated, just his American father. Sunlei said Kiku's father had never married his mother or acknowledged him.

Sunlei and I entered the back room where Junji was staying. It was packed with costumes and stage props. There was Junji laying on a straw matt near the wall. When he rolled over to face us, I was shocked to see the extent of his injuries. His face was bruised and swollen, his arm was in a sling and it was obvi-ous any small movements were painful for him.

"Hai, Naudsan," he mumbled.

"What happened?" I asked

Sunlei explained what Junji had told her. Some thugs jumped him near his home and beat him up.

They said he should stay away from the EM Club or they'll come back and beat him again."

"Junji, did you recognize any of them?" I asked.

Junji winced as he spoke in Japanese. Sunlei interpreted. "They had GI uniforms. One had dark sunglasses with no rim. He was the leader."

Somehow I felt this was all my fault. Baker had to be behind it. I had to do something to help Junji. "Does he have a doctor?"

"Kiku brought him to the hospital and paid for the treatment, but it is too expensive to have the doctor come here," Sunlei explained.

"Look I'll bring his pay out and give you money for the doctor," I offered.

Junji lowered his head and said something in Japanese.

"Junji say he feel sorry to bring these problems to you."

"He's going to get well and get back to work. At least he can still go to school with his pay money."

"Sit down Naudsan. I will make some food."

Sunlei boiled some water in the kettle on a hotplate and fixed noodles for the three of us. Junji had a few mouthfuls then fell asleep.

We sat at a small table in the corner eating and getting to know one another. We enjoyed talking to each other. I told her about what life was like growing up in Manhattan and my folk's constant struggle to keep the family together. She found out I was a New Yorker who didn't really like New York.

Sunlei's mind was a treasure chest of facts and stories, but the thing I liked most was her sense of humor. She smiled easily and enjoyed laughing. In my experience, girls didn't laugh much, especially if they were beautiful. I had heard the reason was they didn't want to develop laugh lines on their faces.

Sometimes, when Sunlei smiled at me. I thought about how nice it would be to make love to her.

We talked for hours. It was getting late and I had to get back to the club. She walked me out onto the fire escape and watched as I made my way down to the back stage door. As I reached it, I turned and looked up. She was still on the balcony. I felt like I was starring in an Asian American version of *Romeo and Juliet*. Suddenly the audience applauded wildly as I closed the back stage door behind me.

I was almost back to the base after being held up for an hour by a major traffic accident north of the imperial palace, near the end of the moat. The cab turned left onto the cobblestone road that ran through the village of Oji. Ahead of us a sudden burst of fireworks lit up the night sky.

"Fireworks Non-deska?" I asked.

"Festival of OBON," the driver explained in broken English. "Each village welcome back spirits and souls of most revered ancestors."

Exploding showers of colored pinwheels and flaming roman candles were still reining down as the cab came to a stop at the main gate.

I paid the driver and thanked him, "Do ma ti gatoe." "You're welcome," he responded. I smiled back at his attempt to speak English and headed through the main gate.

Chapter 20

Second Night of The Miss Tokyo Contest

I could hear the noisy crowd in the club so I knew Surrel must have gotten the contest underway. I changed clothes and hurried upstairs. It was jammed. The smoke was so dense I could hardly see the Little Joes on stage. They were trying to play Jitterbug music but it sounded more like a screeching train wreck. The dance floor was crammed with codebreakers and girls trying to dance to the noise. I was pleased to see all the codebreakers and contestants had come back for the second night of the contest.

Baker didn't seem to care what music Little Joe was playing. He was content to have a tight hold on Umerie as he pushed her around the dance floor in what he probably thought was a foxtrot but he looked more like *Toulouse Lautrec* pushing a lamp post around the floor.

The contestants, from the week before, were scattered around the room at tables with the GIs, enjoying Dehler's photos of the contest that were plastered over the pages of the back section of the Tokyo Daily newspaper.

A couple of waiters had their eyes pressed to the windows watching the Obon Fireworks still reining down on Oji.

"Hey Naud. Where have you been?" Surrel called out. We were afraid you weren't going to show up, he said coming towards me out of the crowd. "We're already up to the third act.

"I got stuck downtown," I answered.

"The contest got a ton of press in the newspapers," Surrel said showing me the pictures of the contestants taken by Dehler. "It's terrific publicity for my company."

I was pleased to see Dehler could do something well, other than be Baker's stooge.

I was still feeling a glow from my moments with Sunlei, and Surrel's enthusiasm was the icing on the cake. Now that I knew where Junji was, there was only one remaining problem. The extra money for the second Miss Tokyo winner.

Surrel starting walking away to introduce the next contestant. "Oh by the way, my company says they will gladly pay for the second Miss Tokyo. You're off the hook for the money." He was grinning from ear to ear. He kept me hanging on purpose, he was waiting the whole time for me to ask about the money.

"There's just one thing Naud," he said.

'Oh no. More trouble' I thought.

"Noriko Sunji's father saw her picture in the paper and refused to let her perform for American soldiers."

"I understand," I said, relieved. I waved Surrel to go on to the mike.

Surrel made his way to the stage. "That's it everyone...dancers off the floor. Here we go with our fifth contestant, Chinku Pansin, who is going to play the Samisen- a traditional Japanese instrument, and sing *Some Enchanted Evening* from South Pacific. Let's give her a big hand."

The GI's applauded enthusiastically for a beautiful, slender, delicate Japanese girl, who made her way to the mike carrying an instrument that looked like a pregnant banjo. She took her place and delicately plucked the strings of the Samisen a few times, listening with her eyes closed, to make sure it was in tune. Then she bowed to the audience with a shy smile and began to pluck and sing. Her voice was small but angelic. The audience was attentive and responsive. though they couldn't understand the Japanese lyrics, most already knew the English version by heart.

Dehler quietly snapped pictures of Chinku performing.

When she finished, her efforts were received in the same manor she delivered them, graciously and politely.

When the applause stopped a sea of GIs flocked to the dance floor corralling their favorite contestant. A few circled Chinku, anxious to dance with her.

A drunken GI headed straight for her, but stumbled over his own feet. Two other guys picked him up and deposited him in a chair, where he instantly fell asleep.

I went behind the bar to help serve the drinks.

Plummer pushed his way through the crowd waving the newspaper at me. "Did you see this?"

"Yeah," I said, handing a drink to one of the GI's, "the photos of the contest is great."

"No, Naud, the front page is all about the Incheon invasion. " He pushed close into the bar and read me the caption underneath a photo of the troops scaling the seawall of Incheon beach on ladders.

"Red Beach on Incheon's north side was assaulted by two battalions of the fifth Marine regimental combat team. Its high seawall required the use of scaling ladders so the assault forces could get ashore from their landing craft. After overcoming the resisting North Korean defenders the fifth marines advanced into the city. Opening the causeway from Wim-do Island so that tanks and other vehicles could cross over and join the action. The marine commanders expect to take the capital by tomorrow night." Plummer was beaming, then he added, "decoded enemy intelligence indicates the north Koreans were taken by surprise."

I shared his enthusiasm, but was too preoccupied to show it.

"Any luck with Junji?" he asked

I nodded yes. "Bakers stooges beat him up."

"How bad?" he asked.

"Pretty bad."

"That son-of-a-bitch," Plummer said shaking his head.

"I'll tell you more about it tomorrow," I said, just as Surrel introduced the next act.

"And now we have Ling Mashikisha with her act, *Husband and Wife*."

It looked like it was going to be a Japanese version of a *Punch and Judy* show. The contestant Ling disappeared behind a 4'x4' cardboard brick wall with an open window In it. Then a female puppet popped up wearing a smart looking kimono with a painted face and her hair full of curlers. She held up a large paddle that had a mirror one side. In a high pitched voice with her lips squeezed tight Ling sounded out the wife's voice. "Good Evening. Me Wife."

The reaction from the crowd was a mix of surprise and chuckles.

The wife puppet began to admire herself in the mirror. "I am really beautiful, aren't I, husband?" There was no response. She called into the empty window again, "Aren't I, husband? And don't lie to me."

A slovenly male puppet with bandages all over his face popped up in the window.

The crowd chuckled.

"Yes, my dear wife, you are the most beautiful woman in the world," he said with a forced grin.

"Are you sure?" she asked.

"Yes. Yes," he insisted again.

Bang! She whacked him with the mirror. Knocking him down below the wall.

"You are a liar. All you do is lie to me."

There was silence.

"What are you doing now husband?"

"I am writing you a love poem," he sounded.

"Let me hear it," the wife said with a flirty grin.

The husband slid up and slouched on the window, with a new bandage covering one eye. The audience laughed.

"Here is the poem. Wife I love you, you are so beautiful. There will never be a more beautiful person than you."

"Are you sure?" the wife insisted checking herself in the mirror.

"Yes. Yes..," the husband answered enthusiastically.

Before he could get one more yes out, she knocked him down again.

"Why do you keep hitting me wife," the raspy husband's voice sounded from below.

"Because you are lazy and keep lying to me."

"If I told you the truth would you stop hitting me?"

"Yes"

"Alright," the husband said as he popped up. "You have a face like a horse."

The audience laughed. The wife was enraged and raised the mirror again to hit him, but this time the husband raised a baseball bat and slammed the mirror into her. She fell down unconscious.

"Goodnight wife," he said pulling the window shade down and vanishing behind the wall.

The crowd laughed and applauded.

Another round of dancing ensued. Corporal Klein latched onto a cute girl who did magic tricks, but she dumped him for getting fresh on the dance floor.

The most memorable display of talent for the evening came from a young lady who called herself, Usako. She wouldn't give her last name. She stepped onto the stage and sat regally at the piano.

From the moment she struck the first key, everyone's ears and eyes were riveted on her. She played Beethoven's *Fifth Concerto* on the tinny, upright piano that probably hadn't been tuned since the last century.

When Usako's last note finally died away, there was only the sound of silence. Then, like a phoenix rising from the ashes, the code guys stood and started to applaud. Slowly at first, but then faster and louder, it became a prolonged standing ovation. The waiters applauded too. The crowd didn't stop, until Usako broke down sobbing.

Pollazzo had studied classical piano for five years in Chicago. He explained to us how good she had to be, to play the way she did. Especially with that lousy piano.

Pollazzo talked to her for a few minutes and persuaded her to dance with him.

Surrel made the announcement that he would be around during the dancing to collect the voting ballots.

After he finished his speech I asked him who he thought would win. He motioned his head to Umerie.

All night Misako Umerie had danced only with Baker. He was busy lobbying for her to be one of the four winners

Half an hour later Surrel came up from the club office with the final tally.

I stepped up to the mike. "Okay, guys, listen up, we got the results of your voting here," I hollered, waving the written list of winners names in the air, hoping to quiet the crowd. I was getting nowhere.

"Quiet down," Surrel called out, trying to help.

"Hey, KNOCK IT OFF," some booming voice from the bar area bellowed.

After some more urging the crowd noise finally dropped to a murmur.

"Okay, here we go, "The fourth winner of the annual Miss Tokyo contest is Ruki Din-san with her ventriloquist act." Greg Surrel was pleased with Ruki's Victory, not only because he wanted to date the lovely girl, but because he hadn't bribed, or lobbied or threatened anybody to pick her. The crowd on it's own had voted Ruki a winner making him feel he was going to win the heart of a special girl.

"The third winner of the annual Miss Tokyo contest is Iko Araki, the origami lady."

The crowd roared their approval. Pfc. Dutton was beaming for Iko Arakii. Since the first night of the contest they had started going out together.

"We have a tie for first place. One of the winners is the girl with no last name, Usako, for playing Beethoven's Fifth." The mysterious piano player Usako rose to acknowledge the crowd's applause. She bowed her head slightly, receiving the applause with the ease and poise of a professional. Pollazzo was especially pleased.

"And the other number one winner is...." I squinted my eyes dragging out the drama. Some of the girls cradled their faces in their hands, praying their name would be called. "Misako Umerie for singing *Tennessee Waltz*."

The crowd stood up, roaring their approval. Some of the contestants, who didn't win, applauded as enthusiastically as everybody else. A few broke down in tears, but were comforted by the GIs around them.

Sergeant Baker wore a sly grin, thinking he had engineered his gal Misako Umerie's victory. His bubble could have been burst by Surrel, who had declared her a winner the first night before she even finished walking across the stage. He knew a girl who looked and moved like Misako Umerie could sell anything to anybody, and he could only win with all the publicity she will bring to the liquor company.

"Here they are our four winners. Let's hear it for our MISS TOKYO's." The crowd cheered loudly as the girls came up to the stage and received their envelopes with the prize money. Surrel stood next to me handing them out, and posing for a picture with each. Dehler snapped away with his camera at Surrel's enthusiastic direction.

When the buzz died down a bit I called into the mike. "And now it's time for the last dance of the evening, to *Until the End of Time.*

Jumbo put on the record as the contestants and girls from Wattanabe's band paired off with the GI's for a slow dance.

A Corporal was pushing his way through the crowd coming my way. He had a pale-gray, pockmarked face. He looked like the walking dead.

"Are you Private Naud?" he asked.

"Why I asked?" I was behind the bar filling drink orders. My first thought was that something terrible had happened to Jessie. Was this guy there to tell me Jessie was dead? I hadn't gotten a letter or heard any more about him.

"I promised Gotman I'd give this note to you," the Corporal said, pulling a piece of paper from a pocket of his Eisenhower jacket. He held out the crinkled dirty page, which had been ripped from a shorthand notebook.

"Is Gotman okay?" I asked, taking the paper.

"He's all over Incheon beach. Blown to hell by a gook mortar," the Corporal said.

The real horror of war had just smacked me in the face. I was horrified and speechless. I looked at the crumpled paper. It was a note scratched in pencil.

Dear Naud,
I'm always felt badly about beating you up at Fort devins. I hope you will forgive me.
Good luck,
Gotman

There was a red streak across the page. I counted the words in the note, twenty-seven. Gotman's life was worth just twenty-seven words. I went up to bed not able to enjoy the triumph of the evening.

Deep into the night, I awoke suddenly and lay there, half awake, listening. I thought I heard something. Or was it only lin my dream? My first concern was for the club money. But it was locked away, and only Toshiko or I could open the safe. All I could hear now was silence. I rolled over, ready to go back to sleep, and noticed that the clouds were gone. Mt Fuji was visible in the moonlight and beautiful as always.

I was just starting to feel drowsy again, when I heard a low grunting noise coming from the other side of the mountain of boxes, by the metal entrance doors. I listened for a moment, trying to convince himself that it was only a mouse. But the grunts were human, and most likely coming from GI's who were there to steal liquor. I recalled Surrel's cautionary tale about one of the Clubs custodians who had been stabbed to death fighting off liquor thieves.

I patted the floor under the bed until I found my bayonet. Then I slid out of my bed and crawled toward the four foot high plywood partition that separated my living area from the rest of the warehouse. I stayed down, hiding behind the wall, as the low grunting noise continued. Quietly, I rose up to peer over the plywood. I saw a hulking grunting shadow, staggering painfully under the weight of some thing boxy and heavy. The fire escape door to his right was open.

I tightened my grip on the bayonet but kept silent. I wasn't about to die for some booze.

The intruder reached the fire escape landing and paused to catch his breath. He balanced the load on the fire escape landing guard rail.

I couldn't see who he was, he was back lit by the moonlight streaming in through the open door. I was crawling to the end of the plywood wall for a better look, when I accidently kicked my table, knocking over the goose neck lamp.

The noise caused the intruder to look back into the warehouse. I panicked. I was certain the guy was coming to get me. I stood up, and in a flash, without thinking about it, I hurled the bayonet at the fire escape door, hoping to scare the invader and keep him at bay. But my aim was off and the deadly blade headed straight toward the ominous hulk.

'Oh God, I'm gonna kill somebody,' I thought.

An instant later, the bayonet buried itself in the door jamb and stuck there, its quivering blade reflecting the moonlight, inches from the intruders head.

"AAAAAAARGHH!!!" the startled thief screamed. He jumped back, bumping the stolen booty off the guardrail. It hurtled toward the ground, five stories below, as the thief fled down the stairs.

I ran to the fire escape door and caught a glimpse of the intruder fleeing into the moonlight. It was Corporal Dehler.

When my heart slowed to where I could catch my breath, I went down to recover what Dehler had taken. I found it buried in the soft dirt. But it was too heavy.

The next morning, it took Jumbo and three other waiters an hour to carry the four hundred and fifty pound safe back upstairs. I didn't bother to explain how it got there.

Chapter 21

Plummers Story

The Miss Tokyo contest was making me a celebrity. Guys around the mess hall were watching me. Some code guy came by to say I was a hero for having brought good-looking girls to the Club. Most of them were used to being around beat up old hookers at the Clubs downtown.

It was 7a.m. when I left the mess hall. Most everyone had finished eating and gone to work. I crossed the assembly area and looked up at the office windows. Toshiko was standing there pointing up, with a smile on his face. I had asked him to move my golf net onto the club's roof. From the smile on his face, I figured it must have been done.

I got my clubs from the secret room in the warehouse and followed Toshiko and his two office helpers up to the roof. There was a warm morning breeze tinged with a scent of tar. I made a mental note for Toshiko to get a half dozen large potted plants to place around the roof, to absorb the smell of tar.

Toshiko had set my rubber practice mat up so I could hit balls into the net ten feet away that he had loosely stretched between to very tall way stack pipes.

I smiled at Toshiko. " Good Job, Tosh."

He nodded back his appreciation and stepped aside, while I chipped three practice balls into the net.

I was setting up to hit a ball with my five iron when I heard the crash of glass coming from the graveyard of bombed burned out aircraft factory buildings to my left. They stood there like an eerie monument to the firebomb raids.

Toshiko spotted three young Japanese boys amidst the rubble, having fun hurling rocks at the few windows left in the twisted steel wreckage. "Over there Naudsan," he said.

I changed to a seven iron and put three balls down on the mat. The windows were about 145 yards away. I struck three quick shots, trying to hit one of the windows to surprise the kids. The first one hit a part of the metal window frame and bounced away. The second and third shattered side by side windows.

The kids froze, looking around to find the source. When they looked in our direction they were blinded by the sun. They ran away spooked.

Toshiko and his helpers smiled and nodded approvingly.

"I have good news Naudsan" Toshiko said holding a piece of paper with Japanese writing all over it. "First time in year Club have ichi bon profit. $2,000."

"No kidding," I said, staring at the list of meaningless Japanese numbers. "Two thousand dollars huh? We can use it for the Bingo prize money."

"Oh No. EM Club law say all profits must go back into club."

I had no reason to doubt Toshiko, he knew the laws backwards and forwards. Then I had a great idea, one that I felt would keep the codebreakers coming. "Slot machines draw big crowds down at the downtown clubs. But I know they cost around $3000 each and can takes months to get from some company in Ohio. Can your friend Black Market Sam get us one for $2000?"

"Hai, Hai. Sam can get machine... maybe cheaper."

"If Sam can buy us a slot machine, get it right away."

"Hai," Toshiko said, as I whacked another ball out towards the windows. "Tosh? I'd like you to buy us a Christmas tree for the Club. A big one, okay?"

"Hai, Naudsan," Toshiko answered. "Christmas is happy time in America?" Toshiko asked.

"Yeah," I said, sounding casual. I suddenly realized how little I knew about Toshiko. We had rarely talked about anything except the business of the Club.

"Do you have a family, Tosh? You know, wife, children?"

"Hai; wife, son, father," Toshiko answered sadly. "Hai. All die in war."

For a moment, I had forgotten where I was and what had happened here. "I'm sorry. I guess you have good reasons to dislike Americans," I said.

"No hate you, Naudsan." Toshiko replied.

"War is a stupid way to die," I said, expecting Toshiko to agree with him.

"War give way to die for what one believes. Give life meaning and purpose," Toshiko said, with pride.

His response surprised me. "Surrelsan says you and the waiters were all Kamikaze," I said.

"Hai," Toshiko answered, quietly.

"I wouldn't be brave enough to be a Kamikaze." I said.

"Ooohh, not all Kamikaze so brave, Naudsan." Toshiko replied.

I found the idea of a cowardly Kamikaze surprising. It brought to mind the image of the cowardly lion in the *The Wizard of Oz*.

"Why you join army, Naudsan?" Toshiko asked.

I was surprised by his question. It was very un-Japanese like to ask a personal question. "I didn't join the army. I was drafted," I said.

"Oohh. Many Japanese soldiers drafted too," Toshiko said.

"What do you think of Sergeant Baker?" I asked, fishing.

"Baker dangerous man," Toshiko observed.

"I heard a rumor he was making the waiters pay kickbacks."

Toshiko's face looked grim. It was a clear answer to my question.

The building suddenly began to vibrate. It was an aftershock from the earlier quake. It quickly became much stronger.

I lost my balance and began bouncing around. The gravel on the roof was hopping about like Mexican jumping beans. I grabbed hold of a tall vent pipe sticking up through the roof and held on. Toshiko looked almost relaxed as he took hold of the same pipe.

The building continued bouncing up and down, and back and forth, violently. It was the strongest quake I had experienced. I was scared but I tried not to show it.

"Tokyo have much earthquakes," Toshiko said, casually.

I couldn't tell if Toshiko's relaxed reaction was an act for my benefit or what, but he never flinched. He never showed any fear. He just hung on to the pipe and looked, for all the world, like a morning com‑ muter on a New York Subway train heading down‑ town to work.

Later that day, I went downtown to bring money to Sunlei for Junji's doctor. We had lunch and spent the afternoon together. When I arrived back at the base that evening, Black Market Sam was there. He had brought a slot machine to the Club. He wanted to be paid cash, nine hundred American dollars. It was illegal to pay in U.S. dollars but I did it anyway. Because the price was right.

"Sam? What are the odds on winning a jackpot?"

"Make as hard as you want, Naudsan," Sam said, as he finished counting the nine hundred American dollars.

"Make it as easy as you can, okay?" I said.

"Ooooh, you make too easy, lose much profits, Naudsan," Sam moaned.

"No, Sam. Good odds will keep the guys coming back," I explained.

Sam's devious mind understood right away. "Very smart, Naudsan. Make easy first, bring GI to club. Then make hard, make more money." Sam opened the back of the machine and moved the wheels and levers to give the players the best possible odds.

I had the slot machine placed close to the end of the bar, near where I usually sat. I was hoping the noise from the machine would help drown out Little Joe's band.

By the end of the first night, a long line of guys were waiting to play the one armed bandit. Misako Umerie dumped a hundred dollars of Baker's money into the machine. He obviously had the hots for her and was willing to pay the price. She gave Baker just enough of herself to hold his interest.

I figured they were two of a kind, both users. But her equipment was sure a lot better than his. And she had more class. But then, anyone had more class than Baker.

"Hey, Naud, could you play some Glen Miller music?" Pfc. Dutton asked. He was dancing with Iko Araki, the Origami lady.

"What's wrong with the Little Joe Band?" I asked, out of curiosity.

"They stink for dancing," Dutton said. Iko giggled and turned away embarrassed by Dutton's candor.

"I'll play some Glen Miller during the Joes next break, Okay?" I said.

From what I had overheard or was told directly, very few guys really liked Little Joe's band, including Sergeant Baker. So why had Sergeant Creamer ever signed them to a long-term contract? Something didn't make sense.

During the next break, Jumbo played a couple of his Glenn Miller records and the dance floor was jammed with couples. And among them were Pfc. Dutton and Iko Araki.

Toshiko figured in another week, if the crowds held up, they would have the cost of the machine back plus a profit. I told him, if that happened, he was to buy another slot machine, right away. 'PT Barnum was right,' I thought. 'A sucker is born every minute.' And they all love to play slot machines. Including the egg-heads from Oji. I turned off the lamp and hit the sac.

A few days later I was riding in a cab, coming back from a downtown trip to have my hair cut and have dinner with Sunlei. I was trying to relax, lying back with my eyes closed, when the cab made a sharp left hand turn. I could feel the bumping of the cobble-stones under the tires so I knew I was almost back to base. I opened my eyes just as the cab suddenly swerved, trying to avoid an Army ambulance, which came roaring around us with its lights flashing and alarm wailing. The cabby pulled to one side and to let the ambulance go by. I shielded my eyes from the glare as I sat up and tried to see ahead.

The cab driver was forced to creep the car through the gridlock of people, bicycles, cabs, and motorcy-cles blocking the road. There was a crowd gathered in front of the Flaming Pisspot. Pollazzo was stand-ing out in the street, tucking in his shirt. Behind him, Mamasan had her arm around one of her Joy- girls, trying to comfort her. The girl was crying hysterically, though her tears seemed as manufactured as they were real. As she hugged the girl the Mamasan was complaining to two American MP's about something she was pointing to in the alleyway.

"Chot-mati," I said, ordering the driver to stop.

"Hey, Pollazzo!" I called out.

Pollazzo came rushing over. "Jesus, Bill," he said, greeting me at the taxi's window. He kept pushing his hair back exclaiming, "You wouldn't believe it! You wouldn't believe it!"

"Well calm down and tell me what happened. I'll believe it," I said.

"Look," Pollazzo said, pointing down the alley." Plummer went through there."

I looked around the side of the crowd so I could see what Pollazzo was talking about. There was an ugly, jagged hole in the wall on the second floor of the Pisspot building. My first thought was that some Commie had thrown a bomb.

"Did you say Plummer was at the Flaming Pisspot?" I said in disbelief.

"Yeah, you're goody two shoes. The virgin who was saving himself for his girlfriend. Bill, it was nutso time. I'm lying there with this girl and suddenly there's a tremendous crash. I look up to see what had happened.... They had flown out of the building," Pollazzo said.

"Get in, we'll meet him at the hospital." I moved over to make room.

Pollazzo told the driver in Japanese to follow the ambulance. He maneuvered wildly through the cobblestone streets until he caught the trail of the ambulance.

As we followed along, Pollazzo went on to explain what happened.

"I was sitting at the bar listening to the *Yanks* playing the *Giants* in the world series, when Plummer came in looking distraught. He asked me to go down to the Flaming Pisspot with him, he needed company. I thought he was joking, but he kept after me. I figured the only way I was gonna hear the rest of the game was if I went with him. When we got there he got this girl Kasua, the most popular Joy-girl at the Flaming Pisspot, she was well skilled at pleasing We were both in the upper room with a girl. I was preoccupied listening to Mel Allen broadcasting the game. I convinced the Mamasan to let me have the radio. The Giants were beating the Yankees 3-0, with runners on first and third, when Hank Bauer hit a base-clearing triple, tying the game up. A couple of minutes later the Yanks went ahead on a missed fly ball catch.

The Yanks and Phillies were tied and it was the last inning. Plummer could care less. He and Kasua had been screwing for three hours and Plummer could no longer get a hard on. The two and a half bottles of sake Plummer had drunk wasn't helping. Kasua was straddling Plummer's waist, and French kissing him while his sex weary legs carried them around the room. He was desperately trying to find some way to make his cock hard again. 'You number-one lover boy,' Kasua said, urging him on between French kisses. 'Plummer-san wild man. Make me much hot,' Kasua said, as she ground her hips in against his trying to revitalize his limp organ. Stubbornly, he kept on, exhausted, and about to fall on his face. Then Plummer made a drunken lunge and they slammed into the wooden post hard enough to jolt the whole house. Guys from other rooms were yelling, 'What the hell's going on in there?' Plummer just kept pumping harder, banging into the post again and again, each time rattling panels all over the second floor. Some frightened voice from the adjacent room thought it was another earthquake. I was trying to ignore the whole thing and listen to the ballgame, it was almost over. The Giants were still trailing by one with two men on base and two outs. All the Yankees had to do to win was get one more out. The Giants batter hit a fly ball towards right centerfield. The crowd went wild as Hank Bauer chased it down. Right at that moment Plummer, entwined with Kasua, trundled past me with a smile on his face, as he charged across the room, figuring once more bang against a post would keep him going. They were too busy French kissing to notice they were moving fast towards the outer rice paneled wall instead of the post. Suddenly, their two lustfully entwined bodies went crashing through the sandalwood panel, smashing violently into the wooden railing, which instantly gave way. There they went, flying off the balcony and sailing out into the star filled night. I heard a horrendous crash just as Mel Allen announced Bauer had dove for the fly ball and caught it mere inches above the turf. The crowds roared. 'How about that!' Mel Allen announced, 'the Yankees have won the World Series again!' I was in baseball heaven. I could hear loud moaning so I rushed out onto the balcony to see what happened to Plummer. Plummer and Kasua were on the roof of the building next door, twenty feet below. They were stark naked but still locked in a grotesque lover's embrace. 'Plummer?' I screamed out. All I got back were pained groans. The girl moved and seemed to be okay. 'Jumping Jesus, I don't believe it,' I just kept saying, and ran to get help. The girl was just shaken up, thankfully. Someone called an ambulance for Plummer. I still can't believe it happened. You're goody two shoes actually took a flying F***!"

I was having trouble believing it too!

We pulled up in front of the downtown hospital at Hardy Barracks. It reminded me of the laboratory where the hunchback, in the *Frankenstein* movie, stole the brain to build the '*creature*'. It was a sprawling single story white wood structure with branches going off everywhere. It took us ten minutes to find the entrance to the emergency room.

Inside the main doors, there were only a few dim pools of light, and nobody in sight. An armed Sergeant seemed to come out of the wall like one of the clay people in the Buck Rogers serial. He really spooked me.

"Show me you're ID, soldiers," the Sergeant said in a deep voice.

I handed over my ASA ID Card. Pollazzo did the same.

"I'm looking for Corporal Plummer. He was just brought in," I asked.

"You'll have to ask at information," the Sergeant said, handing back the IDs. "Down the corner, to the left."

There was a female Corporal all alone at the information desk. She looked like an angry bulldog and was reading a Japanese magazine. "Patients last name?" she said without looking up.

"Plummer. Corporal, Arthur."

She checked the roster sheet for Plummer's name and found it. "Three corridors down, turn left to the ward marked 'P' for, prisoners," she said with an obvious note of contempt.

I went down the hall and found the door with a large yellow "P" on it. It had a small window with half-inch thick bars and was guarded by a giant MP Corporal who was even more frightening, though far less charming, than the *Frankenstein* creature.

"You got firearms?" he grunted.

"No," I said.

"You gotta wait here. They're still working on him."

Finally after about an hour we were allowed to go in.

The creature wasn't taking any chances. He patted Pollazzo and me down for weapons, just to be sure. Then, he unlocked the door. The creaking noise it made as he pulled it open, fit in with the monster-movie feel of the place. "You got ten minutes, soldier," the grizzly guard grunted.

I entered the under-lit ward looking for Plummer and the creature locked the door behind him. Each side of the dreary room had ten hospital beds. Above each bed was a heavily barred window. I could only see three patients. Of the two sleeping on the right, one looked to be in his late thirties or so and the other was around fifty. The third guy was on the left, all the way down. It had to be Plummer. One leg was suspended above the bed in a massive plaster cast and he had his had buried in the sheet.

I eased up to the bed, quietly and whispered, "Hey, Plummer. How ya doing?"

Plummer opened his eyes slowly. It was obvious he had been crying. "Hi, Naud," he said. "I guess what I did was really stupid, I really made a mess of things," he added.

A nurse in her early thirties, with a badge that read LT. Megan, arrived at Plummer's bed with a tray full of food and a smile on her face. She was a plain- Jane type, whose only beauty lay in the genuine caring on her face. "How are you feeling Corporal?" she asked.

"Is the girl, okay, Lieutenant?" Plummer asked.

"She must be," the nurse said, "there was no mention of her in the accident report."

"I saw her, she's okay, just shaken up," Pollazzo offered to make him feel better.

"Your buddy's a very lucky guy," the nurse said, turning to me. "All he got was a broken leg." She placed the food tray next to the bed. "You should try to eat something, Corporal," she urged.

"I'm not hungry," Plummer said.

"Well, I'll leave the tray in case you change your mind," she said. She made a few adjustments to the ropes holding Plummer's leg up and left.

Pollazzo was eying the food, "If you don't want it I'll eat it," Pollazzo asked.

"Sure, go ahead," Plummer said as he shifted his body, looking for his clothes. It was evident, from the look on his face that his broken leg was giving him a great deal of pain. He spotted his uniform draped over a chair on the other side of the bed.

"There's a letter, in my shirt pocket, Bill. Get it will ya?" he asked.

I found the letter and held it out to him.

"No. You read it," he begged.

I had a feeling it was bad news, I was reluctant. But the pain on Plummer's face made it hard for me to say, no. I opened the letter, and found it was an invitation.

"Mr. and Mrs. Parker Lofton, of Brookline, Massachusetts, announce the wedding of their daughter Anne to........" I stopped reading. It was a wedding invitation. It didn't surprise me, but for Plummer's sake, I acted shocked. The girl he had been saving himself for, the one who had turned him into a drunk and caused him to leap off the balcony of a whorehouse, was marrying his father's lawyer.

"I got this today," Plummer said.

Now the story was clear. Plummer tried to vent his frustration and anger in a marathon sex jag and ended up taking a flying leap. I thought the whole thing was funny. And it was. Except for the pain on Plummer's face. The only way I could think to console him was to repeat a line from a W. C. Fields movie, *"Look at it this way, my boy, in fifty years she'll be an old hag,"* I quipped trying to buck him up.

Plummer looked lower than whale shit.

It wasn't working.

"The Colonel warned me, twice, About the drinking. He said I'd be gone if I didn't stop," Plummer confided.

"As far as I know you did stop, until today," I insisted, adding, "look, I'll tell the Colonel what happened. He'll understand."

"Don't, Bill. You'll only make an enemy out of him," he warned. "It's out of the Colonel's hands. They have to court-martial me for endangering the life of the girl. Three years in a stockade. I coulda' killed her, Bill."

The nurse Lieutenant appeared again, pushing a medications cart. She affixed a needle to a syringe and filled it with a clear liquid from one of the vials. "He needs rest," she explained to me. She lifted up Plummer's hospital gown just enough to mask what she was doing from any eyes but her own, and gave Plummer a shot in his buttocks. "He'll be asleep soon," she said.

I watched her push the cart back to the ward door. She was a plain Jane but she had a great figure. The *Frankenstein*-like guard held the door open for her as she wheeled the cart away. When I turned back, Plummer was already out like a light.

The following morning I was having chow. Colonel Macmillan was due back in the afternoon from Korea.

Sergeant Hannigan, one of the guards from the codebreakers building, came off the chow line looking for a place to sit.

"Hey Hannigan," I called over, "there's a seat here."

"Thanks Buddy," he said as he sat down.

"What time is the Colonel coming in?" I asked.

He garbled an answer as he stuffed a pancake in his mouth.

"Say again?" I said.

"He's been in for an hour," he said, almost choking as he swallowed the pancake.

I was gone before he could say another word. I had to do something to keep Plummer's butt out of trouble. I could hear my footsteps echoing all around the marble hallway. Plummer's desk was piled with work to be done and the door to the Colonels office was open.

He was standing behind his desk reading a document.

I tapped on the door.

He looked up. "Come in, Naud."

I entered the office as he returned my salute. I stood in front of his desk. " How's the war going Sir?" I asked flippantly.

"We're kicking their asses, Naud. Whatta you want?"

"I guess you can tell that Plummer is not here, Sir."

"Yes I can see that, Naud. Get to the point," he answered

"Well, that's why I am here, Sir ...to explain why he's not here, Sir."

"Spare me the formalities, Naud. Where is he?"

"I can explain, Sir." I was shaking like a leaf knowing I was about to tell a flat out lie to the base commander.

"It's simple, Sir. Plummer and I were bicycling around the area yesterday. His front wheel must have hit a rock, because he lost control and got dumped off into the gravel. He broke his ankle. He's over at Hardy Barracks hospital."

"Is that the truth?' the Colonel asked as he sat at his desk staring directly into my eyes.

I hesitated. "Ah, well sir, most of it." I was trying to assemble the courage to tell him the whole story, but getting nowhere.

"Let me ask you, Naud . . . How often does Plummer ride his bicycle across the roof of the flaming Pisspot?"

I felt like a kid caught with his hand in the cookie jar, he already knew what had really happened. "I don't know, Sir, but I'm sure he will never do it again.'

"You tell him, we haven't won this war yet. MacArthur's on the move to push the commies north of the Yalu River. The communiqués running through here are vital to his success. I need his ass here right away!"

"Yes, Sir. I'll get him back as soon as I can," I said. I saluted and left.

I went to pick up Plummer at the hospital. He was waiting for me outside of the emergency room. He looked slightly punchy, but okay. I deposited him at his desk. Fortunately the Colonels office door was closed.

"Thanks, Naud," he said as he maneuvered himself and his cast into the chair behind the desk. As I started down the hall he began sorting through the documents on his desk. I heard the Colonels door open briefly.

"Send this up to encryption and have them send it on to the Joint Chiefs of staff," Colonel Macmillan ordered then his door closed again. I could hear Plummer reading it to himself as he typed:

....

Top Secret/ASA OJI Decrypted Communique

Date: October 6 1950

To: JOINT CHIEFS OF STAFF

From: MACARTHUR

Subject: TACTICAL SUMMARY

Synopsis:
   North Korea People's Army ceased to exist as an organized force anywhere in the Southern Republic. Request immediate permission to pursue North Korean forces, North, beyond the 38th parallel and destroy them.

Signed
MAC

....

I was starting up to the office when I noticed a crowd gathered around the company bulletin board. When I got upstairs, I asked Toshiko to focus the telescope on it. I was certain it was some new chicken-shit regulation Captain Cross had cooked up.

Surprise. Surprise. The memo was from Sergeant Baker. Because of the large demand for seats to tonight's movie, *Father Of The Bride,* starring Elizabeth Taylor, there would be two showings one at 1900 and one at 2200 hours.

Pollazzo agreed to take over the club for the evening. I was not about to miss a movie with one of the most beautiful women in the world.

Plummer was wading his way through the work on his desk when a response came down from the codebreakers upstairs. Plummer ripped it off the machine and handed it to the Colonel in his office:

....

Top Secret/ASA OJI Decrypted Communique

Date: October 13   1950

To: MACARTHUR

From: TRUMAN

Subject: TACTICAL PERMISSION

Synopsis:
Permission granted to pursue North Koreans so long as the Chinese stay out of the fight and you have reasonable chance of winning.

Signed

TRUMAN

....

Around 1900 hours, I made my way through the dark auditorium to a seat on the back row as the titles began *Father of the Bride*. I glanced to my left and was surprised to see one of the cooks, Sergeant Cummings was sitting next to me. He was a big man with a strong friendly face with a warm smile when he something to smile about. He was famous for his delicious franks and beans. He usually stood serving in the chow line just to rake in the compliments by the GI's.

"Hey Sarge, I thought you'd gone on emergency leave," I said.

"I canceled it," he said. "There's no way the doctors can tell how long my mother will live. I decided to wait a few months until I rotate out. At least when I get home I'll have enough to pay the doctor bills and give her a really nice funeral." He was obviously distraught by the situation. "But thanks for asking," he added

I was sure it was a hard decision, especially since the army had been his home for more than ten years. It would always be a better choice than working in a nasty coal mine in West Virginia.

A lecherous barking swept through the audience, as the crowd in the auditorium got their first glimpse of a thirty foot Elizabeth Taylor, in a bathing suit. The kind of reaction only beautiful women provoke. It grew louder and louder as she dove into a pool.

The loudest lecherous barking came from Sergeant Dollin, directly in front of me. A voice from the other side of the room chastised him. "Console yourself Dollin. In fifty years she'll be an old hag."

There was a brief burst of laughter that ended abruptly. Not many guys were comfortable with the thought that something that beautiful could ever change.

I went out to get some fresh air. Sergeant Kelly, the gate guard, came out of the mess hall with a pitcher of hot coffee. He rushed up to me. "Hey, Naud. Hold on," he said as he took a folded sheet of lavender rice paper from his uniform pocket. It was sealed with wax and an ornate chop design. "A cab driver left this," he said, handing me the lavender paper.

Sergeant Kelly never missed an opportunity to speak his mind. "You know, Naud, you'de better set a limit on how long a guy can play one of the slots. Some guys are hogging them," Kelly complained. Then he headed back in.

I stared at the package for a few moments then broke the red lilac seal and began reading:

Dear Private Browne.

I would like you to join me for dinner on Thanksgiving at my residence at seven o'clock.

I am enclosing a map for your driver.

Yours truly,

Sunlei Arashi

Chapter 22

Thanksgiving Dinner

I exited the main gate wearing my best class a uniform. I kept the Joy- girls away using my favorite ploy, coughing and sneezing like I had consumptive bronchitis. The girls moved back, opening a path.

I climbed into a cab and handed the driver Sunlei's invitation, which had her address on it and a map showing how to get there. Before I could say another word the cab pulled away, doing the usual lurching and screeching maneuvers. Terrified, I just held on. Telling the driver to go slowly was a waste of time so I decided to try something different. I leaned forward on the seat and held up a note Toshiko had written for me in Phonetic Japanese. I read it loudly at the driver's ear making sure he heard. "HAR·a·ga EYE·ta. No·hi·YA·koo. Hi TE· shi·ma I·so·da," I hollered. Roughly translated, I had told the guy I had a weak stomach and unless he drove very slowly and carefully, I would probably vomit all over him.

He must have understood, because he immediately slowed down.

I felt triumphant as I sat back smiling to myself, feeling relaxed, while the cab moved along cautiously.

We were heading north, and about an hour or so later we were in farm country. The driver turned onto a long straight country road that was lined by cornfields. The afternoon shadows were getting longer. To my right, I watched the setting sun sink slowly in the sky.

As the cab caught up to a tanker truck on the narrow, twisting, dirt road it slowed to a crawl, while waiting for a chance to pass. The "tank" on the back of the truck was actually a giant wooden barrel. There were trucks just like it all over the city. The GI's called them 'honey-wagons', wooden barrel tankers that collected human waste so it could be sold as fertilizer. Either the cab driver couldn't smell the noxious odor streaming back from the honey-wagon or was so used to it he didn't notice.

"Hi-ya-koo. Ee-kee-ma-show," I hollered.

The driver did his best to comply with my order to hurry-up. He found a section of road where he could pass and went around the lumbering truck.

'So much for the fresh, country air,' I thought.

When it was almost dark, the driver came to a stop in front of a beautiful thatched roof cottage with a prim garden that looked like something from a fairy tale.

I paid the driver and started up the front path. There were two expensive motor bikes parked by the porch and a pair of western style men's loafers sitting by the front door. It was obvious Sunlei had another guest.

I stepped onto the porch as the front door panel slid open. The last rays of the sinking sun threw a golden spotlight on Sunlei's face. She was almost angelic in her pink and white Kimono.

"Good evening, Naudsan," Sunlei said warmly.

"If you already have company maybe I should come back later," I said feeling uncomfortable.

"Oh, no, my guest was unexpected. Please come in."

I stepped in, and she led me into a sparsely decorated Japanese style main room. It was encircled by wood framed rice paper panels that led to other parts of the cottage. In the middle of the tami matt covered floor, sat a low black lacquered table surrounded by colorful oriental cushions. A small Bakelite radio was sitting on one corner of the table and was tuned to Armed Forces radio, Christmas music was playing.

A handsome Japanese man was sitting cross legged on the cushions. He was around forty-five and well dressed in an expensive looking Western-style business suit. He rose to greet me.

"I'd like you to meet, Mr. Nobura," she said to me. "This is Naudsan," she said to him.

'How do you do?" I said, offering my hand.

He looked directly at me. "I am glad to meet you, Naudsan," he said, as he shook my hand firmly. I noticed a large gold dragon ring on his middle finger, carved in the center of it were three Japanese symbols.

"Please sit," Sunlei said, gesturing us both towards the table. "I will get us some tea."

"Forgive me, Sunlei," Nobura said, "but I must leave now. I have a party I must attend." Then he turned to me. "I am sorry I don't have time to talk to you now Naudsan. Perhaps another time." He bowed graciously and started out.

Sunlei followed him to the front door where he slipped into his shoes, stepped off the porch, and climbed onto his motorbike.

I could see him through a narrow opening in one of the wall panels, as his motor bike roared to life.

319

He kept revving it up and then pulled away, shifting gears as he headed back down the country road.

Headlights suddenly came on from a nearby wooded area. A small tinny black car pulled out and followed him down the road. It was obvious that someone was keeping an eye on Mr. Nobura.

I was left alone wondering what kind of relation-ship Sunlei really had with Mr. Nobura. The radio announcer began to billboard a selection of popular Christmas classics.

Sunlei returned to the room carrying a tray, with a teapot and two cups on it. "Please sit," she said as she placed the tray on the table and knelt down.

I sat down and slipped my legs under the table, they were warmed by the heat coming from the hot coals in the grated stove below.

"Would you like some tea?" she asked.

"Yes," I said.

She poured me a cup and handed it to me, then poured one for herself. Bing Crosby voice came over the radio singing, *White Christmas,* as she placed the teapot on the table. "Do you like Bing Crosby?" Sun-lei asked.

"Yeah, "I said absent mindedly, I was distracted. I couldn't get Nobura out of my mind.

I sipped the tea.

A wry smile appeared on her face. "You're jealous aren't you," she said, as if she could read my mind.

"No, oh no.," I lied, embarrassed by my own feel-ings.

"We have a saying, 'friends don't lie to each other'," she said.

"Okay. I was jealous," I said.

"I will explain. Nobura is a rich powerful man I used to work for. He came here tonight to ask me to marry him."

I was momentarily stunned. "So, are you going to?" I asked.

She lowered her eyes, politely ignoring my question.

The Christmas music continued with, *'It's beginning to look a lot like Christmas.'*

Her face was pained as she began, "It was a crazy time when the war ended. Junji and I lived in the streets Sometimes we ate bugs to stay alive. That is where I met Nobura. He offered us food and a place to stay, medical help, and a job. Junji and I were just trying to survive. Twice a week I would wonder through the crowds in the Ginza, getting young Japanese men to try and pick me up. Then I would tell them I would meet them later at a party being given by a friend. I would give them a card with an address on it. Each night twenty five or thirty men would show up there, hoping to see me. After serving them rice cakes and beer, Nobura would lecture them on the virtues of joining the Communist Labor Union. He was going against the government, and his father, who owned many steel mills. Though he had worked in his father's steel mills, he didn't like the traditional paternalist way the mills were run. He tried to establish rights for the workers. His father had him arrested by the Tokko, the Emperor's 'Thought Police', and he was put in jail. They tortured him brutally, hanging him by his feet and putting bamboo slivers under his nails. They left him alone for months in a dark cell. He had to sleep in his own waste. But that just emboldened him to fight harder as he does to this day for Communist Unions."

'Nice father', I thought. "Are you a Communist?" I asked gently.

"No," Sunlei adamantly answered. "I don't believe in Communism."

The hurt on her face was obvious but it vanished as she poured more tea. Then I figured I owed her an apology for my attitude. "I'm sorry if I sounded angry. I guess I just felt uncomfortable."

"Why?" she said intently searching my face.

"Because I think of you more than I should," I said.

"I'm glad you think of me," she said. She took her cup of tea and held it up ceremoniously. "We should drink a toast. To the good we hold in our heart when we think of each other,"' she said.

We touched cups and sipped our tea.

"I too, think of you, Naudsan," she confessed. She paused with the cup near her lips.

Now I had to know. "Was Nobura ever your lover?" I asked gingerly.

Her eyes gazed down at the tabletop. "No. But he wanted to be. One night he got drunk and tried to rape me," she confessed.

"How can you even bear to look at him?" I said angrily.

"For a long time I couldn't," she said quietly. "But now, I feel sorry for him. He deals with his guilt by drinking too much. He gave me this house, and he keeps proposing marriage." Her tone was gentle and forgiving, as her eyes lowered.

I stared hard at her. "Will you ever say yes?"

She raised her gaze to look at me. "No. Not now." A tear fell down her cheek.

The radio announcer cheerfully introduced the next Christmas classic. "Now we have *It's beginning to look a lot like Christmas.*"

We both couldn't help but smile.

"Would you like to eat now?" Sunlei said, brightening the atmosphere.

"Yeah, I'm hungry," I answered.

She went into the kitchen.

There was a small silver bowl on the table with pine needles, incense sticks and cherry blossom petals. I caught a whiff of the pungent aroma.

Sunlei returned with a silver tray on which there were two dinner plates heaped with food. "I put that decoration on the table to celebrate the Japanese New Year, *'Show-she-ku-by'*," she said. With an endearing smile she added, "it means, *'a new beginning'.*"

Using a pot holder she placed the food in front of us, then sat down. "Be careful, the plates are hot," she warned.

I was surprised and delighted to have a complete Christmas dinner including turkey, gravy dressing, peas, cranberries, and sweet potatoes. laid out in front of me.

We savored the food and company in silence.

"That was wonderful," I said, finishing the last bite of turkey. I noticed there was the crest of the Imperial hotel on the plate?

"The chef at the hotel did the cooking," she confessed.

I smiled. "It doesn't matter, it was delicious."

She smiled back and poured us some tea. We ate sweet rice cake cookies and talked for hours, mostly about our lives during WWII.

I told her I had always loved to build model airplanes and was fascinated by flying. "When I was eleven years old, I asked a friend to help me build a full scale glider on the roof of our seven story apartment building in Manhattan. I was going to pilot it for the first test flight, but my older brother found out and said if I did he would break my leg. So we strapped a garbage can filled with ashes to the pilots seat and shoved it off the roof, expecting it to sour like a bird. It went down like a ton of bricks. I was glad I wasn't in it."

We both began to laugh.

She told me after the fire bomb raids began, the government ordered all the girls at her school to help with the war effort. Once a week they took them to a factory, where they showed them how to make balloons by gluing together pieces of rubber. When the balloons were finished they would take them down to a beach south of Tokyo where soldiers would inflate them with helium and attach barometric bombs to each. The government knew the trade winds were strong enough to carry them across the pacific to the northwest shores of America where they would explode. She didn't want to see anyone hurt so she would hardly put any glue on the balloons seams, knowing as they rose the increasing air pressure would cause them to break apart and they would fall harmlessly into the sea.

'Not only was she bright,' I thought, but she had a kind heart as well.

"O' Christmas tree. O Christmas tree," came over the radio.

Sunlei stood and went to one of the sandalwood wall panels and slid it open, revealing a hidden garden. There, in the middle, was a six-foot high living Christmas tree, decorated with blue blinking lights and twinkling silver stars.

"It's beautiful," I said. I rose from the table and joined her at the tree. I could feel myself choking up.

She stood close, looking up at me. "I made it for you. Merry Christmas Naudsan."

I leaned forward, touching her lips with mine for the first time. They were warm and moist. I kissed her, softly and she returned the kiss. We kissed again and then again with increasing passion. We were on the verge of not being able to stop, when a car began honking.

"I told the taxi driver to come back," I said, catching my breath.

"Stay with me, Naudsan," she said

The taxi kept honking.

"I have to get back," I said. I knew if I kissed her again, I would never leave.

"Then go, but take my heart with you," she said,

"Show-she-ku-by, Sunlei," I said, and left.

She stood on the porch, watching the cab vanish into the starry night, feeling alive as she probably never had before.

As I road back to base, I felt a mix of conflicted feelings swirling inside me.

When I arrived back at the club it was crowded and noisy. I had left Pollazzo in charge while I was at Sunlei's. People were dancing and some new guys were in on R&R from Korea. Everybody looked home-sick and slightly bedraggled.

Sergeant Cummings had been kind enough to prepare a special Thanksgiving dinner with all the trimmings for those who wanted to eat at the club. It looked like they had all finished eating.

Pollazzo was behind the bar, serving the liquor like a well oiled machine and really enjoying it.

"Hey Pollazzo. How's it going?" I asked.

"It's my kind of work!" he responded with an exaggerated joy.

"Mind closing up ...I'm tired. Going to bed."

"Go right ahead," he answered.

Plummer was at the end of the bar reading a letter from his mother. I moved down towards him. "What's your mom have to say?" I asked.

"She says Anne has been over to see her a couple of times to tell her how sorry she was for doing what she did, breaking our engagement. She went and had the marriage annulled when she realized she made a mistake. She asked my mom if she thought I would talk to her, so she could tell me herself how sorry she was for the trouble she created," Plummer said, looking disgusted. "I don't want to talk to her. It's all a lot of bullshit. She made her own bed," he said bitterly.

But he wasn't fooling me I could see he still cared about her.

I ordered some root beer. Pollazzo brought it over. Wattanabe and the Stardusters were the band for the evening and they were playing Glen Miller music. Sergeant Baker would have loved it, but he and Deh-ler were busy, out following Umerie around to all the clubs downtown, along with the other Miss Tokyo girls and Surrel. Surrel was having a ball because he was still getting a lot of publicity for his company.

Before going to bed I went down to take a shower. The steady stream of hot water from the nozzle was relaxing. I lathered the shampoo into my hair. I thought about Sunlei and the Christmas dinner and Sho-she-ku-by, the new beginning. How different our worlds were and how lovely she was. I rinsed the stinging soapsuds from my eyes, wishing I knew more about her.

I hustled back up to the warehouse, locked the door, shut off the light, then groped my way around the mountain of whiskey crates to my bed. I hurried to get under the covers, the room was frigid. In my haste I knocked a letter left on my pillow to the floor. Toshiko always left my mail on the pillow. With the help of a GI flashlight, I kept by the leg of the bed, I managed to retrieve the letter.

As I expected it was from my mother. I snuggled under the covers and read it.

The first part of her letters was always about my brothers. My younger brother, Bob, was working as a part time dress designer for Nat Kaplan, a well known fashion house. My older brother, Tom, had just been made associate producer on the *Today Show*. The biggest news was that mom was promoted to an executive secretary at a Wall Street firm and was doing well. She knew how much I missed being home for Thanksgiving. It was my favorite holiday. To me it was the only time when the family got together, just to be with each other, not expecting to get a present. I had nothing against Christmas or presents. The problem was I never had enough money to buy the gifts I wanted to give. But even if I had all the money in the world, I wouldn't be able to give my Dad the one gift I wanted to, his health.

Mom wrote about their last visit to Dad at Rockland State Hospital. They had taken him a turkey leg with some dressing. She and my brothers sat with him, on a bench outside, while he ate. She noticed how hungry he seemed and asked one of the hospital orderlies on his ward if he was getting enough to eat. He assured her, in an overly officious manner, that 'Mr. Naud most certainly was.' Tom didn't like the orderly's manner. Neither he nor my mother believed him, but they were afraid to make waves for fear it would only make my dad's life there worse. She ended the letter by sending their love, as usual.

I snapped off the flashlight and put it on the floor with the letter. I lay there in the darkness thinking about the tortured life my father was living. Three years earlier, he had suffered a massive stroke, which destroyed his memory. So if you asked him a question, you could see him struggling to find the answer, and a minute later he couldn't remember the question. The stroke had also reduced his field of vision to a narrow tunnel, a condition the doctors called *hemianopia*. The irony was he didn't look sick. He still had the bearing of a distinguished 52-year-old successful Wall Street broker.

My mom had tried to care for him at home, but she ran out of money, and had to work to keep the family going. She wound up committing him to Rockland State Hospital, a publicly supported mental institution forty minutes from New York City. To me, it was a snake pit for deranged, twisted, and lost souls, who were too poor to afford anything better. Dad deserved a better life but we couldn't provide it.

The only contribution we could make, was to visit him at the hospital on Sundays. To me it wasn't enough.

My brother took on my fathers role in the family in many ways and was vigilant about going out to visit him. My brother thought I didn't give a damn about our father because I didn't visit him that often. But I did care. I just cared so much I couldn't bear to see what dad had become. All the things that I had admired most about my father were gone. I especially missed his air of dignity. But most of all, I missed my dad's sense of humor. If God had to take away the best of what my father was, I couldn't understand why he didn't take the rest of him as well, take him to a place where he could be at peace.

The warehouse was dark and quiet. I lay there recalling the last image I had of my father from my visit to the hospital; a somewhat disheveled man in wrinkly blue pajamas, sitting on a bench in the hospital ward's recreation room, looking alone, lost and frightened. As the bus pulled out of the hospital gate, I had the feeling I would never see him again. That had been the day before I left for Korea.

I was mentally tired from thinking about my dad and the confused feelings I had for Sunlei.

I fell off into an unsettled sleep.

Chapter 23

Phone Call From Home

Plummer and I left the main gate at 10:30 a.m., heading for downtown. He had asked me if I would go with him to the Army's Telephone exchange, for a call coming in from his mother at 12:30. It was obvious he needed some moral support, so I said yes.

Our tinker-toy cab was halfway down A-street, running along the moat of the Emperors castle, when we hit traffic. Then it got worse, until we finally came to a dead stop. It was 12:10 and I was worried we were not going to make it. I got out of the cab to look down the lines of traffic to see where the blockage was. This time it wasn't ducks crossing the road. But a line of trucks and buses, displaying banners that read, 'Labor Rally'. They had stopped in front of MacArthur's headquarters and were blocking the road. Muscular labor workers with white cloth headbands, carrying strike signs demanding their labor rights, were jumping off the vehicles only to be met by MP's pouring out of MacArthur's Headquarters building. It was an instant riot.

The MP's were trying to slug the workers into submission, but more and more joined the melee. The chanting crowd kept getting larger and gathering around a flatbed truck on which there was a podium and a microphone.

Soldiers with carbines in their hands formed an arc in front of the headquarters building. A whole company of MPs and security troops arrived to control the crowd and traffic. As they fanned out the crowd was informed over loudhailers, that 'they were illegally blocking the road.'

"What's going on?" I asked Plummer.

"Looks like another strike by the commies in the Labor movement. They're a real thorn in MacArthur's side. The fact is MacArthur runs this country. A few years back he passed a law making it illegal to strike, in order to quell the economic chaos. It's ironic, he would rather prop up the paternalistic family-run businesses that go against democracy. But at least it helps keep stability among workers in the country," Plummer explained.

The speaker the crowd was waiting for, blared his rant of workers rights over a microphone. A chill ran up my spine. The voice sounded very familiar.

The impatient honking and hollering of the traffic was reaching a fever pitch and nobody was going anywhere. Plummer had only fifteen minutes to get to the telephone exchange a mile away.

"Look Plummer, if we're going to get your call we've got to do something now." I pulled out a twenty dollar bill. "Tell the driver this, when I say go, I want him to drive onto the sidewalk and go as fast as he can, trying to avoid whatever gets in his way, until we get past this mess."

He repeated my words in Japanese to the driver as I held out the twenty dollar bill. The cabbie grabbed the money.

"Alright Go!" I yelled but he had already pulled onto the sidewalk narrowly missing pedestrians who were frantically scrambling to get out of his way.

A couple of minutes later we were past the blockage and back on avenue A. The brand new two story steel and marble telephone exchange building was just ahead. The cabbie pulled up to a stop.

"You go in and get the call," I told Plummer as I paid the driver. Plummer still had the walking cast on so he hobbled in, using a crutch to help him walk faster.

I followed a moment later. The exchange was a cacophony of noise, guys were rushing from the cashiers counter to their assigned ringing phones, as other guys were babbling emotionally on wall phones and in booths.

"Arthur Plummer... paid telephone call on wall phone 63... Arthur Plummer ...wall phone 63..." came over the loud speakers,

Plummer was awkwardly making his towards wall phone 63 when I caught up. He grabbed the phone. "Hello MOM?"

I could hear his mother's voice as loud as if I were talking to her.

"Arthur is that you?" she said

All of a sudden he became more confidential, and leaned in to the phone, talking in a hushed tone. "Yes mom. How are you?"

"Arthur there is someone here who wants to talk to you. Don't say no," she begged.

Before Plummer could react, a sweet girl's voice came over the line. "Hello Arthur."

Plummer got all choked up.

"Arthur, are you there? Say something, Arthur," she pleaded sweetly.

But he still couldn't say anything.

"Arthur, there's no way I can say how sorry I am for what I did. I hope you will forgive me," she said.

Plummer was still silent.

"Arthur please say something," she pleaded

"I'm listening Anne," Plummer said softly.

"I know what I did was wrong, but I still love you. That's all I have to say. Here, I'll give you back to your mom."

"No, stay on the phone, Anne, Please," Plummer insisted, as he wiped a tear from his eye.

"Arthur, I guess it's hard for you to say you want anything to do with me now. Can I ask you one thing?"

Go ahead," he said, choking on his emotion.

"When you get home would you consider dating a girl who did what I did, Arthur?"

Plummer took a moment to compose himself.

"No," he said.

"I understand," Anne said and started to sob.

Then he added, "only if the girl was my wife."

I could hear Anne break down in sobs of joy.

Plummer's mom came on. "When are you coming home Arthur?"

"In a couple of months ... I'll see you two then."

"BEEEEEP Beeep." The connection was cut off.

Plummer rubbed the tears from his eyes.

We started back to the base in silence. The driver took the long way back to avoid the protesters.

During the drive, I asked Plummer to do me a favor, to find out what he could about a communist labor leader named Nobura. He looked at me expecting me to explain why. But I didn't.

"The fact that you didn't tell me why, means you don't want me to know. How do you spell his name?"

"N-O-B-U-R-A-." I said.

He wrote it down.

Chapter 24

Otas Beating

The club was closed. The waiters had just left. I was sitting at my desk in the office and had just finished writing a letter to my mother. I made up fun stuff, I had to, the reality was the war in Korea was turning bad and I didn't want her to worry about me. I had sealed the envelope and addressed it when the phone rang. Everything on the base was closed so, I decided to let it ring. But it just kept ringing until I felt I had to answer it.

It was Pfc. Clapper calling from the front gate. Clapper was one of the Club's board members, not a bad guy. He would sit at the bar drinking his beers, railing about the taxes the government was imposing on his father's small farm in Tuscaloosa, Alabama. According to him, the government didn't plant seeds, cause anything to grow, or know how to do anything on the farm, but they were always there with their hands out.

I agreed with him. But he wasn't calling me from the front gate to complain about taxes, he wanted me to know that the waiters who had just left the base did not get on their usual bus for downtown. He said they had turned right outside the gate, and headed toward the bombed out factory area. He saw them putting on capes and funny looking cloth bomber hats. It sounded like a meeting of the Japanese Klu Klux Klan. Whatever it was they were doing, he thought I should know about it.

"Where are they now/" I asked.

"I guess somewhere inside the bombed out factory area," he answered.

"Thanks," I said and hung the phone up. I turned the antique telescope around so it focused on the bombed out factory. I scanned the area until I spotted some flickering lights in the middle of a twisted and tangled steel structure. It was the same area where the Japanese kids liked to throw rocks at what was left of the glass windows.

Fifteen minutes later I was going by Clapper at the main gate. He opened the walk through door for me.

"Hey, Naud, It's the middle of the night. If you're going looking for them, you'd better be careful. I've heard some strange noises coming from out of there."

"Don't worry. I'll be fine," I said. I made my way down the cobblestone road to the bombed out factory area.

I was working my way through a section of the barbed wire fence, when I heard a slapping noise and a cry of pain. I moved quickly in the direction of the sound, picking my way through a tangled pile of rusty machinery and weeds. Suddenly I was startled by a bat darting past my face. As I flinched out the way of it, I cut my leg. It flew up through the twisted steel skeleton of the factories shattered roof and disappeared. Right below its path, a hundred yards ahead, I could see a dim flickering light through one of the smashed out windows.

I sneaked up closer trying to see inside. The closer I got, the louder the slapping noises and grunts of pain became. As I peered into the broken window, what I saw unsettled me. The waiters were standing in a very large circle, wearing ritual looking cloth caps and capes, chanting and mumbling in Japanese. Ota was standing in the center of the circle, with his hands bound together and strapped to a beam. His back was exposed and bleeding. It was obvious he had already been struck numerous times and I doubted his crumpled body could take much more.

Toshiko stood nearest Ota, holding a four foot long object resembling a flat baseball bat made of strips of bamboo, bound and wrapped tightly together. I watched as one of the waiters stepped forward and bowed to Toshiko, as he was presented the bamboo bat spattered with blood.

Ota had his hands clasped tightly in front of his face in prayer, readying himself to withstand the next hit. The waiter bowed to Ota, then swung and delivered a hard blow to his bleeding back. Ota slumped over, gasping for air, writhing in pain.

"Stop!" I called out almost involuntarily as I came out of the shadows, pushing my way through the circle of men. Everyone froze.

"What is going on here?" I demanded to know, searching their faces.

No one spoke. Most of the men lowered their heads.

I glared at Toshiko.

Toshiko looked reluctant to speak up.

"Look. If something happens to this man I'll be held responsible. If they're gonna hang me, I want to know why?" I insisted.

Toshiko explained. "Weeks ago I find out many CID people visit clubs in Tokyo area. Try to catch Japanese waiters and bartenders stealing. Only a few get caught but all Japanese get fired in those clubs. So my men take pledge of honor. No stealing. Ota broke that pledge. It is Kamikaze code. Kamikaze who dishonor himself dishonor fellow warriors, must pay consequences."

I was stunned to discover Ota was stealing. Toshiko told me he was the first pilot to volunteer for his Kamikaze squadron, and how profoundly disappointed Ota was, when his mission was canceled and he couldn't sacrifice his life in honor of the Emperor. Whatever reason he had for stealing, he wasn't going to pay with his life on my watch.

"So long as I'm in charge here, they'll be no more beatings. Break it up," I hollered out.

Nobody moved.

"No. Very sorry Naudsan. Men must complete punishment to bring honor back." Toshiko's response was resolute.

'This is crazy,' I thought. It was obvious Ota was on his last legs. "How many more hits, Toshiko?"

"One," Toshiko replied.

I thought for a moment, then agreed. I had an idea. I took up a position with my back to Ota's bloodied back. "Go ahead," I said.

The final warrior came forward to receive the bat. He and Toshiko bowed to each other. It was Noki. They had saved the biggest and toughest for last. He was only 5'8", but he had the muscles of a gorilla. He choked way down on the bat and kept trying to find a solid stance that would allow him to deliver a harsh blow to Ota, without hitting me. At last, the best he could do was a short punch punt to Ota's hip.

Knowing the last blow had been delivered, a wave of relief swept through the waiters. Their honor had been restored. Ota was back in the fold.

"We will talk about this tomorrow," I said to Toshiko, then made my way back through the forest of twisted steel and vines to the main gate.

"What was going on out there?" Clapper asked as he opened the gate door for me.

"Just a good luck ceremony or something. Good-night," I replied nonchalantly.

The following night I went up to the club about fifteen minutes early. On my way up, I discovered 8 or 10 guys in on R&R waiting at the club doors.

"Hey buddy whens the Club open?" one of them asked.

"In about ten minutes," I responded.

"Thanks."

I unlocked the doors and went in. The waiters were still busy setting the tables and chairs, wiping them off, and putting out ash trays.

In view of what happened to Ota the night before, I walked around nodding hello, trying to make them feel at ease. Most of them smiled back. It seemed like we were back to normal.

Jumbo and Ota were behind the bar washing and drying a ton of glasses. Ota was slightly hunched over and moving slowly, averting his eyes from the other waiters, so they couldn't see how much pain he was still in from the blows they had inflicted. He didn't resent them. All they had done was their duty.

I leaned on a bar stool and asked Ota to hand me a ginger ale. I took a few sips and slid down to the end, next to the slot machine. The 'OUT OF ORDER' sign was still on it.

Toshiko came in through the fire escape door with a case of C&C, and took it behind the bar, opening it and stacking the bottles on the shelves below the counter.

"Did Black Market Sam finally fix the slot machine?" I asked Toshiko.

"Yes, slot machine is fixed," Toshiko said, giving me a knowing glance.

I patted my pocket looking for something to put in the machine. I couldn't find anything. "Hey, Ota, hand me one of those coins in the fish bowl below the counter."

He turned to me without raising his eyes. "No coins left Naudsan."

"Have you got one?" I asked.

He patted his pocket, and produced a coin, and offered it to me. I ignored his gesture, while I finished taking a slug of my ginger ale. He was still holding it in the air, when I told him to go ahead and play the machine.

"Go ahead, put it in. Let's see if it works," I said.

"No gamble Naudsan. Must save money," he adamantly replied.

"Play it anyway. If you lose, I'll pay you back. Put it in. I gotta check that it works before I have another riot on my hands."

Reluctantly Ota stepped around to the front of the machine and put the coin in. I listened as he pulled the handle down. The wheels spun. Rabble. Rabble. Clunk! Clunk! Clunk! Bing! Bing! Bing! It lit up like a Christmas tree, and a moment later the one armed bandit was spitting a stream of coins out at him.

Ota jumped back, trying to get out of the way of the flood of the gold pouring out of the machine. The flood became a deluge. He stared, wide eyed, at the deluge of coins piling up on the floor.

"I think you hit the jackpot," I said. "I guess the slot machine works fine now."

Toshiko brought a fish bowl over and we began filling it with the coins.

"Ota, it looks like you've got enough here to pay your wife's doctor bills," I said.

Toshiko repeated what I said in Japanese. The joyous thought registered on Ota's face. He was trying to thank me, but he was too choked up.

"Tell him to take his winnings and go home to his wife, and stay home for a couple of days to rest his back."

Ota took hold of the heavy fish bowl filled with gold coins, and rose. From the look on his face he was somewhere between agony and ecstasy as he headed out, going home to show his wife what he had won.

Toshiko walked him downstairs.

The men on R&R started pouring in. I pulled off the out of order sign from the slot machine and a line quickly formed.

Surrel appeared and found me standing at the bar with a glass of ginger ale and a broad smile. "What's wrong with you?" he asked.

"I'm happy, that's what's wrong. I just lost four hundred dollars," I replied.

It was late, Little Joe and his band were finishing up, and most of the customers had gone home to bed. Misa was huddled with Baker and Dollin at the Board of Governors table. Plummer and Pollazzo spotted me and hurried to the bar to talk to me.

"Bill we got a problem," Pollazzo confided with a clear note of desperation. "Dollin and the motor pool guys just got their new orders, they're are going to Korea, right after New Year's," Plummer said.

"I saw the orders today," Plummer added.

"If we don't get the Coca-Cola Lady for Dollin, he's gonna give the Colonel a letter implicating everybody involved in the black market furniture switch for Mulvey. We'll be breaking rocks for the rest of our lives," Pollazzo said.

I sighed. "OK. I'll talk to Misa, again. But you know what she said." I had spent a nice day with Sunlei, but now I was back to wondering if I would make it through this whole thing without going to prison. Dollin was acting like a petulant three-year-old, he wanted to nail me because I hadn't booked the Coca- Cola Lady like I had promised him the night he issued us the trucks. Who was this woman, anyway? I kept forgetting to ask Plummer. What the hell is a Coca- Cola Lady?

Misa was approaching me. "Good evening, Naud-san," she said. She was wearing yet another elegant and expensive silk dress.

"You look very nice, Misa," I said.

"Do-ma-te-ga-toe," she said.

"Toshiko go home sick. No pay Joes. You pay?" she asked.

"I'll go down and get it," I said.

To me, paying the Little Joes was like paying to be tortured. I entered the darkened warehouse, groping around for the light switch. But before I found it, I stumbled over the pile of extra drums Joe always left there. I lost my balance, banged my knee, and scattered drums all over, as I tried unsuccessfully, to keep from falling on the floor. I thought the whole thing was funny, except it hurt.

"Damn it," I said, grunting in pain. I hopped around, holding my aching knee, until I found the light switch. As I began gathering up the scattered drums and stacking them back in a neat pile, I realized how unusually heavy they were. I tapped one of the drumheads. Then another. They all sounded dull, dead. Something was keeping them from vibrating freely.

I unscrewed the chromium bolts on one of the drum faces and discovered the secret. The drum was packed solid with cartons of American cigarettes. I locked the warehouse door to make sure no one came in while I examined the other drums. All the drums were filled with cartons of cigarettes. I estimated their worth on the black market at more than three thousand American dollars. Misa Manissa, the happy, smiling, well-dressed agent, was into more than the talent business, she was up to her base drum in black market cigarettes.

A few moments later, Misa sat at my desk counting the money I gave her for the Joes, while I stood at the window watching the band loading the drums onto the Army truck parked below in the Parade Ground.

"If I double your fee for the Coca-Cola Lady, can you get her for me?" I asked.

"Oh, not possible, Naudsan," Misa said, as she finished counting. "Coca-Cola Lady much popular act," she added, signing the receipt. "Maybe you get in six months," she said, stuffing the cash into the money belt she wore around her slender waist. "Thank you, Naudsan," she said. Then she bowed and vanished down the stairs.

I waited until she had gone before picking up the phone.

"Connect me with the gate, please," I said.

The gate guard came on.

"Kelly? This is Naud at the Club. Do me a favor, when the truck with the Little Joes gets there, hold them, okay?"

Kelly was reluctant at first, but finally agreed.

I hung up.

Plummer and Pollazzo had been waiting outside. When they saw Misa leave, they came into the office to find out what she had said.

"She said, 'No'." Then my face showed a sly grin. I loaded a piece of paper into the typewriter. "But she might change her mind."

"I don't get it. What's going on?" Plummer asked.

I finished typing, yanked the sheet of paper from the typewriter, and headed down the stairs. Plummer and Pollazzo followed right behind.

"You didn't answer," Plummer hollered. He was not the kind of guy to be led around blindly.

"Plummer? I want you to do some translating for me," I said.

"Of what?" Plummer asked skeptically.

"A letter," I said.

The truck hauling Misa, Little Joe, his band, and all their equipment, was parked near the guard booth. The band members were sitting in the truck, smoking and talking. Misa was pacing around nervously.

Corporal Damion, Kelly's partner, was stationed at the front of the truck with his carbine at port arms.

Sergeant Kelly came up the hill to greet me. "What's going on, Naud? You know it's against regs to keep vehicles parked at the gate."

"I paid the lady and got the wrong receipt," I said. Kelly could tell I was lying, but he let it go.

"I just need to talk to her alone, okay?" I pleaded.

"Five minutes. But no more," Kelly warned.

"Misa, can I talk to you?" I called out.

"Hai, Naudsan," she said, coming over to me.

"Look, I, uh, gave you the wrong thing to sign," I said, leading her away from the group. Plummer and Pollazzo followed along. "I need you to sign something else, OK?" I said.

"Dijob, Naudsan," Misa said.

"Plummer here will read it to you in Japanese," I explained. I gave the piece of paper I had typed to Plummer, who translated it into Japanese while Misa listened.

```
Dear Misa Manissa,
Someone has placed one hundred cartons
of American cigarettes in the drums
aboard your truck. If the guards should
happen to search and find them, you, Joe,
and the band will wind up in jail. In
view of my willingness not to mention
this unfortunate fact to the Guards, I
should like you to do the following:
(1) Cancel the Little Joe contract, as
of this moment and
```

(2) On a night of my choosing, New Year's Eve, provide the Club with the services of the Coca-Cola Lady.

Agreed to and accepted _____
Misa Manissa

Plummer and Pollazzo were both surprised and amused to find out what I was up to. But Misa gave no indication of what she intended to do.

"Tell her if she agrees to the terms of the letter, just to sign it," I said.

Misa spoke enough English not to need a transla-tion. She took the pen I was holding. "Right where it says, 'agreed to and accepted'," I said, in English. I was like a cat with a mouse, caught in my trap.

Misa showed no signs of discord. She just cheer-fully signed the paper and handed it back.

"Time's up, Naud," Kelly said.

"No sweat, Kelly," I said.

"Do-ma-te-ga-toe," Misa said, bowing me.

"Genki Puti-Puti," I said. It meant, "You're wel-come."

Misa got back in the truck's cab. Kelly nodded to Corporal Damion, who stepped back out of the way. The truck drove through the gate, turned left, and headed down Oji's main street. My knee still hurt from where I had stumbled over the drum, but I walked a few steps out of the gate to watch it go. With one lucky break, I had dumped the Little Joes and had eliminated the threat Dollin posed to my health and well-being. I smiled sardonically to myself and shook my head. I still didn't know what the Coca-Cola Lady did.

Chapter 25

Bad News and Good

It was a Saturday and I was up on the roof the day trying to give Surrel a golf lesson when a bugle, calling the company to general assembly, blared over the loud speakers. The troops began pouring out and assembling in front of the company headquarters. Baker emerged and barked "Company Atten-hut."

The troops snapped to attention as the orderly room door opened and out came Captain Cross. Cross returned the salute. "At ease men," he snapped. The formation relaxed.

I had heard Baker was going to call a special assembly to give Captain Cross a chance to say goodbye to the troops. Most of the guys, including the eggheads, were sorry to see him go. He had been tough on them, but fair. In spite of my initial feelings that Cross was a 'gung ho prick', I had come to respect him especially the way he softened his stance on the armies VD policy.

"Men I've only been here a short while, but I've learned one important thing about the ASA and especially the codebreakers. There's been a new chapter added to the military code of conduct, and I think it was written by you men. I'm prepared to concede, when it comes to a difference between ASA officers and enlisted men, the codebreakers view is likely to prevail. In plain English, you're helping us fight this war, YOU'RE way. "

The men all whistled.

Cross let a smile slip out then snapped back into serious military mode. "I want to thank you for your help these past months. I hope you will give Captain Ephrom the same consideration. Good Luck."

He signaled Baker he was through.

Baker probably didn't think the Captain's speech would be that short, he was caught off guard chewing on a hangnail. "Company Atten-hut," he barked.

The men snapped to attention like cadets at West Point. Cross was impressed and returned the salute, obviously moved by the gesture. "At ease," he commanded and went back into his office.

I went back to giving Surrel the golf lesson when I heard the clunk, clunk of peg leg Plummer, coming up the steps to the roof. He looked like he had something serious on his mind.

"Cross got a fine send off," I said.

"Yeah. He turned out to be a pretty good guy. I heard when he gets back to the states he's going to help his father with his Senate campaign."

Plummer sat down on a chair to rest his aching leg. Surrel shanked another shot into the net. I knew how hard he was trying, so I said nothing to him.

"Hey Plummer how come there was no inspection of the company property with the change of command?" I asked.

Plummer coughed ironically. "Well when you're talking about a guy who is about to get the Congressional Medal Of Honor, the rules change a bit. By the way, today's board meeting has been cancelled. The Colonel had to go downtown for an emergency briefing, 300,000 Red Chinese just crossed the Yalu river and are pushing us south. It looks like the Chinese are in with both boots. The Colonel was really rattled. He's a man accustomed to dealing with crisis, but fighting the whole Chinese army is more than even he bargained for. Take a look at this." Plummer handed me a piece of paper.

```
Top Secret/ASA OJI    Decrypted Communi-
que

Date: 26 November 1950

To:  JOINT CHIEFS OF STAFF

From:  MACARTHUR

Subject:  TACTICAL SUMMARY

    Synopsis:
    Chines attacks hit the 8th Army's
center and right at Changjin Reser-
voir.  UNC positions have crumbled.

    Instructing general Walker to with-
draw as necessary.  X-Corp moving to
East Coast Port of Hungnam, north of
Wonsan to ready for evacuation.

    Estimate Chinese combat troops now
300,000.  Chinese are in the war with
both boots.

    Signed

    MAC
```

It was chilling news.

Plummer started hobbling away, "I have to get back to my office."

I called after him. "Any word on Nobura?"

"Check out the newspaper," he responded.

I picked up the newspaper he had left on the chair, and tried to read it, but it was in Japanese. As I thumbed through it, I found pages of photographs of the labor riot at MacArthur's headquarters a few days earlier. I spotted Nobura in a couple of them. In one he was being handcuffed by some American MPs. "That's him alright. I met him last week."

Surrel read the caption beneath the picture. "'Communist Labor leader has been arrested for deliberately fomenting labor unrest.' It's a serious crime according to the Japanese Labor authority." He stared at me with a serious look of concern. "If I were you, I'd stay a millions miles away from him. "

I was immediately worried about Sunlei. I hoped she was alright but I had to find out for sure. "I know a girl that used to work for him. She could be in trouble." From the look on my face he could see I was seriously worried. "Surrel I need a favor. Can you take me out to her house so I can make sure she's okay?"

He agreed to take me out to Sunlei's cottage. I figured it would be more inconspicuous to go out there in Surrel's car, which resembled a black Japanese police vehicle, than an army jeep. I scrounged up the envelope from her Thanksgiving invitation that had the address on it.

An hour later we were in the residential area where she lived, with its hilly, sharply winding roads.

The jeep was bouncing wildly as it snaked its way up a another steep hill.

Finally Surrel skidded onto the long, straight, dirt road leading down to Sunlei's house. Then he stopped short. All we could see at the end of the road was a smoldering pile of ashes. The house had been practically burned to the ground and was still smoking.

"You sure that's it?" he asked.

"Yeah, that WAS it," I said with an empty feeling in my stomach.

We pulled up closer and stopped in front of where the porch once was. I moved my flashlight from one smoking mound of rubble to the next, trying to recognize something familiar. I spotted a sake cup and a dish. The radio we had listened to during our Christmas dinner was a melted blob. 'Show-she-ku- by. A new beginning,' I thought. I aimed the flashlight's beam into the garden and searched with it until I found the Christmas tree. It was a black stump. All the decorations had melted.

"The bastards left her nothing. They didn't have to do this," I said, my voice thickening with emotion.

Then my flashlight caught a reflection of something shiny in the ruble. The tami matts, beneath the dining table we had eaten Thanksgiving dinner at, had all burned away, exposing the wood planking beneath. As I focused my flashlight on the cracks I caught a glimpse of a small metal box below. There was a crow bar in the back of the jeep, I grabbed it and used it to pry the charred boards loose boards away. Then I reached down and recovered the small metal box. It was scorched from fire and still warm.

Inside I discovered a small pink diary. It was Sunlei's, and surprisingly, it was written in English.

Then we heard a vehicle, and looked back down the country road, a headlight from a motorbike was coming toward us. As I rose to greet whoever it was, I slid the diary into my fatigue pocket.

It was a local Japanese policeman coming to check what had happened.

Surrel explained, in Japanese, that we were friends of the owners and were saddened by the destruction. The policeman seemed satisfied with the explanation, but told us we must leave. He was calling in the fire on his radio as we climbed into Surrel's car and pulled away.

"Can you find your way to the Kabuki Theatre? I know a friend of hers who might be able to tell us what happened to her."

"Sure, Bill," Surrel said.

The traffic and the air thickened when we reached the downtown Ginza area and arrived at the Kabuki Theatre. I had the feeling that the police might be watching, so we parked around the corner. I sent Surrel in to speak with Kiku, just in case.

He came out ten minutes later carrying a small piece of paper. "She left you a note."

I unfolded the delicate rice paper and read it by flashlight;

Dear Naudsan,

My heart is very full for you but you must not try to find me for your own sake. It is too dangerous. I suspect they will try to use me as evidence against Nobura. I am hiding in safe place.

Sunlei.

At that moment, I realized how deep my feelings went for her. I didn't care what the risk was, I had to try and help her.

Later that night as I lay in my bunk I thumbed through the pages of her diary.

June 26, 1941

Mother and father and I took our pictures together at one of those booth places on the dock in San Francisco. In two hours we will be sailing back to Japan. In another week we will be back in my homeland, as mother and father call it. But I feel like America is my real homeland.

Everything will seem so strange and different in Japan. I am sure I will eventually like it. Father seems to be worried all the time.

PS. Tonight I am seasick.

July 9, 1941

Today we arrived in Tokyo and I was reunited with my brother, Junji, after four years of separation. He is now 12 years old and, like father, he is handsome.

All he talks about are Japanese customs and traditions. Seeing him in his Military School Uniform makes me sad. Mother is sure a war is coming. He may have to go to fight. She is so frightened about what will happen to our family. I still miss America and my friends there. Father thinks it is unwise to write them any more letters. But for now, we are a happy family once more.

December 6, 1941

Mother was right, a war has begun. We have attacked Pearl Harbor. Father told us it was a glorious victory. It just made me sad. He does intelligence work for the Navy and knows about Pearl Harbor but he can't speak about it. Tonight, Father told us that he wants to serve aboard a battleship. Mother cried herself to sleep.

January 5, 1943

Father left today to serve on a cruiser. He couldn't say which one. The father of my best girl friend is a Captain on a cruiser. Mother says the authorities lie to us about how the war is going. She is working downtown at the NHK Radio Station.

May 4, 1943

It makes tears come to my eyes to hear mother crying at night. She misses father so much and is so afraid for him. I am too. I wonder what my school friends back in America think about me now. I wish I could write them letters and find out.

December 11, 1943

We have not heard from father in three months. Mother has gone to work in a hospital downtown to keep herself busy. She cries at night, often. Mother works hard trying not to think at all. I feel abandoned.

January 9, 1945

Junji has joined the Kamikaze against mother's wishes. He is 16, just a child.

It seems so stupid to send a child out to die, but he seems glad to go. Tadashi has many friends who feel the way he does.

August 7, 1945

I am filled with hate for those who have taken what I love away. Last night the American bombers came. They dropped firebombs and killed Mother at her hospital job. The police said she was alive and now they say she is dead.

Tadashi came home for a day. He has finished his Kamikaze training.

He cried and I cried with him. I feel so helpless. My family is almost all gone.

September 5, 1945

The radio says the war is over. People from the Navy called and told me father died an honorable death. "An honorable death."

It is such a vain stupid thought.

October 11, 1945

The Americans have occupied the country. I live in the streets and eat vermin in the ashes of this once beautiful city. There is no sense to life. I wish I had the courage to die.

November 13, 1945

Junji returned home. He is sick with fever but at least he is alive. He is all I have left to live for.

American soldiers are everywhere but I avoid them.

A man named Nobura offered me food and a home if I would get young men to come to his meetings. He is a communist who wants to change the Emperor system and make all citizens equal. He gave me a paper, which says, "WIN THE YOUTH AND YOU WIN THE FUTURE." I told him I would accept his offer but only if I could bring Juni and he would get medical help for him. He agreed.

February 22, 1946

I walk the streets getting young men to come to Nobura's communist meetings. I do well for him and he has gotten Junji medical help

August 15, 1946

Today I am sixteen. Mr. Nobura tells me I am his best recruiter, I have gotten him fifty new members.

I think the idea of communism is a dream. He says people are paid according to their needs. Such a foolish idea. Who decides my need? And what if people are selfish?

September 9, 1947

Mr. Nobura told me Junji has to help recruit young men to come to the communist party meetings or go live someplace else. Junji moved out.

I moved into the small house behind Nobura's. I feel safer from him back here.

March 21, 1948

Nobura wants me to be his lover. I told him, "No".

I am concerned about what he will do. He is drinking a lot.

August 30, 1948

Last night, Nobura broke in and tried to rape me while I was sleeping. He was drunk. I clawed his face and screamed and he stopped. I am afraid that, if I tell Junji, he might kill Nobura. It was a horrible experience.

I felt like a peeping Tom reading her private words. I couldn't imagine dealing with the sad events she had to in her youth. At sixteen all I cared about was getting a ride in my friend's shiny new family car.

Chapter 26

Christmas

It was my first time away from home for Christmas, and it looked like I might be spending a lot of time in jail the way things were going. Sure Misa agreed to book the Coca-Cola Lady but it wasn't for free. If I didn't get the money to pay her fee, Sergeant Dollin was going to blow the whistle on the trip slip I signed authorizing the use of army trucks to transport Black Market goods. The court martial lawyers wouldn't care why I did it, only that I had broken the law.

I needed three thousand dollars and if what I had in mind worked out, I might get it. If Not?? I was terrified of, IF NOT. I was out of time. At least this latest problem, was taking my mind off worrying about Sunlei.

I slipped into a Santa-red golf shirt and khaki slacks, combed my hair in the mirror behind the locker and headed up to the club. It was jammed with people laughing and drinking, knee deep in Christmas revelry. A load of new fresh faced troops had just arrived from the states. They were a stark contrast to the burned out guys, who were in on R&R from Korea. I wished Jessie had been among them, but I kept up hope he was okay.

I looked around the club trying to spot Bakers CID guys. I casually wandered around the Club from group to group wishing everyone a Merry Christmas, as I tried to spot them, but it soon became obvious they weren't there. At least not yet. I was becoming paranoid. Surrel had told me they were arresting club custodians all over Tokyo for crooked bingo games and missing club funds.

I called down to Hannigan at the main gate. "I think Bakers bringing in CID guys to sniff around the club to find something to get me in trouble. If you see any unfamiliar snakes coming in, call me."

"You got it," He assured me.

Then for a change, I sat at the opposite end of the bar to avoid the sound of the slot machine.

Captain Ephrom was on stage leading his twenty man choral group. He loved his choir, he made them sing like angels. Their harmonious voices filled the room with Christmas carols. Some of the guys sang along with the group, but most just listened. I let the familiar Christmas melodies stir happy memories of past holidays back home.

"It's sure a beautiful looking tree, Naud," a Corporal in from Korea said.

Everybody liked the fifteen-foot high Christmas tree sitting on the stage. I had shaped it and sent Toshiko to the Ginza to buy strings of colored lights, and loads of tinsel and ornaments to decorate it. Cummings, the cook, made a twelve-inch star from a tin cookie sheet, which I put on the top. I had guys hang their Christmas cards on it too. The tree was picture perfect, it deserved all the attention it got.

Ephrom's choral group had just finished and was leaving the stage, after a standing ovation, when Pollazzo, who had been watching the Parade Ground below, cried out, "Santa is coming. Santa is coming."

I had promised Sergeant Baker we would introduce him as Santa Claus. Even if I hated Leroy Baker's ass, I couldn't disappoint Santa Claus.

Baker took the ovation as a joyous heralding, he entered the club dressed as Santa Claus, carrying a sack of presents slung over his back. He was the spitting image of a Norman Rockwell version. I thought Baker's Santa costume was better looking than the ones I used to see on the guy at Macy's department store. I heard Baker had rented the expensive costume downtown and had spent hours spirit-gumming the white beard and hair to his face.

"Ho, Ho, Ho," he bellowed in a low tone, as he made his way through the crowd, smiling and waving. Then he dropped his sack down on the stage.

Surrel entered the club just behind Baker. He was staring at Santa Baker with his mouth wide open in disbelief.

Dehler was sitting at the Board Of Governors table nearest the stage. He snapped loads of pictures of Santa's arrival. Umerie was sitting to his side trying to unsuccessfully light a cigarette. She had no idea who the jolly man in the red suit was supposed to be, and why everyone reacted with such reverence to him. Misa Manissa was also at the table along with Bakers stooges, Hartung, Mula, and Zinger.

I joined Santa Baker at the stage as he gleefully shuffled through the sack of gifts. I figured I would help him orchestrate the show.

"Have you been good boys and girls," he playfully asked the crowd.

The men answered with a quiet, but mischievous yes.

"I didn't hear you," Baker goaded them.

"Yes!" they loudly yelled in unison.

I couldn't believe it was really Baker.

"Whadda you want Naud," Baker said out of the side of his mouth with a chilling tone. "I'm gonna give out the gifts by myself."

"Nothing. Just Merry Christmas," I said and headed back to the bar to join Surrel and Plummer. It was still hard for me to believe, that a guy like Baker could have a shred of a generous giving spirit. All I could figure was he was trying to make up for all the lousy Christmases he had in his life. Only Baker knew why Christmas gave him the excuse to be the person he always wanted to be.

On the table, in front of Dehler, was a bowl with 30 or 40 chits with the names of GI's written on the backs.

"My assistant will pick out names. If your name is called, come up for a gift. If not you'll get a ticket for a free drink," Santa Baker explained to the crowd in a forced jolly tone.

With a sour looking face Dehler, Santa's assistant, stuck he hand in the fish bowl filled and took out a ticket. . "Let's see who gets Santa's first gift," Baker said, hamming it up.

"Pfc. Hayes," Dehler read aloud, with no evidence of enthusiasm.

"YOOO," a voice hollered out. Pfc. Hayes jumped up and rushed toward the stage.

"Ho, Ho, HO, Merry Christmas," Santa Baker said as he reached into his bag to find him a gift.

Plummer had told me Baker bought all the Christmas gifts with his own money. I scoffed in disbelief. If Baker bought anything, for anybody, with his own money, the gifts would have to be junk or cheap crap he got from Black Market Sam.

Pfc. Hayes's face lit up as he waved his present in the air for the crowd to see. "It's a seventeen jewel Bulova wrist watch. Thanks Santa!"

The crowd 'oohed and ahhed.'

My mouth dropped open in surprise. That wasn't the junky crap I had expected.

"Who's our next GOOD LITTLE BOY," Baker called with a belly roll tone.

"MEYER. MEYER?" Dehler called out, double-checking the name on the ticket.

"YOO," Meyer answered, excitedly heading to the stage to get his gift.

It was nothing but a plain envelope, which was in my mind, more like Baker's style. He probably planned to give out one good gift and then give out plain white envelopes with something really useless in them like a coupon for a free dance lesson at *The Arthur Murray Studios* in Newark, New Jersey.

"Hey, thanks, Santa," Meyer said, cynically, trying to mask his disappointment.

"What is it?" somebody screamed out, "toilet paper?"

Meyer opened the envelope, read the white paper, and broke into a smile.

"It's a weekend trip for two to Fuji," he hollered out. "Hey, thanks, Santa."

Everyone cheered.

I was floored. And so, the gifts went. Besides tourist trips to Fuji, watches, jewelry and movie tickets, there was softball equipment, earrings, perfume, telephone calls to home, free laundry, several three day passes, skis, etc., etc. There were lots of gifts, expensive gifts. They must have cost Baker a pile.

Everywhere I looked I saw happy, smiling faces. It gave me a warm feeling, the kind only Christmas can give, though I was sure there was only one reason Baker would give such nice gifts, to make himself feel better. Certainly, if anyone needed to feel better about himself, it was Sergeant Baker.

"Next," Santa Baker chimed.

Dehler called out, "Ukie Umerie."

She was startled hearing her name, but elegantly made her way up to the stage. Baker warmly placed in her hand a 4"x4" package brilliantly wrapped in gold foil with a giant bow.

"Open it!" he crowd called out.

She pulled off the box cover and gasped at what was inside.

"What is it? "some in the crowd called out.

"It's just a ring for the good little girl," Baker said playfully.

Umerie said nothing. With an odd smile on her face she quietly went back to her seat.

Surrel moved up to the dance floor to get a closer look at the ring, Umerie had placed it on her finger. He came back to the bar with a sour look on his face. "She has too much class for him," he grumbled, lighting another cigarette.

'Me thinks he protests too much' I thought. He obviously had some feelings for Umerie.

I went to the microphone to move things along. "Okay folks we'll have thirty minutes of dancing and then we'll start the Super Bingo."

Wattanabe and his Stardusters began to play. Minutes later, a sea of dancing couples crowded the floor including Santa Claus awkwardly clomping about like a bull pushing the decked out lamp post, Umerie, around the floor.

Wattanabe tried a zippy rendition of *White Christmas*. Some guys had tears in their eyes, which wasn't surprising. It was Christmas Eve and their families were halfway around the world.

The phone at the bar rang. Nakijima handed it to me.

"Two snakes on their way up," Hannigan said and hung up.

A moment later S.S. Dalton, Bakers Cid buddy, and his cohort, entered the Club, and made their way to the bar where they ordered a drink.

Ota came through the crowd with the large cardboard box, which was used to carry the bingo cards around. He handed it over the bar to Jumbo, along with the money from the card sales.

"How many cards did we sell, Ota?" I asked.

"Almost sell all," he said, smiling.

I was lousy at math, but I ran a quick computation. We were selling the cards for twenty-five bucks. Tonight's final Super-bingo game could be worth around five thousand dollars:

I went onto the dance floor and grabbed the mike. "Listen up...' I said, gesturing to the band to stop playing. "Dance time is over. It's BINGO time!"

As the stage cleared, I pulled the bingo table and equipment into position. Everyone settled down to their tables with their boards in front of them, hoping they would have the *'luck of the Irish'* on Christmas eve.

I caught Dalton and his buddies trying to melt into the crowd looking for the best vantage point to surveille my every move.

"The first four games will be worth $100, the fifth Super Bingo game will be worth $5000. "

A rush of whistles and ahhs rippled through the crowd.

"Let's get started," I said. I cranked the arm on the cage until a ball rolled down the chute. "Our first number is, B-9, B-9," I called out.

"BINGO," some joker screamed.

The crowd booed.

I went along with the joke. "Bring the card up and I'll check it," I said.

The guys erupted into laughter.

I finished cranking again, when another ball fell out. "G-52. G-52," I said holding it up high in the air for everyone to see. Then I placed it in the cigar box to my right along with the first ball.

Six balls later, I called "N-19, N-19,"

"BIN-CHO, Bincho" the pretty Japanese girl with Pfc. Hayes enthusiastically called out. Hayes ushered her up to the stage to help her collect her money.

I checked the numbers on her card, as the crowd grumbled, more interested in getting on with the next game.

"Let's go, Bingo... Let's go, Bingo!" they chanted.

"It's official, we've got a winner here," I announced. The Japanese girl was all smiles, bowing her thanks as I presented her with the one hundred-dollar prize. She and Pfc. Hayes returned to their table.

Four more games were played, with S.S. Dalton and his buddy watching my every move like a hawk.

"Now we're going to take a short break before we play the $5000 SUPER BINGO Round. Don't forget to get you're extra Super Bingo cards from the waiters for $20 each."

I joined Plummer at the bar. "Nakajima? I got a bingo card on a shelf behind the bar there," I said. "Hand it to me," I added.

Nakajima found the card.

"Give that card to the guy sitting alone by the window over there. And do it quietly."

"Hai, Naudsan," Nakajima crawled out from behind the bar and moved slowly through the smoky crowd.

"Don't do it, Bill. Please," Plummer cautioned. "Baker will be watching like a python."

Plummer had finished his fifth glass of ginger ale and couldn't put off taking a leak any longer. It was go now or piss in his pants. Jumbo was back behind the bar serving drinks. "Hey, Jumbo, save my spot. I'll be back," Plummer said, sliding off the barstool onto his good leg. He grabbed his crutches and made his way through the crowd heading toward the front door. He had to hurry to be back in time for the Super-bingo game.

The chants began loud and clear, "Super Bingo! Super Bingo!"

I headed for the table by the stage and grabbed the mike. "Alright it's time for Super Bingo," I announced.

A bold cheer went up, then the room quieted to a hush, in anticipation of everyone's chances of getting rich.

Plummer came rushing anxiously back into the club just as I was about to start.

Baker and his cronies scanned the room like they were trying to find a shill on their radar screen.

I took hold of the crank and spun the cage around. "Listen for the sound of the lucky ball falling," I said goading the crowd.

Plummer noticed Santa Baker was focused on the guy he presumed had the winning card, sitting over by the window. Plummer figured I was about to do exactly what Baker had done in the past, conceal the winning balls in the cigar box on my lap.

"HOLD IT, HOLD IT," Plummer screamed, before he had even realized what he was doing.

Suddenly the room froze and everyone's attention shifted to Plummer.

"Listen, everybody. Hey, listen up," Plummer bellowed out. "It's Christmas, right? And who gives presents at Christmas time? Santa, right?" He didn't wait for an answer. "Well then, shouldn't Santa pick the winning balls?"

Plummer started a chant. "SAN · TA, SAN · TA."

"SAN · TA, SAN · TA," the crowd picked it up.

The call for Santa finally got so loud Santa Baker had no choice but to join me at the table.

"Ho, Ho, HO," he said, waving to the crowd.

I had no choice but to go along. I moved the bingo cage towards me into the center of the table. "Okay, here we go," I said, cranking the cage full of balls around and around, until one fell through the hole in the bottom of the cage, and rolled down the metal trough to a stop.

There was dead silence. "What's the first number, Santa?" I said, pointing at Santa Baker, who picked up the ball from the bottom of the chute, and showed it to the crowd.

"It's B-7. B-7," Baker announced into the mike.

I caught the look on SS Daltons face. He was staring hard at Baker trying to spot the scam.

I cranked the cage around again. The balls bounced and clanked until another one fell through the hole.

Baker grabbed it. "N-23, N-23," he called out.

Plummer looked like he was feeling more relaxed. In his mind, by a stroke of good fortune, he had saved me from hanging himself.

I was frustrated, as I cranked the cage around slowly and deliberately. The balls tumbled over one another until one dropped through the hole. "Alright ball number three," I said, as it hit the bottom of the chute and bounced out. But Baker caught it before it fell off the table.

"Good catch Santa," I quipped.

Baker held the ball up high. "G-29.G-29," he called out, then tossed it into the cigar box that held the other called balls. He looked like he was trying hard to figure out if there really was a scam going on.

Half of the guys were calling out the numbers they needed to win.

"Calm down. ' I called out." "Let's get the next number." I started to crank slowly. Someone in the crowd yelled, "Faster! Faster!" So I went faster. A ball fell. A second later another ball fell.

Baker picked up the first one and called it out." O-27.O-27." Then the second one, "B-43."

Now all the guys were raucously shouting out the numbers they needed to win. I finally had to make an effort to quiet the crowd. "Hold it down!" I shouted.

I noticed SS Dalton was on his feet moving around the club checking the faces of the crowd, trying to see who might be sitting on the golden egg. He kept eying Baker, who just shrugged ignorance.

I started to crank, and a ball quickly fell through the hole. Baker picked it up and called out, "N-21. N-21."

A voice screamed out, "BINGO, BINGO," from the far side of the room, like a bolt of electricity.

The crowd let out a collective groan, angry with the winner because it wasn't them.

"Bring the card up and Santa will check it," I said.

Plummer was happily surprised and relieved, it wasn't the guy sitting by the window, whom I had sent the card to.

The winner was Cummings, the popular cook from the mess hall.

Sergeant Cummings arrived at the stage and showed Santa and I his card. Baker called off the numbers, while I checked them against the called numbers on my board, under Baker's watchful eye. They all checked out.

"Ho, Ho, HO, we got a BIG winner here," Santa Baker announced with phony enthusiasm. There was some applause while others moaned and groaned their disappointment.

Plummer was pleased that the winner was Cummings. Everybody knew Cummings was heading home soon to see his dying mom. Plummer was sure the money would help.

I was down in my office paying Sergeant Cummings.

"Good Luck, Harold," I said, handing him the envelope with the prize money. The cage with the bingo balls was on my desk.

"Thanks, Bill. Make sure to call me if you ever get to Dayton, huh?" he said.

Plummer came in as he was leaving.

"Good luck, Harold," Plummer said.

"Thanks," Cummings said.

Plummer waited for Cummings to leave. "Look, Bill, I know you're probably mad at me, I only came down to apologize for lousing up your plan."

"Hey. No sweat. I understand. You were just trying to help," I said. You were smart insisting Baker call out the balls."

Plummer spotted a bingo card lying on the table, and picked it up. "Isn't this the winning card?"

"Yeh," I said.

"Sergeant Cummings, should take it and have it bronzed," Plummer said. "I wish to heck I'd gotten it. I never win anything," he added.

"Well, maybe it's still got some luck left in it. Give it a try," I urged.

"Why not?" Plummer shrugged.

I cranked the cage full of balls around and around. Five came down and Plummer checked them against the card. "Bingo," he quietly exclaimed.

I put the balls back into the cage and snapped the door shut.

"Wanna try again?" I asked with a straight face.

"How'd you do it?" Plummer asked. He was completely mystified.

I showed him. I had sanded the balls with the winning numbers, until they were a thirty-secondth of an inch smaller than all the others? Then, I made the opening at the bottom of the cage, where the balls fell out, a thirty-secondth of an inch smaller, so only the smaller balls with the winning numbers could fall through.

"That's clever, Bill. Really clever," Plummer said, chuckling as he said good night.

I replaced the rigged bingo balls with a fresh set and fixed the opening in the cage.

I now had the money to pay the Coca-Cola Lady. 'Merry Christmas to all, and to all a good night,' I thought as I went into bed.

The next day Plummer told me he had tried to sleep, but couldn't, because he couldn't stop smiling.

Chapter 27

HAPPY NEW YEAR

It was New Year's Eve. 1951 was just four hours away. I had been hoping to spend it with Sunlei, but there was no news from Junji on where she might be.

The EM club was a boisterous smoke filled jungle of both ASA code guys and their shell shocked buddies in on R&R from Korea. They couldn't wait to explode into the new year wearing silly cone hats, drinking, laughing, and blowing horns through a storm of confetti and balloons. I guess the promise of a fresh start was as appealing to most people as it was to me. It was something like starting the back nine on a golf course, after shooting ten over on the front nine.

On stage, Wattanabe and his Stardusters were playing Nat King Cole's *Unforgettable* for the third time. Some of the dancing couples were so close that, to quote Grouch Marx, *'If they got any closer, they'd be behind each other'*.

I moved through the crowd wishing everyone a Happy New Year. Surrel was behind the bar following my orders, plying Dollin and his three motor pool drivers with generous glasses of free whiskey, trying to get them smash ass drunk. I gave him a thumbs up as I made my way to the windows at the back of the club. I reached them just in time to see the truck carrying Lucinda and her all girl band come to a stop in front of the building.

Lucinda got out of the cab and opened the doors at the back of the truck. Misa Manissa was with her. Lucinda directed her fifteen girls, dressed in band costumes and carrying their instruments, into the building's lobby, toward the elevator. One of those girls was our three thousand dollar guest, but I couldn't tell which one.

I started down to the warehouse, feeling butterflies in my stomach. It was the same sensation I got going over the top of the Coney Island Roller Coaster. I entered the warehouse, locked the door behind me, and made my way through the maze of liquor crates to the heart of the secret room.

Toshiko, Pollazzo and Jumbo were impatiently waiting for my final briefing.

At one end of the room, a large sheet hung across the front of the Industrial sized Ammunition Elevator. On it I had drawn a detailed floor plan of the fifth floor office warehouse and the club above.

The elevator came up from below and bumped to a stop at our floor. The doors squeaked as Toshiko pulled them open, and Lucinda and her band emerged from behind the bed sheet. Lucinda was aware of what we were doing with the Coca-Cola Lady, so she hustled the girls out of the warehouse and up to the Club to change places with Wattanabe's band. A few moments later Wattanabe's twenty piece band, sounding like a herd of elephants, made their way back down to the office.

While the Coca-Cola Lady stayed in the elevator, dressing for her performance, Misa came out with a small record player and placed it on the table next to the elevator door, then plugged it into the wall.

And for the third time she asked me, "You give me Coca-Cola lady money now?"

I responded firmly, "Not until she finishes her act."

A disgruntled Misa vanished back into the elevator.

There was a knock-knock, at the door. I made my way out through the maze to answer it. Knowing Plummer's secret knock, I opened the door just enough to let him in. The reception area was jammed with Wattanabe's band milling about wondering what to do.

Langon stuck his head in the door. "What about these guys?"

"Sit as many as you can up against the door to block it."

"Got it," Langdon said, adding, "by the way you gotta get this mob of GIs off the landings in the stairwells. They're a fire hazard. "

"Just give me thirty more minutes, please, Langdon," I pleaded.

"Okay," he said reluctantly.

I pushed the door shut and locked it.

Plummer was anxious to give me his report. "They must know what we're doing. A couple of minutes ago Baker, Dehler, the CID guy with the dark glasses, two MP's from Hardy Barracks and the OD Captain Ephrom came out of the headquarters office and quietly made their way across the compound to the base of the fire escape. They're down there now, waiting."

"Follow me," I said. I headed toward the fire escape door. It was blocked with sheets of plywood, heavy crates of liquor and the safe. I pointed at a large pipe with a valve coming out of the wall to the left of the fire escape door.

"Stay here," I told Plummer.

"And do what?" he said, looking mystified.

"If you hear anyone coming up the fire escape, open this water valve all the way. Toshiko and I have connected a piece of hose to the outlet on the roof. We stuck it over the edge and affixed it, so it's aimed down at the fire escape. When you turn it on, they'll feel like they're being hit by Niagara falls."

Plummer shook his head. "You really love this intrigue stuff, don't you, Naud."

I guess I did, but I didn't answer him. I just hoped the plan would work so we wouldn't all end up in Leavenworth Prison.

I returned to the secret room, ready to resume my briefing. The guys were seated at a line of cocktail tables facing the elevator. They were staring bug eyed, mesmerized by the almost naked silhouette of the Coca-Cola lady being projected onto the sheet by the light bulb in the elevator.

I shoved the elevator door closed and pulled the sheet down. As I stood before the guys I felt like General George Patton, about to finish briefing his men on a super-secret mission, even when the enemy already knew what they were going to do.

"Listen up. Here's the plan. Plummer is on the water hose, Langdon is guarding the warehouse door, Toshiko will be in charge of the elevator and light switch. When Surrel gets down here with Dollin and his guys, he'll stand behind Dollin at the first table, Pollazzo will be behind McGourdy, Jumbo behind the pimply guy, and I'll be behind the fourth guy. Our job is to keep Dollin and his guys plied with liquor. "

I checked my watch. "In about four minutes, Lucinda and her band will start playing loud noisy Jitterbug music, and she'll keep playing it until I tell her to stop. That'll cover the stripper ladies music. At the same time Toshiko will turn off the warehouse speakers. At one minute of ten, Misa will put on the Coca-Cola ladies record and Toshiko will turn off the lights. At exactly ten o'clock, approximately, the Coca-Cola lady will begin her act. You got it?"

My two Japanese warriors, Jumbo and Toshiko, gave a sharp nod, while Pollazzo lackadaisically waved a limp hand at me in the air.

I told Jumbo to go up to the Club and get Surrel, and bring Dollin and his crew down. He was gone like a shot.

I could hear Lucinda and her band, over the warehouse speaker, playing Somewhere over the Rainbow. *It was coming in loud and clear. Then they* suddenly stopped and broke into Glen Millers *Tuxedo Junction.*

There was a knock, knock, at the warehouse door. When I opened it, Surrel and Jumbo ushered Dollin and his staggering buddies into the secret room, and seated them according to the plan. I locked the door.

Dollin and his motor pool guys may have been blottoed but they were wide eyed and hyper anxious to witness what they had waited so long to see. As they sat at their respective tables, staring at the elevator doors, Surrel and Jumbo poured them each a glass of whiskey, per my instructions.

Everyone and everything was working like clockwork.

Dollin downed the first glass and coughed, almost choking on the strong whiskey. "Hey when's this slant eyed bitch gonna start."

"As soon as she's finished dressing," I answered.

"Who wants to see her dressed?" McGourdy called out in a drunken slur.

The four of them laughed raucously.

At exactly ten o'clock, Toshiko turned the warehouse speaker off. Misa stuck her head out of the elevator. "Coca-Cola Lady ready, Naudsan," she announced. Then she sat down next to the table with the record player. She put the needle on the record. Misa turned the sound up as loud as she could get it.

Toshiko snapped off the lights as Dollin and his guys hooted and hollered, "Take it off! Take it Off!"

A scratchy hissing noise filled the darkness of the secret room then the Plink Plink, Plank Clink, Clank Clank, music began. With a flourish, the Coca-Cola lady opened the elevator doors and slid into the room, sweeping the beam of her flashlight, up, and down, and all around her body as she strutted back and forth with an alluring smile in front of the tables, presenting her assets.

She was met with animal hoots, hollers and horny gestures, as Dollin and his buddies studied her luscious body with their mouths hung open. Even Toshiko's eyes bulged. He had never seen such large, well-shaped breasts.

She suddenly thrust her breasts into the face of Dollin, but before he could grab one, she moved on to McGourdy and the others. They were all mesmerized.

I thought the Coca-Cola Lady had two things going for her; the first was her giant pair of tits, the second was a willingness to show every inch of her body.

She kept writhing her hips and twisting, as she bent over, placing an open bottle of Coca-Cola on the floor. Then with each erotic turn of her body, she lowered her vaginal orifice toward the bottle, like an elevator on its way down. Her moves kept perfect time with the bumps and grinds of the music.

Then she turned her back to the audience. Punctuated by some drum banging, she bent over sticking her ass up in the air to provide a spectacular view of her most private parts. She further taunted her audience by focusing the flashlight beam on it.

It was more than horny Dollin and his buddies could take. They pulled party snappers from their pockets and began firing them at the obvious bull's-eye, like a machine gun. After several shots, the pimply guy, who was built like an ox, made a direct hit. The sudden pain caused the Coca-Cola Lady to leap away, knocking the record player and Misa to the floor. The record was shattered into a dozen pieces.

Dollin and his guys were still firing at the irate Coca-Cola lady, who was scrambling to get to her feet. She turned off the flashlight and started cursing loudly in Japanese.

"What's she saying?" I asked Misa.

Misa lit the area with her Zippo lighter. "She feels degraded. She says, she refuses to deal with animals and she's quitting," Misa interpreted.

I heard banging and slamming at the fire escape door. "They're trying to get in," Plummer screamed. A moment later, I could hear the deluge of water pouring down on the fire escape. "It worked." Plummer screamed. "They're backing down the fire escape, giving up!" He was barely audible over the Coca-Cola ladies ranting.

'Giving up hell,' I said to myself, Baker wasn't that kind of guy.

The Coca-Cola continued cursing as she groped around in the elevator, for something to put on.

Dollin and his buddies were firing a hail of party snappers at the elevator, while complaining loudly that they were being cheated. I warned them frantically about the snappers and they finally stopped, slumping down in their chairs like scolded children.

I hollered in Misa's direction, "Tell her, they're sorry. They're very sorry and won't do it again."

Misa told the Coca-Cola what I said, but she still refused to continue.

"She says she can't dance now because she has no music," Misa said, holding up a broken piece of the record. "Normally, a twenty-piece orchestra plays while she performs."

I saw the Coca-Cola Lady's sheet music sticking up in Misa's carpetbag purse. I pulled it out. "This is her music right?" I asked.

"Hai," Misa nodded yes.

"Tell her I'm gonna get Lucinda's big band upstairs to play it. She'll hear it over the warehouse speakers. "

Misa told her in Japanese.

The Coca-Cola lady responded with a series of grunts.

"What did she say," I asked Misa.

"She say $500 more money and no snappers."

"Tell her okay," I said, anything to get the show finished.

Then, with a petulant toss of her head, the Coca-Cola Lady stopped pacing and agreed to go on.

"You heard her Dollin," I warned, "no more snappers or she's out of here. Cough 'em up. ALL of them!"

The guys bitched and moaned a little, but they gave in. Jumbo and Surrel collected the rest of the snappers.

Toshiko turned the warehouse speaker on, as I raced upstairs. "Excuse me," Excuse me," I said, climbing over the piles of lounging bodies on the stairs.

The dance floor was jammed with GIs and their girls, happily bobbing, stepping, and twirling to the rhythm of the jitterbug music.

Lucinda continued leading her band as I tried to explain what I wanted. "Look," I said, waving the sheets of music at her. "You play this music and don't stop till I say so. No matter what. DOZO! Please!"

Lucinda finally understood. "Hai." She brought her orchestra to a sharp stop, and handed out the sheets of music. Her girls looked at the notes on the sheets, but were totally befuddled.

I had no time to explain. "Just tell them to play it," I insisted. "And NOW."

The band began playing the Coca-Cola Lady's music.

The crowd on the dance floor was trying to pick up the beat. "Bing Bing. Bonk. Clunk Clunk Zoop." But there was no beat to follow. The music just sounded like a collection of quirky sound effects. They started complaining, but Lucinda and her band kept playing.

As I picked my way through the mob blocking the stairs, I could hear Baker, Dehler, and his entourage, at the bottom of the stairwell, battling to come up. When I finally got into the warehouse and locked the door, I could hear the Coca Cola ladies music loud and clear through the warehouse speaker. She had resumed her act with renewed energy, twisting, bumping and grinding her naked body.

Dollin and his buddies were slumped over the tables, watching bug- eyed as she swung her mammoth breasts, left then right. Then she brought her gyrating hips, lower, and lower over the open bottle of Coca-Cola on the floor, until, finally, she squatted on it. She tightened the lips of her vagina on the bottle's neck and stood up to the beat of the music, bringing the bottle up with her. Then she bent over backwards as far as she could, and put her hands on the floor to steady herself, then she shook her hips like a belly dancer faster, faster and faster, causing the coke in the bottle to foam and spew, until the pressure got so great, the bottle shot out of her vagina like a daredevil being launched from a circus canon. It barely missed Dollin's head, struck a whiskey crate and landed on the floor spinning like a top. It slowed until it came to a stop with the foaming coke dribbling out.

It was the highlight of her act. Even I was awestruck. Dollin and his buddies sat there, still as statues, their mouths agape.

I could hear the crowd upstairs over the speaker. The GI's were chanting, "WE WANT DANCE MUSIC. WE WANT DANCE MUSIC," louder and louder, as they began to stomp the floor.

Captain Ephrom, Sergeant Baker, Dehler and the rest of the entourage had reached the outside of the warehouse door and were slamming it with their bodies trying to knock it off its hinges. "Open this door!" Ephrom yelled.

"Naud! Open this door!" Baker kept screaming as they continued their assault. When it finally gave way, Baker and the Captain stumbled into the darkened warehouse.

"Naud! This is Captain Ephrom," he called out, "we know what vile things have been going on in here! Naud, do you hear me? Now turn on the lights!"

The lights came on. I was standing there to greet them.

"Naud, we know what's been going on here and YOU'RE in a lot of trouble," Ephrom threatened.

"What for, Sir?" I said innocently, playing dumb.

"You know what for!" Ephrom shot back.

"We're just having a party for Sergeant Dollin and his motor pool drivers. They're going to Korea tomorrow, Sir."

"That's Bullshit Captain," Baker barked.

"There's no need for vulgarities here, Sergeant," Ephrom bristled.

Baker leaned in to the Captain. "There's a secret room inside those cartons of whiskey, Captain, and that's where the stripper is."

Ephrom stood tall and determined. "Let's tear a hole through that wall of boxes and get in there," he ordered, shaking his hand in the air.

I watched as the entourage tore into the wall of whiskey boxes. In a couple of minutes they had cleared open a passageway four feet wide into the secret room.

Captain Ephrom picked his way in. The overwhelming smell of whiskey, and the sight of the unconscious men lying face down on the tables, seemed to sickened him, and fill him with righteous indignation. "What's wrong with those men?" he demanded.

"They're drunk, Sir. I told you. They're blowing off steam before they ship out tomorrow."

"Oh, is that so. I know what's really going on here," the Captain responded skeptically. "Now, where is that strip teasing harlot, the Pepsi lady?"

"There is no Pepsi Lady, Sir," I said innocently.

"Don't smart ass the Captain Naud," Baker chimed in, "you know he meant the Coca-Cola Lady." Baker was ready to kill. "Now where the hell is she?" he angrily demanded. "You tell me boy, or I'm gonna bust your smart-ass, New-York butt, understand?"

Captain Ephrom's face became beet red. "I warned you Sergeant about using that vile language. Now knock it off."

"Yes Sir," Baker said. But he wasn't retreating. He started to search the room, mumbling under his breath, "She's here. I know she's here."

Dehler was preoccupied, staring at the disturbed dust around the elevator. It was like a light bulb went off in his head. "I think I know where she is. Sir. She's in the elevator. That's where she is," Dehler announced.

"Then Open it up!" Ephrom commanded.

'That's it,' I thought, 'we're sunk.'

Dehler hurried to pull the elevator door open, with Baker joining him for the search.

"Well?' Captain Ephrom questioned.

Baker and Dehler became deflated. "She's not there sir," Dehler answered sheepishly.

I let something out, far beyond a sigh of relief. I looked at Toshiko for some clue as to where she was. He just remained poker faced.

The Captain looked up at the ceiling. It was vibrating, and the sounds of an out of control brawl were pouring out of the warehouse speaker, getting louder and louder.

"What in heaven's name is going on up there," Ephrom yelled.

"It sounds like a riot, Sir," I said naively.

Before Captain Ephrom had a chance to think of what to do next, a herd of angry ladies carrying musical instruments came through the pile of debris into the secret room. They were joined by their leader Lucinda. She could see I was in trouble. She glared at the Captain and at the top of her lungs she began railing angrily about what her and her band endured up in the club. She went on screaming an endless litany of complaints in Japanese, as Surrel translated with an equal vigor.

"She says that she and her girls have been attacked by a sexual herd of American Soldiers, "he explained.

Captain Ephrom was dumbfounded by the whole episode.

Lucinda kept on mumbling, as she ordered the band into the elevator. When they were all aboard she closed the door.

The assault on the Captains nervous system left him dazed and shaken. He just stood there watching the elevator start slowly down. Then the intense sounds of the riot coming through the speaker, snapped him back to his command presence.

"Alright, now listen men. Let's get up there and get that riot under control. Naud, you stay here with your people and straighten out this mess. And that's an ORDER!"

The Captain, a cowed Baker, Dehler and the rest of their entourage tromped out over what was left of the warehouse door and hurried upstairs to the club.

I looked at Toshiko. "Where did she go?'

He opened the elevator door. I looked down the shaft at the elevator car that had almost reached the lobby. The Coca-Cola Lady and Misa were sitting on top of it.

I smiled at Toshiko. He smiled back and locked the elevator door.

Pollazzo was still bug-eyed from the Coca-Cola Lady's performance. He volunteered the following observation, "I've never seen so many moving parts on a woman.

Plummer who had made his way back to the room just in time to catch the last part of her act commented, "I'm sorry I saw it. I'll never be able to get it outta my mind."

Surrel had too much class to comment. He was just glad it was over.

"Everybody do something to look like you're cleaning the place up. I'll be right back," I said and left. I hurried to get downstairs, picking my way over the piles of passionate bodies entwined in the stairwell, busy trying to swallow each other up.

When I reached the lobby, the elevator cab had been lowered enough to allow Misa and the Coca-Cola Lady to climb off. They were racing out of the building towards the back of the truck.

I stepped outside just as they were boarding. Misa glared at me. "You give me Coca-Cola money now!"

I reached out to hand Misa the envelope of money, but before she could take it the Coca-Cola Lady grabbed it away, while mumbling what I was sure were Japanese curse words.

For no apparent reason I looked up at the club windows and saw Baker and Dehler looking down at me. Bakers face was boiling mad and in an instant he was gone from the window, I presumed heading my way.

Lucinda and I locked the truck doors. No sooner was Lucinda in the cab, then the driver made a sharp U-turn over the crunching gravel and roared towards the gate.

I stepped back into the shadows, as Baker came out of the building like a snorting bull.

"Stop that truck!" he bellowed. The few people within earshot were drunk and could care less. Baker rushed back into the building and picked up the lobby phone. I could hear the gate phone ringing busy. Baker let it ring a few times more, then he threw the phone at the lobby wall and ran out of the building, continuing toward the gate. I watched him round the bend, then vanish.

I ran to the top of the hill just in time to see Baker arrive at the gate.

There was no truck.

Baker rested his head against the gate and started to sob.

After the secret room was passably straightened, Plummer, Pollazzo and I headed back up to the Club. Pollazzo jumped onto the stage, causing the horn blowing and confetti throwing to suddenly pick up a notch. "Hey, folks, We got five more minutes left to midnight. Are you ready?" Pollazzo said, into the mike.

There was a chorus of, "Yeahs", mixed with blasts of horn blowing.

I was sipping the overflow from a fresh glass of ginger ale when someone edging in to the bar for a drink, bumped me accidentally. I looked up, annoyed.

"CALLAHAN," I hollered, surprised, and delighted to see him.

"BILL," Callahan answered back, equally surprised. The last time we had seen each other was four months ago, at the main gate on our way to Korea. I noticed the bandage on Callahan's left hand.

"Hey, It's great to see ya, I hear you run this place," Callahan answered.

"Yeh. What's with your hand?" I asked.

"I lost a couple of fingers. It's okay," Callahan said, making light of it.

"Two minutes to go folks," Pollazzo's announced from the stage. The horn blowing and crowd noise were growing so loud, I had to scream to be heard.

"Jessie was supposed to be here, too" I hollered, sounding disappointed.

Callahan looked startled at those words. He started to say something but stopped.

"Whatsa matter?" I hollered.

"I'm sorry, Bill," Callahan hollered back, looking pained. "I thought you knew."

"Knew what?" I said.

The answer was already on Callahan's face. A morbid chill flooded through my body. "Oh, Jesus, No. Oh, Christ," I anguished. I pulled Callahan to the end of bar where we wouldn't have to scream.

"It's true, Bill. Jessie is dead. I was with him," Callahan said.

"What happened?" I asked. .

Callahan took a drink and started. "They sent us across the Yalu to test the enemy resistance. The river was frozen. Then all of a sudden, Chinks were everywhere. They chased us back across the ice, right into a minefield, Most of the squad got it there.

Jessie, me, and a guy named Adam were the only ones left. The gooks had us surrounded. We started running back to our lines. I got hit, so did Adam. Jessie picked me up and carried me back to our line and then went for Adam. A sniper got him and he fell on a ridge. Three Chink soldiers came up and kicked him over to see if he was dead. He slid down into a ditch filled with water."

"You're sure he was dead?" I said.

"Yeh. I hid behind a dirt bank, watching him until it got dark, hoping for a chance to crawl out and see if he was alive. He never moved. He was a hero, Bill."

"Okay, folks, here we go," Pollazzo said, checking the second hand on his watch. "1951 is coming up in........ Ten seconds ......" The crowd joined in, counting down, "Nine... Eight... Seven... Six... Five...Four... Three... Two......'" "Happy New Year," Pollazzo bellowed into the mike.

Watanabe and his Stardusters began playing 'Auld Lang Syne'. The room erupted into a cacophony of blowing horns and exploding balloons as everyone hollered or screamed, "Happy New Year."

"Jessie wrote you this letter. I was gonna leave it in your office," Callahan said. He put it on the bar and vanished into the smoke-shrouded chaos.

I had to get out of the club, so I went up on the roof to open the letter.

Dear Charley,

I hope you are still my friend. I didn't write you because I was ashamed of what I did. Callahan and me are in the same unit and hang around a lot. Sometimes he talks too much, but I don't care.

I hear you're doing well running the Club. I'm glad. I often think of all our adventures especially the transvestite in Oakland. My dad is still in Europe. He's had a heart operation. He says he's okay but I'm kinda worry about him.

You're a real friend. Take care of yourself and I'm sorry for any trouble I caused you. It's not so bad here, honest. I asked Callahan to bring the letter and tell you I'll be there around New Year's.

I hope.

Your friend,

Jessie

Still in shock, I looked up at the clear star filled night sky. A white comet shot across the darkness. I was hoping it was Jessie going home.

....

Top Secret/ASA OJI   Decrypted Communique

Date: 31 December 1950

To: JOINT CHIEFS OF STAFF

From: MACARTHUR

Subject: TACTICAL SUMMARY

   Synopsis:
   Chinese forces have attacked Seoul.
General Ridgeway reports that holding the line at the 38th parallel is
dependent upon the 8th Army confidence.
I have told the troops, "We must wage
a war of maneuvers: fighting delaying
actions when the enemy attacks and
slashing at the enemy when he with-
draws."

HAPPY NEW YEAR

Signed
MAC

....

Chapter 28

NBC Calling - Standing By

I was sitting on my bed polishing my golf clubs, when Surrel showed up for another golf lesson, this one on the course at Kogene. I had been promising it to him for several months, and now at last we were going to do it.

"I'm going to turn you into Ben Hogan," I said.

"I'm glad to see one of us is optimistic. Okay let's go," he replied sarcastically.

We took our clubs, left the warehouse, and headed downstairs. Toshiko appeared at the head of the stairs and called down to us. "Naudsan, telephone call, NBC."

I put the clubs down on the staircase and hurried up to answer the office phone. "Hello," I said, as Surrel came up to the Office door.

I put my hand over the mouthpiece, "Where's NHK Studio?"

"Near the South end of the Imperial Palace," Surrel answered.

"Okay I'll be there," I said into the phone and hung up.

"So is our lesson canceled? " Surrel asked.

"No. My brothers calling me from New York at nine this morning. He works for NBC as a producer on the TODAY show. We'll play golf after I talk to him. Okay?"

"No sweat," Surrel said.

As we drove downtown to the NHK studios, I was hoping to see the mama ducks and her ducklings again near the Palace, but they didn't show up.

"You'll be heading home soon," Surrel said. "What are you going to do about Sunlei?"

I don't know, "I answered. It was a question I wished Surrel hadn't asked. We continued our ride in silence. I was confused about my feelings for Sunlei to begin with, and not knowing where she was made it worse. Rather than think about it, I forced myself to concentrate on the passing scenery.

The NHK radio building was located about a mile south of the Imperial Palace. It was a ten story, grey stone-block building. On the roof was the tallest and most powerful transmitter in the far East, visible from anywhere in Tokyo. Surrel told me it was where Tokyo Rose made her propaganda broadcasts during World War II.

It was a few minutes past 9 a.m. when we entered the building. Garrick Utley was waiting in the lobby. NBC rented studio space in the building and Utley was their number one Far Eastern Correspondent. He was a slender guy in his early thirties, wearing a business suit, and an academic smile.

Surrel decided to wait in the lobby and look around. Utley led me down a hall past a wall of celebrity photos, which included Tokyo Rose. Then past a series of windows that looked into small studios the size of a master bedroom. They were lined with white acoustic panels filled with holes. Metal bar stools, music stands, microphone booms and cables were neatly placed around the walls. Each had a glassed in room where technicians were busy at work.

I found it all exciting, and a little bit intimidating, to think I was about to talk to my brother in NY, half-way around the world.

When we got to Studio B, Utley directed me to sit on the metal barstool in the middle of the room. An engineer came in and adjusted a mike hanging at the end of a long metal arm over my head. "

"Do you know my brother Tom Naud?" I asked Utley.

"Yeah, he's doing a great job producing the Today Show, should be a hit.' Utley said, then left and went into the control room.

"Okay, Mr. Naud. Say something," a voice requested from the control room.

"Something," I said. I kept saying it, because I couldn't think of what else to say.

"Okay, Hold it. They're gonna patch us to New York now and you'll talk to your brother. Stand by," Utley said.

I watched the engineers plugging wires into a panel that looked like a switchboard.

"Be sure you keep your head up and talk into the mike," the technician reminded me.

The engineer took his seat at the control board. "Stand-by," he said.

Utley was standing behind the engineer, monitoring the events.

"Coming up in ten, nine, eight," the engineer counted down. "Three, two, one......."

"Bill? Are you there? This is Tom, in New York."
His voice was coming from the studio speakers as
clearly as if he was in the room.

"Hi, Tom. Yeh, I'm here," I said. "Can you hear
me?"

"Yeah, I can hear you fine. You okay?" Tom asked.

"I'm fine," I said.

"Mom and Bob want to say hello," Tom said.

I was surprised to hear that my mother and
brother, Bob, were there too.

"Hello dear. How are you feeling?" my mother
asked. I could sense tears in my mother's voice.

"Hi, Bill," Bob said.

"Are you okay, mom? What's wrong?" I asked.

"She's okay, Bill," Tom said. "It's about dad," he
added. "'That's why we're calling this way, instead of
writing a letter," Tom said.

"What happened?" I persisted.

"Dad passed away," Tom said.

The news devastated me.

"He just went to sleep, and didn't wake up," my
mom said.

"Bill? You still there," Tom asked.

I was having trouble speaking. "Yeah,"' I said
softly. The engineer was waving his hand motioning
for me to speak up into the microphone.

"We took dad up to New Haven and buried him
yesterday," my mother said.

"It was a very nice service," Bob added.

"I'm sorry, mom," I said. My voice was starting to
break. "He didn't deserve it. It doesn't seem right."
Tears were rolling down my cheeks.

"I'm sure, he's better off where he is now," my
Mom said with a quiet finality.

"Bill? We gotta get off now," Tom said.

"We love you, dear. We miss you and we'll see you very soon," my mom said.

They all said, "Goodbye" together.

"Bye," I said. My voice was barely audible.

The hum in the studio speakers suddenly went dead.

"Are you okay, Naud?" Utley's voice inquired from the control room.

"I'm okay," I managed to get out, but I was lying. I took a moment to dry my tears and compose himself.

The control room door opened and Utley came in. "I'm sorry to hear about your dad," he said.

I thanked him, shook his hand and said goodbye.

Surrel was waiting in the lobby. I didn't mention my dad's death. As we drove off in silence, the sky suddenly became grey.

"Maybe it's not such a good day to play golf. Looks like it might rain," Surrel said.

"Yeah, I don't feel much like golfing."

"Sure," Surrel said, without the slightest protest. "I'm sorry about your dad," he added.

I looked at him, wondering how he knew.

"That Utley guy told me why your brother was calling," he said.

I turned my attention back to the passing scenery. "At least he's out of that snake pit," I said.

Surrel was sensitive enough not to ask what I meant by "snake pit".

I got back to the warehouse around noon.

I sat on the bed and started a letter to my mom. I wanted to share my memories of my dad with her, and tell her what he had meant to me. I could still see my dad's smile, and hear his laugh, and see him drinking his cup of tea. I wrote a few lines. But when I read them back, they seemed empty and inane. I tore the paper up thinking that maybe a second try would bring better results. But it didn't. I finally realized that words couldn't say what I needed to say. How do you capture, in words, the love a son feels for his father? I remembered the last gray day at Rockland State Hospital, sitting on the bench with my dad, wondering if my father understood when I told him I loved him.

I cried myself to sleep.

Toshiko entered the warehouse and woke me. "What time is it, Tosh?" I asked, sitting up.

"Nine o'clock, Naudsan," Toshiko said.

I sat up on the bed thinking it was nine in the evening, but when the bright sunlight hit my face, I realized I had slept a whole day away.

"Sorry to hear about Naudsan's father," he added.

"Thanks," I said. "Has Junji found out anything more about Sunlei?"

"No Naudsan. I'm sorry," he said with obvious sadness.

I took my bathroom stuff and glumly headed down to take a shower. When I got back I fell into a restless sleep. Then I started having a nightmare;

I had arrived in the middle of the night at the Flaming Pisspot and was greeted by Mamasan. She told me she had made me a statue and led me to her garden. But there were no statues there, just beautiful flowers. She left alone saying she would be back after she had talked to the Emperor. While I waited in the moonlight, grotesque warrior statues appeared like magic and filled the garden. They came to life.

"We have come to warn you," they said like a Greek chorus. "About what?" I asked, then realizing the statues looked like the waiters. Before they could answer, black clouds covered the moon and the garden turned dark. Bolts of lightning exploded from the sky, striking the statues, causing them, one by one, to burst into flames and melt into the ground. I covered my face to protect myself from the fires and intense heat. Then, from out of the flames, Sunlei appeared. "Help me. Help me," she begged. Then she told me she had defied the Gods of thunder to come see me. She warned me, I would be destroyed if I tried to steal the warrior statues. Then a powerful lightning bolt suddenly struck Sunlei, exploding her into a million bloody pieces. The garden began to shake violently and I awoke.

I sat up in bed. My nightmare was interrupted by a real earthquake. I was waiting for the aftershocks, which always followed. The warehouse was dark and cold. I rarely ever dreamed, and this one was so strange and horrible I wanted to forget it right away. But now I was left awake worrying about Sunlei.

Chapter 29

Resurrection

It was a weekend night; the club was packed and smoky. I had to get some fresh air so I went out for a walk around the parade ground.

"Hey Naud," Dalton, the gate guard, called to me. "Someone wants to see you at the gate."

As I approached, I could see a young Japanese girl waving to me. I figured she was one of the Joy-Girls. "Mister. Someone want to see you."

"I'm not interested, miss," I said firmly shooing her away.

"No not me," she said, discreetly flashing a note crumpled in her hand. I took it through the iron gate and read it.

I was shocked. "Where's the guy?" I whispered.

"Him go down street," She said.

I looked down Oji's long cobblestone street. Nobody was in sight. When I turned back, the girl was already running away.

"Hey, come back," I hollered.

"What's wrong, Naud?" Damion hollered from his booth, my call to the girl had caught his attention.

"It's okay, Damion," I said, stuffing the paper in my pocket. If the note was for real, I didn't want to discuss it with an MP or with anyone else.

The Jitsu bar was a quarter of a mile down the cobblestone street. It was very late, the people of Oji were asleep.

I kept to the middle of the deserted road in case the note was a ruse to lure me into a mugging along the way. A sudden screeching noise startled me, and I jumped. I felt a little foolish when it turned out to be a parrot in one of the shop windows. When I reached the end of the quarter mile, I stopped opposite the Jitsu bar. I could see by the dim red lights inside that the place was empty, except for the bartender.

"Bill! Over here," a voice whispered.

I turned to see a hulking figure lurking in the dark shadows by the side of the building. 'Holy Christ,' I thought. It was Jessie taking a quick drag on a cigarette. His fatigues were filthy and he looked desperate, like a lost child. 'I must be seeing a ghost,' I thought.

I joined him in the darkness between the buildings. "Callahan said you were dead, Jess."

"They're trying to send me back to Korea, Bill. I won't go. I'd rather die here," he said, blowing smoke out, as he checked up and down the street for any sign of movement.

"Callahan told me about the other guy and the ditch and all. What happened?" I said.

"I woke up, crawled back to our line and collapsed. They sent me to a hospital in Osaka," Jessie explained.

"Didn't you tell them you were with the ASA?" I said.

"Yeah, but the ASA said they never heard of me. They wanted to send me back to a combat unit as an infantryman. So I went AWOL," Jessie explained.

"You gotta talk to the Colonel. Get him to tell 'em I'm ASA. If he does, they can't send me back," Jessie pleaded.

"Okay, I'll talk to him in the morning," I said.

"You gotta talk to him now. If the MP's catch me, I'm dead," Jessie insisted.

Jessie took a Forty-five from his fatigue pocket. I could sense he would use it if he had to. "I'm not going back," he threatened

"Okay, I'll talk to him now," I said. "But you gotta give me the gun, Jess."

"No way, Bill. Anybody tries to take me back, they're dead, or I'm dead. It doesn't matter now. I don't care anymore," Jessie said.

"I care, Jess. What about your father?" I said.

"If they send me back it won't make any difference to him if I was killed by an MP's bullet in Tokyo, or by a gook at the Yalu," Jessie was fighting back the tears.

I realized nothing I was going to say would change his mind. "Okay, I'll go talk to the Colonel," I said. "If I'm not back in thirty minutes, take off." Then I added, "Remember, Jess, if you or anybody gets hurt with that gun they'll hang me too."

I had just turned and started out of the alley, when Jessie's hand grabbed me.

"Bill?" Jessie said calmly, "Go ahead, take it." He held the Forty-five by the barrel and handed it to me.

I stuffed the gun under my jacket where the guards wouldn't see it.

"Wait behind the building," I said.

I told Damion, the gate guard that my trip down the cobblestone street was to give one of the Joy-

Girls from the Pisspot some money. The guards didn't see the gun.

I stopped by some bushes and stuck the forty-five deep inside the thick leaves where it couldn't be seen.

Oakley was on duty at the Bachelor officer Quarters desk, he was working on a crossword puzzle.

"Hey Oakley, ring Colonel Macmillan and tell him I have something very important to talk to him about."

"Jeez, Bill. Do you know what time it is?" he answered, showing me his watch.

"It's very important," I insisted.

"Okay, it's your ass buddy, but you owe me some free drinks," he said, shaking his head as he picked up the phone, and woke the Colonel.

Ten minutes later an irate Colonel Macmillan emerged. He was still tying his bathrobe when he reached the bottom of the stairs. "I hope this is important Naud", he moaned, as he followed me into the darkness of the doorway entrance to the building, for privacy. The orderly was trying to ignore us, he went on pretending he was reading.

"Sir it's very important." I said, keeping my voice down.

"You got two minutes, GO," the Colonel said.

"Sir, when I came here, you asked me to do something with the Club and I think you'll admit I did it very well. And now I need your help," I said, my mouth was as dry as a blotter.

"This agency isn't run on a quid pro quo basis. Get to the point, Naud," he barked.

The Colonel's abruptness was rattling me. I had a case to make for Jessie that was life-or-death and I felt that I had a right to be listened to.

"Bonato needs help, Sir" I said.

"Bonato?" the Colonel exclaimed, recalling him with disgust. "The screw- up who shot-up the Flaming Pisspot?"

"That screw up went and became a hero, and got himself wounded. They put him in a hospital in Osaka, and now they want to send him back to Korea with an infantry unit. He told them he was ASA, but the agency says they never heard of him. He went AWOL to get your help. All he wants is to get back into the Agency." I wanted to put it all on the Colonel's conscience, so he would bear the guilt for whatever happened next.

"Once you reveal you are with the agency your automatically out. That's SOP and you know it," The Colonel said.

"I don't care about SOP. He deserves your help," I insisted.

"Naud, you're way out of line! " The Colonel was fuming. "We're ASA, but we're soldiers first. Soldiers do what they are told," the Colonel angrily reminded me. "Where is he?"

I was reluctant to answer.

The Colonel glared at me. "You're bordering on being insubordinate, soldier. If YOU don't want to end up in Korea, yourself, or in a stockade, you better answer my question, Now," the Colonel ordered.

I knew I had no choice but I felt that at least the OJI ASA guards would be less likely to injure or kill Jessie, than if he was caught on the run by some MP's. It was a choice between something bad, and something really bad.

"He's waiting down behind the Jitsu bar," I said

"Is he armed?" the Colonel asked.

"No, Sir. His Forty-five is outside in the bushes," I said.

"Now get your butt out of here, Naud," the Colonel barked as he picked up the phone and called the Sergeant –of-the-guard. Just stood there listening.

"Sergeant, there's an AWOL named Bonato at the Jitsu bar, down in Oji. Get yourself two or three hefty guys and put him in the lockup," the Colonel said. Then he glared at me. "That was an order I gave you Naud. Get outta here."

I was heading back across the Parade Grounds in a blind rage, when I saw the Sergeant of the guard and four men running out the main gate toward the Jitsu bar. I heard the MPs wrestling with Jessie trying to put hand cuffs on him. I had guessed wrong about the Colonel. The bastard was sending Jessie back to hell. And I had helped him do it.

Chapter 30

Dark Side of The Moon

The sun was going down as Surrel stopped the jeep by one of the railroad overpasses. He looked back to see if we were followed. He had been glancing in his rear view mirror the whole way, just to be sure.

Until eleven o'clock that day I had no idea where Sunlei was hiding. Then Langdon, the gate guard, brought me a sealed envelope that a cab driver had left with for me. When I opened it, I found a card with two words on it, *'sewing lady.'* I knew instantly what it meant, it was where Sunlei was hiding. I remembered from her diary the passages about living with a woman who had a sewing factory in Kasawagi, north of downtown Tokyo. I called Black Market Sam and asked him to get me a bicycle for two right away.

Surrel and I took the two-seater bicycle off the roof and stood there smoking, waiting for the darkness to close in. We both wore dark shirts to blend in with the night. I was suddenly shaken by a screaming steam engine that roared past overhead.

"Let's go," I said, mounting on the bike. We started peddling into the darkness.

The area we were in was known as the *'dark side of the moon'*. It was one of several bombed out sections of the city, about a mile square each, that had been cordoned off to prevent traffic from entering. It was littered with signs showing a football shaped bomb symbol with a lit fuse. They read, UNEXPLODED ORDINANCE-DANGER-DO NOT ENTER. An irregular roadway had been plowed through the piles of exploded debris, like a dangerous maze.

The whole place really did eerily resemble the pockmarked moon. There was no electricity and no lights. People were living in the ruble below ground and in tunnels using candles for light, and hibachis to heat their food as well as themselves.

It wasn't safe for anyone to be living in this desperate jungle, especially not Sunlei. We kept peddling around, in and out of alleys, until we hit a wide path. I spotted a partially intact building, but there were no signs indicating what it once was. Suddenly out of the darkness came two bicyclers, they rode past us, disappearing as quickly as they appeared.

Then out to my left, I saw a flash of light. Then another out to my right. We stopped for a moment, studying the directions they were coming from. I was worrying it might be the police tracking us. We waited a few moments until the lights were gone, then we moved along slowly onto the widest path we could find.

Up ahead about a half mile I saw a bombed out two story building with a crumpled thin metal advertisement sign on the roof. There was a faded sewing machine painted on it.

We headed towards the building. In front there was a bombed out cement truck whose contents were scattered around. I whispered to Surrel, "this must be it. When you get opposite it I am going to slide off, and crawl under the truck, then get down into that trench that runs along the sidewalk. You just keep going."

I started to sweat badly, as I counted out loud. "4,3,2,1." Off I went into the pile of sand and under the demolished truck.

Surrel kept going.

I crawled through the sand and across the sidewalk, and slid down into the trench that ran alongside the building. There was a three foot long piece of pipe lying at the bottom. I grabbed it and made my way along like an alligator until I felt I was safe. There wasn't a sound, so I stood up and slowly made my way to the only connecting trench I could see that led down the basement door of the building

Suddenly, a flash of metal came at me from the side, but before it hit me I landed a solid blow with the pipe, on the head of my attacker. The act made me lose my balance and I fell forward onto him, as together we slammed to the ground. I was wobbly and desperate to get to my feet, so I pushed myself up off him, grabbing his ski cap and pulling it off. To my surprise, my attacker wasn't exactly what I expected. It was a woman, with long black silky hair. The shock jolted me to my feet. She came to, and grabbed at my ankle with one hand, as she blew into a whistle on a cord around her neck. Suddenly three other figures dressed like her came rushing towards me in the trench. An air raid warning started to sound, and sweeping lights came on, heading our way.

Surrel was waiting for me up the block. When he saw me leaving the trench, he frantically peddled up to me. I jumped aboard and away we went.

We circled the piles of debris, hoping we could shake the police car following us. After a few moments of chase, we made a sharp left, skidding into a pathway littered with broken glass. Luckily we maneuvered around it, and safely kept going. The police car rounded the same curve and tried to miss the jagged pile of glass in the narrow alleyway, but couldn't. One of the tires blew out and it flew out of control, flipping and slamming into one of the trestle arches, and into an ordinance warning sign. I could hear the screams of the men as they climbed out and ran away, just as the car blew up and became engulfed in flames.

People started coming out of the piles of debris to see what happened.

We quickly pulled away, peddling back around the alleyways until we found a place where we could safely watch the sewing factory. A squad of police cars had surrounded the building. It was lit up like a Christmas tree.

My only hope was that I had gotten the address wrong, and Sunlei wasn't in there, but moments later, I watched in horror as they brought her out in handcuffs and led her to a police van. The door slammed shut behind her and they pulled away.

I couldn't help her, and it pained me to think in some way, I had helped put her in jail. 'What the hell did they want with her,' I thought. All she wanted was to be a young woman, designing dresses.

We headed back to the jeep and rode back to the base.

"Sorry, Naud," Surrel said. The rest of the way we rode in silence.

Chapter 31

The Last Mission

I had just finished my favorite lunch, SOS, shit on a shingle. The chilling winter air somehow made the after taste better. I crossed the compound and went up the stairs to the fifth floor. Toshiko was waiting for me. From the look on his face something serious had happened. Before I could ask what, he blurted it out.

"Sergeant Baker called an emergency Board of Governors' meeting at 12:30."

I looked at my watch. That was in fifteen minutes. I thought Baker had given up trying to nail my ass to the wall, especially since I was going home soon. But now I realized I was wrong.

"He wants the Colonel to appoint Dehler new Club Custodian."

"Over my dead body," I shot back. I knew Toshiko and the waiters were afraid of the cruel treatment they would have to endure under Dehler. But my words did not reassure Toshiko. I also knew I had a better chance of coming up with the meaning of life than a way to stop Baker.

Toshiko gestured for me to follow him into the office. The phones were ringing off the hooks. The waiters were answering them and scribbling something down on little slips of paper, then hanging up.

Toshiko hustled me to the antique telescope.

"Naudsan, look," Toshiko said.

I didn't have time to watch a lot of wacko, bicycle riders trying to kill each other. "I've already seen those crazy bicycle races," I said.

"You look again, Naudsan," Toshiko insisted, sounding strangely resolute.

I looked through the eye piece focusing on the riders who were ready to go. They were dressed for war, wearing ¾ pants, heavy leather gloves, knee pads, elbow pads and heavy leather donut shaped cloth bands around their foreheads. Every inch of their clothes was covered with Japanese symbols. One represented a tire, another a bicycle, which told me they must be promoting somebodies products. There was a crowd of about ten thousand Japanese people in the stadium watching.

Toshiko shifted the head of the telescope to the left to focus on a big green board with Japanese writing on it, just like the ones you find at a racetrack. I recognized several numbers 1, 7, and 5. It was a tote board. It took me a moment to put it all together.

I looked at Toshiko. "This is an illegal gambling operation right?"

He lowered his eyes, but didn't say no.

"ATTENHUT!" Sergeant Baker's voice bellowed from the club above.

Toshiko and I raced up to the club and took our places at the conference table.

Plummer wasn't there yet.

Baker greeted us with a cloud of cigar smoke from across the table.

Colonel Macmillan was at his place at the head of the table looking tired and drawn, and in no mood to tolerate anything.

"Alright, Baker, we'll make this informal. What have you got that's so damn important."

Baker had his elbow on the table holding up in his hand an 8'x10' envelope, like a snake coiled up ready to strike. I had no idea what he was going to do.

By the look on Toshiko's face, he obviously did. He had his own 8'x10' envelope in hand and the resignation of a Kamikaze on his final mission.

Baker smugly started," Sir I believe we have evidence here of a major impropriety going on, on the part of the club custodian Naud."

"Well what is it?" Macmillan demanded impatiently.

"Take a look at these, Sir," Baker said. He started to reach over to pass the envelope to Colonel Macmillan.

But I grabbed it from his hands, protesting, "Colonel I believe I have the right to see the evidence against me, before any judgment is made."

"That's fine. Take a look, Naud," Macmillan said with irritation, just about to lose his patience with what he saw as petty squabbling between Baker and myself. He went back to reviewing his war reports.

Like a card player trying to protect his hand, I held the envelope close to my chest and took a glance at the contents. I was shocked to see there were five old photos, taken a couple of years earlier, of Sunlei and Nobura. The sixth photo was taken recently, at Thanksgiving, of Nobura arriving at Sunlei's house. The seventh photo included me, standing on Sunlei's porch, kissing her goodbye. The consequence of collaborating with a known communist was a court martial. Baker was out to get me locked away.

"Come on Naud. Give that stuff to the Colonel," Baker barked with agitation.

Just at that moment Plummer clumped his way into the club. "Sir, this reply communiqué just came in," he said handing a top secret envelope to the Colonel. Plummer was obviously shaken as he sat down next to me.

"Christ, MacArthur wants to blow the ass out of China with atomic bombs, " he whispered.

Macmillan's face went dead white as he stared at the communiqué.

Toshiko removed one of a stack of documents from his envelope and held it out in front of Baker.

"Maybe, you show these to Colonel too, Sergeant," Toshiko said.

Baker glanced at the paper, then he started a choking cough, jumping to his feet and spitting the cigar out of his mouth. It landed on his crotch. He kept jumping up and down trying to brush the pain away.

I asked Toshiko what was in the envelope.

"Betting slips and deposit slips for Bakers Safety Deposit Box," he whispered, showing me a slip.

"Whose is the other signature on the slips?" I asked.

"Black Market Sam," Toshiko answered.

The records in the folder documented Baker's secret bookie operation. Baker's signature was on everything. Toshiko had been paid to run the betting operation, and now he was using it all to blackmail Baker. He was putting himself in danger, to help me.

"Alright," the Colonel barked. "Where are we now? Let's wrap this up. "

"Sir," Baker started peevishly, "It has been brought to my attention that the evidence against Private Naud is obviously fabricated and inconclusive."

The Colonel looked at him with disgust. "You mean this whole meeting is a damn waste of time. Is that what you're telling me Sergeant?"

I jumped in and answered, "No, Sir. Sergeant Baker wanted to make sure he got in his recommendation for Pollazzo, as the new head Club Custodian. "

"Is that right, Baker?" the Colonel snapped.

"Yes Sir," Baker answered, slumping down in defeat.

Dehler's head went down and made hard contact with the table.

"Let the record show, Corporal Pollazzo, will be the new club custodian after the departure of Private Naud. Now I've got more important things to do. Meeting adjourned."

Colonel Macmillan rose to his feet and strode out, not bothering to return our salutes. A beaten Baker and his stooges followed him out in silence.

"What's going on Naud?" Plummer asked.

"It looks like we won the Baker war after all," I said.

Toshiko was beaming. He had found the courage to lead his last mission and it was a glorious success.

I still had one more mission, to somehow help get Sunlei out of jail.

....

Top Secret/ ASA OJI Decrypted Communique

Date: February 4 19...

To: JOINT CHIEFS OF STAFF

From: MACARTHUR

Subject: AUTHORIZATION

   Synopsis:
   I am proposing four retaliatory
measures:

1. Allow diversionary operations
   by Nationalist Troops against
   Mainland China.
2. Blockade China Coast
3. Destroy China's War Industries
   with Naval and Air attacks.
4. Reinforce troops in korea with
   Chinese Nationalist Forces.

Signed
MAC

....

Chapter 32

Last Golfing Lesson

Plummer, Surrel and I, were hitting practice balls on the Kogene driving range. The morning was clear and sunny. It was going to be hot.

In eleven more days, Plummer and I would be going stateside. We would be discharged, and then head home. I desperately wanted to see Sunlei, but she was still in jail and her case wouldn't come up until November, another five months away.

Surrel had gotten Sunlei's diary to Rorshack, hoping it could somehow help her case, but I hadn't heard a word back from him about it. All I knew was that bail had been set at four thousand dollars. It didn't matter. Even if I some how got the money, I was sure Baker would have S.S. Dalton watching me. It was obvious now that I was never going to see her again.

I had suggested we play one last round of golf, mainly to cheer myself up.

As we were getting ready to start our round, we heard a familiar voice coming from the bar. "Bring me a scotch on the rocks," the Champ ordered. Make it a double," he hollered as the waiter was leaving. He spotted us. "Hey, Surrel. Why do you keep making a fool of yourself?" he chided.

Surrel looked at him, puzzled by the remark.

"Golf, ole buddy. It isn't your game. Why don't you give it up," the Champ said.

I couldn't stand the Champ, a friend of Rorshack's, and I was in no mood to sit there and listen to his bullshit.

"You know, Champ," I began in a saccharine way, "Plummer here has never even played eighteen holes and I think he can beat your ass."

I had punched the right buttons, threatening the Champ's self-esteem. He leaned forward resting his arms on the table, snorting to do battle.

"Yeh? Whatta ya want to bet?" the Champ said, looking at Plummer.

The waiter arrived with the drinks. The Champ paused long enough to throw down the shot of scotch before turning to me. "How much, Naud? What's it gonna be?"

I took a slug of iced tea, as a scheme took shape in my mind.

"This Bean Town bum couldn't beat a blind man," the Champ said, trying to needle Plummer.

Plummer continued to ignore him. Plummer had no interest in playing golf with the Champ, especially a money match.

Surrel was on the verge of leaving.

"We want four to one odds and four strokes a hole, and we'll even play SCOTCH RULES," I proposed.

"What are you talking about, Bill?" Plummer protested.

I just sipped my ice tea.

"What the hell are 'scotch' rules?" Plummer asked.

"The winner of a hole has to drink a water glass of scotch," the Champ said. "Okay, you're on."

"Our hundred against your four hundred dollars," I said, trying not to sound too eager.

"Bill? I'm not gonna play him," Plummer said, realizing the bet was serious

I was drinking the ice tea, thinking if the Champ won the first six holes, he would have to drink six glasses of scotch. Between the scotch and the boiling sun, he would probably be so drunk that Plummer wouldn't need to win by low strokes.

"Whatsa matter, Bean Town? Trying to fink out?" the Champ said, chewing on ice cubes from the empty glass of scotch.

Plummer's back was up. "Okay, I'll play."

We were standing on the first tee ready to tee off. The day was already hot and on its way to getting hotter. The little bit of breeze that had been blowing earlier was gone.

The girl caddies cost three dollars, plus tip. Yoko, Rorshack's regular caddie, was on hand. She was a wiry, sharp-faced woman with muscles of steel and eyes as sharp as a hawk's. She liked the Champ's winning attitude. Having been on the losing side of World War II, Yoko was ready to do whatever she could to make the Champ a winner. Besides, the Champ was a big tipper.

"Let's do it," the Champ said.

"Okay, Let's be clear. We're playing Summer Rules, right?" Surrel said.

"Summer Rules" meant nothing to Plummer.

"The rule is you gotta play all eighteen holes or you lose," Surrel explained.

"We wanna raise the bet," I said.

"Name it," the Champ said, taking another picture perfect practice swing.

"Two thousand dollars," I said.

The driver suddenly flew out of the Champ's hands and sailed off down the fairway.

Yoko rushed away to recover it.

"Whatsa matter? Chickening out?" I taunted.

"It's a BET," the Champ replied, as Yoko returned to the tee with his club.

"Bill, where ya gonna get two thousand dollars?" Plummer whispered.

"Same place I was gonna get the hundred," I said. Plummer thought I was nuts to bet money I didn't have. That is, until it dawned on him that the Champ had no way to collect. We would be gone, back in the States. At four to one odds, I could win enough to post bail for Sunlei.

"Okay, Bean Town. Ready? I'm gonna whip your ass," the Champ said. He teed up his ball up and took his stance.

"Better check that shaft, Champ I think it's bent," I said.

The Champ checked the shaft and couldn't see a bend, but decided this was no time to risk using a defective driver, so he switched to a three wood.

It was exactly what I had in mind.

To make up the distance lost by not using his driver, the Champ swung hard, lunging at the ball and topping it. It went fifty feet down the fairway.

I smiled, complimenting myself on the success of my ploy.

I teed Plummer's ball up and whispered some last minute instructions.

Plummer took his stance and when I said so, he swung and topped the ball down the fairway close to where the Champ's ball was.

"I think Plummer out drove you, Champ," I quipped, needling him.

Our group headed down the fairway, with me carrying Plummer's clubs. As we walked we could hear the five bottles of Johnny Walker Red label scotch clinking in the Champ's golf bag.

The Champ's second shot landed in a trap by the green.

I whispered instructions to Plummer, who then hit his second shot.

He swung and his ball hit a tree, and a pathway, and bounced onto the green, finally stopping ten feet from the hole. For a lousy shot, it had turned out great.

The Champ was pissed at Plummer for what was obviously "pure luck". Plummer's good luck had put a kink in my plans, too

The Champ hit his ball out of the trap, twenty feet from the hole. Yoko helped him line up his putt. He sank it for a par four.

"There's a spike mark in front of your ball," I whispered to Plummer. The ball was a foot from the hole, a literal tap in. "So be sure you hit the ball HARD," I added.

"Why HARD?" Plummer asked.

"Why? So the spike mark doesn't deflect it. Remember HARD," I told him firmly.

Plummer hit the putt HARD. It went roaring over the hole and off the green into a trap. He wound up taking a total of twelve strokes.

"We lost, but we won," I consoled Plummer as we headed to the next tee.

"I don't get it," Plummer said.

"You will," I said.

The Champ was beaming from his unexpected victory as he sat on the bench and downed the glass of scotch Yoko had poured for him. Having seen Plummer take a twelve, from a foot away, the Champ was sure that he was on his way to victory. Yoko put the bottle of scotch away. The Champ rose briskly from the bench to tee off. He took one step and fell on his face. The scotch, the punch, and the heat were beginning to take their toll.

"You okay?" Plummer asked as Yoko helped him get up.

"I'm okay. I'm fine," the Champ insisted.

I figured the scotch the Champ had downed at lunch was helping to speed things up. At this rate the Champ would be out of the match by the fifth hole.

By the time we reached the sixth hole, my plan was working. Plummer was six down. The Champ had drunk six large glasses of scotch whiskey, plus the one he had downed at lunch. The sun was boiling hot and he was yawning constantly. I figured he couldn't last much longer.

On the seventh tee, after another glass of whiskey, the Champ fell asleep on the bench. Yoko had to shake him awake. He stood up long enough to hit his tee shot, while humming, *Somewhere over the Rainbow*.

The ball flew down the fairway and bounced hard left into a shallow pond. Immediately, the Champ sat back down on the bench and fell asleep. Yoko shook him awake and dragged him down the fairway like a bag of wash. The Champ ignored his ball in the pond and lay down on the bank. He fell asleep. Yoko found the ball then dragged the Champ into the pond by his shirt, sloshing him around in the water like a washing machine. The Champ began choking and coughing on the water. In a few minutes he was wide-awake and ready to go.

He hit a five-iron to the green. The ball stopped twenty feet from the hole.

Yoko glared defiantly at me as if to say, 'take that, you Yankee dog.' With Yoko willing his ball in the hole, the Champ sank his putt and ended up with a six. Plummer six-putted the green and lost.

Yoko had the Champ drink the scotch standing up, so when he fell asleep, she could get a good grip. Which she needed to drag him along.

I kept complaining about Yoko dragging, but Surrel kept insisting it was legal.

The Champ would hum as he hit the ball, drink the winner's glass of scotch, and pass out on Yoko's shoulder. Yoko would drag him to his next shot, as he slept, then she would wake him long enough to hit the ball again and on they would go. It was a scene from Ripley's "Believe It or Not".

"I'm dormie, ole sluddy," the Champ reminded me in a drunken slur.

Plummer had no idea what "dormie" meant.

I explained it simply. "Dormie" meant that there weren't enough holes left for Plummer to win the match. If he won them all, the best he could do was a tie

"Let's quit and get out of the sun before we melt, huh?" Plummer pleaded.

My only hope was for the Champ to pass out and not be able to finish the match. I insisted that Plummer was going to win. I 'had a vision'.

Plummer knew it was bullshit. But he kept going for my sake.

By the last hole I knew the match was over, but I was determined to play it out until the end. All the Champ had to do was finish and he would win. With Yoko carrying him, there was no way he could lose.

"Slow down. Take plenty of time on each shot," I whispered to Plummer.

"Why?" Plummer asked.

"You wanna win don't you?"

"We've already lost. I just wanna get out of here."

"Do it for me, please." I begged.

Plummer couldn't refuse the desperate look on my face.

The eighteenth fairway had no trees or shelter of any kind. I could see the heat rays rising from the fairways, making everything shimmer. The sun was at its peak and it was steaming hot.

Plummer hit his Tee shot down the center of the fairway. The Champ's ball stopped twenty yards ahead of him.

Plummer hit his second shot. It stopped on the green six inches from the hole. Plummer started for the green, glad the whole thing would soon be over.

The Champ's second shot to the eighteenth took a bad bounce and rolled into a deep trap at the back of the green. Yoko grabbed him before he could hit the ground and began hauling him down the fairway. She dragged the Champ down into the trap to find his ball, and set him up to hit the trap shot. Then she climbed up onto the green to hold the flag.

The trap the Champ was in was so deep nobody could see him. But we did see his ball come flying out. Yoko pulled the flag out of the hole, thinking the ball was going in. But it stopped a foot away.

Yoko headed over to rake the sand in the trap. She stopped on the edge of the trap and looked down. Then she mumbled something in Japanese.

Plummer and I went over to the see what was wrong.

The Champ was lying face down on the sand. Yoko kept railing in Japanese.

"She's saying the Champ is sick," Plummer told me.

I could hear the Champ snoring. "He's not sick. He's asleep," I called out with glee. "He's gotta finish the hole or loose the match," I declared.

"That's the rule," Surrel said, hollering. "Hey Champ, wake up Get up."

"How long do we have to wait?" I asked.

"I guess, until the next foursome arrives," Surrel said, looking back down the fairway. Two groups were backed up, waiting for the green to clear.

Yoko jumped down into the trap and began shaking the Champ, trying to wake him.

My faint hopes for victory were being dashed as Yoko dragged the half- conscious Champ out of the trap and across the green to his ball. She stood him up in position over the ball and placed the putter in his hands.

"*Hi-Ho. Hi-HO, it's off to work we go,*" the Champ began humming weakly.

Yoko was aiming his putter blade square at the center of the hole.

"Champsan must do it himself," I said, warning her.

Yoko made a final check of the Champs' putter alignment. Then, carefully and slowly she backed away. But not before she checked to be sure he would stand on his own. "NOW, PUTT, CHAMPSAN," Yoko commanded, in her deepest voice.

"*We're off to see the Wizard*," he hummed, swaying over the ball.

I held my breath watching the Champ drag his putter blade back.

"FORE. FORE," the chorus of impatient voices screamed from down the fairway.

The Champ's putter blade stopped at the end of his back swing.

It seemed frozen in space.

Then, like the Wicked Witch of the North, the Champ, ever so slowly, began to sag, humming, "*We're off to see the Wizard*."

Yoko watched him come to rest in a heap on the green. Quietly, he started snoring as he fell fast asleep. Tears welled up in her eyes.

"FORE. FORE," the screams kept coming, getting louder and angrier.

"That's it! We win!" I declared, giving in to the pressure from the waiting golfers.

Plummer, Surrel and I carried the Champ into the clubhouse.

I had won the match and shook Champ awake so I could get my winnings.

He just started to laugh, "I haven't got a dome ole buddy."

I was stunned. Plummer had won the match but I had won nothing.

Chapter 33

Sayonara

Six days later, Surrel arrived at the base, and took Plummer and I to Kogene air field for trans-shipment to the United States. Surrel went to make a phone call as Plummer and I sat on our duffel bags wait- ing to be called to board our plane. Our names were called, while Surrel was away.

We headed toward the gate hoping he would make it back in time to say goodbye. Just as we were about to climb the steps up to the DC –4, Surrel came run- ning towards us with a big smile. "She's out, Naud," he said excitedly. Sunlei had been released from jail. Rorshack didn't know all the details of why but he was sure the diary I had given him had helped.

There is no way to describe how I felt. She was free and in some way I had helped.

I thanked Surrel for the good friend he had been, and promised we would stay in touch.

Plummer and I climbed aboard the plane and took seats near the galley. The stewardess, a pretty gal, the first American woman I had seen in six months, closed the door and sealed it.

The pilot taxied out to the runway. Once we were given clearance, the engines roared and we picked up speed. I hated to fly, and had an empty feeling in my stomach as the wheels came off the runway and we climbed into the sky. Our adventure in Japan was over; we were heading home to return to civilian life.

On the flight back to the States, I tried writing Sunlei a letter. But the words I wrote couldn't express what I was feeling, so I gave up.

The girl with the cobalt blue eyes was a dream come true. But now the dream was over. I realized Sunlei was probably gone from my life, forever.

Chatting with the stewardess kept my mind off the rest of the flight, as did thirty six cups of coffee.

Thirty-three hours later, with a brief stop in Wake Island and Hawaii, our wheels touched down at the Oakland California air base. We were back in the U.S.A.

Two weeks later, I was discharged from the Army at Fort Monmouth in New Jersey. Coming back across the George Washington bridge, I noticed the expansion joint I had last seen on my way west, almost a year ago.

A week later, on a gray overcast day, I took the train from New York to New Haven to visit my father's grave, and say "goodbye".

The cemetery in the south side of the city was old and quaint.

The only marking on my dad's grave was an eight inch square stone with a number 52 on it. The family couldn't afford to buy a headstone.

"I love you, dad. I'll miss you," I said, as tears streamed down my face. "I'm sorry I never really had a chance to know you well." I wiped the tears and left the cemetery.

On the way back to Manhattan I thought about Japan, Sunlei, Baker, the Colonel, Plummer, Toshiko, Surrel, Arrowsmith, and all the others. I would never forget any of them, especially Sunlei. I wondered if I would ever find another girl like her.

I looked out the train's window at the Hudson River going by. The gray clouds vanished leaving the Hudson Valley area flooded in sunshine.

Epilogue

All this must come to an end but the story kept going on. Shortly after getting home, I received good news regarding Jessie Bonato. The Colonel did not send him back to fight in Korea, he sent him back to the states with an honorable discharge. He was safely at home in Brooklyn, New York.

For my part, I was going to college at NYU in New York.

A month after I arrived home a set of golf clubs were delivered. There was a note from Colonel Macmillan. They were Arrowsmiths. He had saved me from the front lines in Korea but he couldn't save himself.

Two months after I left OJI, to my surprise, Sergeant Baker resigned from the army and went back to his home in Bristol, Tennessee, to wait for his beautiful bride-to-be, Misako Umerie, to come over from Japan.

Misako Umerie did come to the United States, but was met by Surrel who had returned to Carmel, California, to complete his last year of law school and open a small liquor distribution company. Umerie and Surrel fell madly in love, married and were expecting a child while Baker was still waiting for her in Bristol Tennessee.

Dehler left the ASA four months after I left and became a full time station news reporter in Omaha Nebraska and a part time rancher.

Plummer married his gal Anne, completed his college degree and began teaching history at a boys' prep school in Brookline Massachusetts.

Toshiko resigned from the EM Club at OJI and was replaced by Jumbo. Toshiko and Black Market Sam opened a swank restaurant in Tokyo, Japan.

Junji immersed himself in law school.

Pollazzo continued running the club and was loving every day of it.

Captain Ephrom remained the company commander.

Colonel Macmillan remained the base commander and was waiting for the conclusion of the Truce talks.

Nobura was still agitating the government with Communist protests.

Captain Mulvey's wife had an operation and was beginning to walk again, and was expecting a baby.

I never heard from Jessie Bonato again.

Last but not least, Sunlei bought out the dress shop at the Imperial hotel and was designing and selling her own dresses there with much success.

Somehow in my heart, I knew I would never see the girl with the cobalt blue eyes again.

·1952·

Made in the USA
Charleston, SC
01 December 2013